The COLONEL'S DAUGHTER

Occupied Germany 1946 *to* 1949

Jean Walters Gayle

THREE HORSES PRESS

This Book Was Published by Three Horses Press 1998
Copyright @ 1997 by Jean Walters Gayle
All rights reserved under International and Pan-American Copyright Conventions.
Published in the United States by
Three Horses Press, Washington State
Distributed by Three Horses Press,
P.O. Box 104
Montesano, WA 98563
360 533 3490
ISBN 0-9661536-3-4
LC 97-091156
Manufactured in the United States of America
Published May 1998
First Printing 1998
Germany-History,Range 1945-55

*D*edicated to:
My Dear Friend, Marilyn Roberta Oars

ACKNOWLEDGEMENTS

I wish to thank those who took the time to read and critique this book:

Princess Gunilla Fugger-Babenhausen
Countess Paula Clary-Aldringen
Count Markus Fugger-Babenhausen
Marilyn Oars
Donald Oars
Vera Stewart
Isabelle Lamb
Holly Emerson
Ralph Emerson
Ralph Emerson Jr.
Maxine Pace
Brent Goeres
Billie Roberts
Ken Roberts
Janie Kay Richardson
Terry Stevenson
Dan Ayres

Special thanks to the reference people at the Aberdeen Library....Martha, Sandy, Emily and Tim

Without my friends I am a stranger.

PHOTOGRAPHS

CONTENTS

The author in 1946

CHAPTER I

GETTING STARTED

The time was April 1946. The place was Eugene, Oregon, following the end of the second World War. I was a college student finishing my Junior year at the University of Oregon. My father, Eugene Paul Walters, was an officer in the United States military government in Karlsruhe, Germany, and was attacking the red tape required to get me to Europe. This was to enable him to have a home and me to have the experience of my life. I had already met with Senator Wayne Morse in Eugene and was assured that my papers would be processed "soon," allowing me to set sail by September 1946.

My sorority sisters were green with envy. My mother and grandmother were hesitant, but knowing nothing would stop me, were trying to help. A long- standing feud existed between my divorced parents, but my brother and I were rarely aware of it. My mother had chosen a small town life for us, while my father had headed for Hollywood. I had a deep attraction for my father, and would spend summers with him until the war. Life in Hollywood was full of excitement, movie stars, wealthy friends and homes, and all the glitter that was gold. Dad was a handsome, charismatic, tall man who always knew important people wherever he went. I loved being in his shadow, and managed to adopt a more metropolitan air than my brother, Charles, or so I thought.

THE COLONEL

Eugene Paul Walters was born in Spokane, Washington, in 1896. His father was a self-ordained (hell /fire) minister and they lived on

Colonel Eugene Paul Walters

a 40-acre hillside without water or electricity. They were the *poor kids* at school. Grandfather Walters drove himself and his family at a hard, unrewarding pace. When Dad was seven, his mother left the family. She went to California supposedly to die of *consumption*. We now know this illness as tuberculosis. Little was ever mentioned about his mother. She is buried somewhere near San Francisco.

Grandfather Walters was left with the two children, Aunt Monta who was five, and Dad. Grandfather had immediately hired a live-in lady, Florence. He later married her to be *Christian*. She was a simple,

honest woman, who tried to show the children some kindness. After several hard years, Grandfather moved the family down the hill to a small farm where they had lights and water. The soil was rocky and the climate unbearably hot in the summer. I am sure my father decided early in life that he would never live that way when he grew up.

He ran away from a home he found too punitive and isolated when he was fourteen. Somehow he managed to get to his Uncle Colonel Ades in Tacoma, Washington. The family took him in and he remained estranged from his father for the rest of his life. He completed high school and then enlisted in the US Cavalry at age eighteen when the 1st World War started. Dad was injured, superficially, during the war. A bomb had landed nearby and left him with shrapnel in his knee and eye.

Despite the wounds, he continued fighting. He became a Lieutenant in the cavalry, was a superb rider, and saw action throughout Europe. When he returned home, he entered college at the University of Oregon in Eugene, Oregon. Later, he attended and graduated from Oregon State at Corvallis. He became a member of Beta Theta Pi fraternity, and was considered the top catch on campus. Dad supported himself by selling insurance and working at clerical jobs. He could sell himself to others, and could be comfortable in any group.

While attending Oregon State College, my mother, Eunice Romilda Haines, from Everett, Washington, met Dad. She was bound and determined to *catch* him, as he was considered a very eligible bachelor. Mother was a first year student, a sorority member, but still a small town girl.

They were married despite angry reactions from her parents, the Dean of Women, and her friends who were set against the union. Dad was seen as a ladies' man who loved to party. Life in those days was postwar and parties. My mother was a *flapper*, a name given to the young socialites who bound their bosoms to appear flat chested. They were partying during prohibition as liquor was illegal and had to be purchased from the *bootleggers*. At that time there were *Speak Easy* clubs where they danced, smoked, and shared, or bought, illegal alcohol. Life changed for my mother when she became pregnant and had my brother Charles. Nevertheless, Dad was still pursuing his need to get away from restrictive life and was not the best husband. When I came along, there were already serious problems in this five-

year marriage. Mother was trying to hold things together and Dad
was wanting to *live.*

After graduation, Dad tried to settle down and he became a full-
time Life Insurance Agent. His fraternity brothers were always to
help him along the way. One especially, Z. Wayne Griffin, was offering him connections in Hollywood. It must have seemed irresistible
to the boy from the dirt farm in Spokane. I was just five and my
brother, Charles, was seven when they sent us to live with my Aunt
Monta in Hawaii, and the divorce was imminent.

One day Dad was flying with two friends and the plane crashed.
He was left for dead, his head resting on the dash with his skull
cracked in half. The rescuers removed the still living pilot and other
passenger. At that point, they heard Dad moaning and realized he
was still alive. They rushed him to the hospital where he was to spend
several months recuperating from his injuries. I think this close
brush with death stirred the old need to live and get the most out of life.

He left Mother and moved to Hollywood, near some of his fraternity brothers. Recuperated from the accident, he sold insurance and
then went to work for a large company providing trainloads of sugar
to ice cream and candy factories. By now, he was in the Hollywood
crowd and was well accepted. We would spend our summers with
him and just have the time of our lives. Beaches, movie stars, freedom, and sunshine. What a contrast to our life with mother's family.
The drudgery of school, discipline, and routine. My grandmother
and grandfather Haines were wonderful people, well monied, until
the depression, but Victorianly strict.

Dad went into the service again, at the beginning of the second
World War . He had to accept the Special Services Branch because of
his age and health. This bothered him as he wanted to see active
duty. Later, he was to become a member of the military government
that ran the occupation of Germany. He had been a member of the
Army Reserve Corp. between wars and so entered as a Captain. His
visits during the war at my sorority house, Alpha Phi, were always a
thrill for me. He was so handsome and I had always dearly loved this
man. Dad was not a great father, rarely there for us, often critical of
us, but I was swept along with the romantic nature of his personality.

As the war was ending, he entered Germany, just behind the
fighting troops, as a member of the Occupying Forces. Dad was first

stationed in Memmingen, then Karslruhe, and then Stuttgart where he was the Assistant Director of Military Government for Würtemberg/Baden. It was when he first went to Stuttgart that he had decided to have me join him so he could have a house there. Only officers who had dependents could have private requisitioned German homes. Dad lived in Germany until 1957, eventually leaving the War Department to join the State Department and then to civilian life.

It was while he lived in Germany that he met, and later married, the Countess Paula Clary-Aldringen. They had been friends for several years before her husband, Count Marcus Clary-Aldringen, returned from Russia where he had been a prisoner of war. Following her eventual divorce from Marcus, and the death of Dad's second wife, Bebe, in 1956, they began to see each other again.

He had married Bebe Jorgenson of Pasadena, California, in 1955 in Frankfurt. She had been his great love when he was married to Mother, and one reason for the divorce. Unfortunately, Bebe was quite ill when they married and she died after a year or more. From her estate, Dad bought a fishing resort in Mexico, Rancho Buena Vista, on the Baja peninsula. He developed the resort from a shack and a few buildings into one of the most popular fishing resorts in the area. Here he was the *grand patron*. The little boy from Spokane had finally made it. He was quite wealthy and famous people were his guests and friends. He died in a California hospital in 1977 at age eighty-one. To the very end he felt he would never die.

I was spending the summer of 1946 at home in Everett, Washington, when the final papers came allowing me to sail to Germany. It seemed like a Hollywood script at the time. Dad had arranged for me to meet with members of the Ritter family in Hollywood, California. The Ritters were owners of several large newspapers, including the Los Angeles Times. They wished to repay him for rescuing their sister, Frankie Leuttich in Germany, by entertaining me. This would be a slight detour on the way to New York. Preparing for the trip, Mother and I went shopping in Seattle for my wardrobe. We had our usual argument over styles. She had always wanted a fussy, femme fatale daughter, while I was strictly tailored. With luck, an understanding clerk managed a compromise and we were both happy. I felt beautifully outfitted and could hardly wait for the trip to begin.

Countess Paula Clary-Aldringen

On August 16, 1946, just after my twenty-first birthday, I was packed and ready for my new world. It was a tearful goodbye for my grandmother, Edith Haines. It was also one of the rare times I had seen her cry. Mother drove me to the train station in Seattle. I really do not remember what we talked about. I can guess though, as she was a very supportive lady. It was difficult saying goodbye to her. I felt such a mixture of *getting on with it,* and yet a reluctance at leaving her

for such a long time. The length of the trip was couched in terms of *one year*. My mother could be as stoic as Gram so she kept us from losing our composure. Nevertheless, I knew the minute I was out of sight she would have her cry. When I was finally seated in the train, several people asked if the lady waving from an overpass belonged to me. That was the only time tears came as I saw my mother blowing kisses and also her nose. Nevertheless, I was off to see the world.

At the stop in Portland, my two ancient Aunts, Ina Mayer and Becky Haines, were there to greet me. They were waving while hanging onto each other for support. Bless them as they had made the supreme effort to be sure to wish me well. Aunt Ina had lead a colorful life, for such a diminutive sister of my grandmother Haines. She had left her husband, Uncle Bill, to marry a world traveler named Goober. How she had made it past the name was always a mystery to the family. What made him worth leaving Uncle Bill was also beyond all of us. Perhaps we both shared a need to broaden horizons. They had traveled to Africa and gone deep into the jungle to some tribe. There they had both come down with a fever and Goober had died. The natives loved Aunt Ina and had brought her out of the jungle to a doctor. After recovery, she was shipped home where she remarried Uncle Bill, the wanderlust out of her system. I am sure she identified with me on this trip.

Aunt Becky was not too well known to me as she seemed to stay aloof from family ties. She was the sister of my maternal grandfather, Charlie Haines, deceased. She was a very likeable lady, who had never married, and had supported herself by secretarial work. Aunt Becky would visit Aunt Ina, but that was about it. Later, in the early fifties, Mother and I went to find her and we were shocked at her deterioration. She knew Mother however did not seem to recognize me, and this was to be expected. Nevertheless, this proud, independent lady was tottering, dirty and unkempt, and living in a foul smelling one-room apartment. It was so bad that when she mentioned going to lunch, Mother and I made some weak excuse and took an early departure. We both forever felt guilty about this and the fact that we could not help her.

Back on the train, I waved to the elderly dears and wondered if I would ever see them again. Two days later Nellie Hiersch's chauffeur met me at the station and drove me to her lovely home in Holly-

wood. Nellie was a sister of the Ritters. She had a dinner party for me that evening that was really enjoyable, as the guests took such an interest in my trip. They seemed to be wondering, as I did, what lay ahead. Next morning the maid brought me breakfast and a message that Nellie and I were going shopping. It seems the family felt I should have a fur coat (my first) to fit into the European social milieu. I was really being well primed for the life I would lead for the next three years. We drove to one of Hollywood's finest fur salons where the models paraded their coats. I tried them all on and then chose a lovely full-length Russian dyed squirrel, with the approval of the models. Mink was there, but extremely costly due to the war. The coat I chose cost nine hundred and twenty-five dollars. That was a large down payment on a modest home in those days.

That evening several movie producers entertained us royally, one even offering me a position on his staff. However, nothing was going to stop my trip. Well, perhaps if he had offered me a role in the movies! But he did not. In the next few years there were to be many exciting offers that would have changed the course of my life. I cannot help but wonder what might have been different if I had accepted anyone of them.

CHAPTER II

NEW YORK

The next morning, August 20, 1946, we drove to the train station for my trip to New York. As I write, I wonder why I was not flying. My best guess is it was due to my father's thriftiness when it came to his children. Nellie had the maid prepare a huge basket of fruit, cheese, and crackers for me that carried me almost across the country. Nellie was a lovely woman with a generous heart. I learned later that she had upgraded my coach ticket to a roomette where I spent a comfortable three days and two nights. On the train, my daydreams were filled with castles, nobility, and the wonders of war-torn Europe. What would it be like? The days passed rapidly, the nights slowly as they did in those little roomettes. The porter was my best company as he was well versed in history and could tell me about Europe. He told others about my coming trip so, when I ventured out, I was immediately involved in discussions of what I might find in Europe.

Dad met me at the New York Train Station on August 23 and gave me a rare compliment-Nellie and her friends had liked me! Perhaps he was surprised! I do not remember the name of our hotel in New York, but we were on the 21st floor. A great view of this busy city in 1946. Fifty taxis to one car and some old trucks still going on hard rubber tires. The business and activity on the streets was staggering. Even then, traffic was heavy all night. Arriving in my room exhausted, I took a short nap. Afterwards, Bill Bender, (one of Dad's old sergeants) and his wife joined us. We joined a Major Bee and his wife, the Countess Eleanore (Nora) Fugger (pronounced Fooger), for drinks at the Savriani Cocktail Lounge.

Nora was the cousin of the Prince Friedrich Carl Fugger, a friend of Dad's in Europe. I suppose I was interested in meeting this Countess. However, Dad had friends in Hollywood who went by the titles of *Count* or *Baron* and everyone knew they were not real. Nevertheless, Nora was a real Countess. She was a friendly, unpretentious person and somehow the title fit her comfortably. I was later to meet her two sisters, the Countesses Rosemarie and Sylvia (Pinki) Fugger in Germany. Rosemarie and I became good friends during my stay in Europe. She later attended college here in the United States. After cocktails, we went on to Bender's home for dinner and an enjoyable evening around the piano singing old songs.

Bill took the next day off to drive us around to see the sights of New York. We had lunch at the St. George Hotel, a monstrous but beautiful building. We also drove out to Fort Hamilton to check on our embarkation and learned that everything was in order, much to my relief. Next, we enjoyed a tour of Coney Island for some knishes at Feltman's, one of the oldest restaurants on the very noisy and crowded walkway. Staten Island was next, then Chinatown with its then totally foreign atmosphere and then on to the Bowery with its shabby buildings and shady pubs. Finally, a tour of Grenwich Village where our artist cousin Bob Ades had started his career.

Back at the hotel, I telephoned a Beta boyfriend, Merlyn Nelson, from college who was attending the Yale Law School. He and I went out on the city to a marvelous dinner, and then a play starring Ingrid Bergman. Could life offer more? Indeed it would, but it was nice to be with Merlyn and remember old times. That night we wedged Merlyn into Dad's room's hallway on a little cot, as it was too late to send him home.

The next day Merlyn and I toured Radio City and the Plaza. From the top of Radio City Tower we could see New York for miles around. A very stirring view. We then walked through Central Park to see the zoo and to sit on a bench and watch the people go by. Such a pleasant man. I cannot imagine why we are not still together. Later, we had dinner at Longchamps and then, after fond farewells, he left for home.

The following day Dad and I again went to Fort Hamilton for further clearance procedures. Afterwards, Dad went back to the hotel while I had to stay for my third series of shots. For the second time,

I had misplaced my papers! I had never been one to organize and later was to have some difficult times without necessary ID. These were painful shots! You might think I would learn something from this! I felt then that I must be protected for life from smallpox and whatever else they gave me. My first solo trip on the subway was an experience, but I made it back with a feeling that I could now find my way around the world. Subways are like that! One thing though, a person does have to be adept at getting in and out of those subway doors in a hurry.

That evening Dad; one of his girlfriends, Virginia Kincaid of Washington, D.C.; one of his captains, Owen Martin from Stuttgart; and I went to such places as Samuel's Bowery Follies where the old stars of Vaudeville still entertained. This was *slumming*, as we called it then. The names of this motley group of old actors and actresses were vaguely familiar. Nevertheless, they were young in spirit although old in face and voice. We soon had a table surrounded with many legends of the past and were sorry when it was time to move on. We then went to Billy Rose's Diamond Horseshoe Club for the floor show, which lacked the mood of the Bowery. Owen and I left the others and headed for the famous Stork Club. I had seen it so

New York, Sammy's Bowery Follies, author, Captain Owen Martin, Virginia Kincaid, Colonel, and some old vaudevillians.

often in the movies. It was everything that Hollywood said it would be, glamour and famous names at every table.

Later, feeling the *spirit*, martinis in hand, we talked a milkman, (it was early morning) into taking us through Central Park. This was a slight variation from his route in his horse drawn truck. This was much more fun than hiring one of the many horse drawn taxis standing there. The park was well lighted by the street lamps and the coming dawn. Horseback riders were already having their morning hacks. In those years, there were no joggers or runners. I think the park police would have taken after them assuming they were running away from some *evil deed*. It was all very beautiful, not like the dangerous place of today. It was romantic.

The date was now the 27th of August and we were anxious to begin our trip, but we were also enjoying New York and looking up old friends. Julie Carpenter Jones, of Medford, Oregon, and her very handsome husband took us to dinner at Luchow's. Julie was my sorority sister. In fact, she had been responsible for my pledging Alpha Phi sorority at Oregon. Our dinner was of fine German food and I decided I would enjoy German cuisine. After a good time of sharing memories of college, Dad and I returned to the hotel for some needed sleep.

The next day, supposedly our last in New York, we shopped, wrote letters, and called home to reassure the family that I was on course. On the 29th, in a flurry of excitement, Dad and I were met by Bill Bender and driven to Staten Island for our departure time and to start the process of boarding our ship, the S.S. Holbrook. Dad did most of the paperwork and we boarded the ferry to Terminal Island. It was a beautiful day looking back at New York, watching the busy ships, tugs, and barges. Nevertheless, the most memorable moment was seeing the Statue of Liberty. In those days, we were very proud to be Americans and we had won the horrible wars on both sides. We were winners, life was good, and it had direction again. This statue represented all of these feelings and more. We all were silent as we sailed past her.

What a sinking feeling upon arrival at the embarkation point as they told us that we would not sail for another four or five days. What a blow, as we had checked out of our hotel and now could not find any decent rooms in New York. Dad had arranged for us to be bil-

leted at Fort Hamilton. That night we had dinner at the Officers' Club with a Colonel Bonds, a friend of Dad's. Afterwards, I was to have a liberal education through the thin walls of my room at the barracks. I was in the women's barracks where I found myself in immediate trouble as an officer's dependent. Oh Nellie, I needed an *upgrade.*

I am not a snob-never believed I had a reason to be. However, instantly I found myself typed as *upper classery.* It did not help that they assigned me my own room while the other women were all sharing one large barracks room. I stayed in my room, a coward, and began to write a journal to entertain myself. However, their words were impressive with profanity and sexual reference. I learned a lot about these women who had not seen their husbands for several years.

Sleep helped, but it was soon dawn. The boarding authorities surprised us by escorting us to the ship, our S.S. Holbrook. The government had converted her from a smaller trade vessel to a troop ship. As we boarded, the excitement was overwhelming. This was my first trip on a ship since my brother and I were sent to the Hawaiian Islands when our parents were separating. Our Aunt Monta Chamberlain from Maui had come to get us to ease the shock of the separation of our parents. I do not think we really understood what was happening and thoroughly enjoyed the trip. I was five and my brother, Charles, was seven. Strangely these were the same ages as Dad and Aunt Monta when their mother left them. We were two waifs who spent a year as natives on the island before returning to our mother. The memories came alive again, but now I was twenty-one and free to make my own decisions. Although my father would try to reverse that many times.

Dad was led first to his cabin where he was to share the space with three other officers. Then they showed me my quarters for the trip. Down in the hull, under the water at times, was a large barracks-style room. Some three dozen women and children would be settling into double bunks bolted onto steel floors. They were not to arrive until the day before we sailed. That was all right. I could choose a lower bunk, and I was preoccupied with the coming voyage rather than our Spartan quarters. The showers were at least private, although cold water only. We had narrow lockers for our clothes, but most belongings remained in our trunks or suitcases. Despite the quar-

ters, this ship seemed a beauty to me, although dwarfed by the other liners nearby.

The next day we decided we could not just sit on the ship with so much yet to do, so we caught a train to Washington, D.C.. There we were met by Dad's friend, Virginia, and her father, Commander Kincaid. They were a lovely and energetic family and we felt quite at home with them. The city was so quiet in contrast to New York, and beautiful. This was a place to be very proud of as an American. Dad and I stayed at the Wardman Hotel that night, a sedate place full of politicians. We had an early breakfast and then went to the lobby to meet our cousin, Bob Ades.

Bob had always been my brother's and my favorite. He had lived with us in Hollywood at one time. He was a great artist and in Hollywood lived as a Bohemian, dressed in sneakers and torn clothing. He was an early day hippie, but with morals and a work ethic. I remember that he always fell in love with his lady subjects. When he finished the painting, he would be devastated as the *affair* was also finished. Bob never had money and also stole from our piggy banks, but we loved him.

It was a shock to see him as he was now working in the United States Consulate and wearing a suit, tie, and shoes! Someone had ruined him! He informed us that he was in the process of transferring to Paris, France, with his family and then to the American Consulate in Spain. We were sure to be seeing each other. Underneath the business demeanor he was still the artist. What a relief! It was a joy to tour the art museums with Bob and remember old times.

Later we had cocktails and laughs with the Kincaids and their friends. Dinner was at the Army and Navy Club and we had swordfish steaks and champagne. We went on to the Statler Cocktail Lounge for dancing and an evening of fun.

On the 1st of September we breakfasted with the Kincaids and then went off for a tour of the city. They drove us around the Capitol, Rock Creek Park, Million Dollar Bridge, Lincoln Memorial, Mount Vernon, and the Washington Monument. Also, we went through the very beautiful National Art Museum, and many more sites. Very impressive for me! We had dinner that evening at a Chinese restaurant and later played bridge at the Kincaids. Again, a lovely family and we were so appreciative of their rescuing us from

the spartan ship. It was also the first time that I had played bridge with my father and we did quite well despite my sorority style bidding.

The next morning we said goodbye to our friends and returned to the ship. We were a bit apprehensive that it might not be there, but there she was and we boarded for the last time. Dad had been complaining about having to sacrifice a comfortable trip back to Germany by plane. By coming with me, he was having to put up with eight hundred or so women and children. Still, he was certainly the popular officer helping the ladies with their questions, etc. I thought perhaps I might be the bored one.

We had come back to a little excitement. Two women were already in the brig for drunken conduct. They seemed to have lost their control with the crew around and had been found in the lifeboats with sailors. Other ladies were seasick even before leaving port. It was going to be an interesting trip. Dad and I rummaged around and found a little confiscated coffee in the galley. We enjoyed some conversation with a military police lieutenant and two new lady friends. However, the commanding officer, a full Colonel, came in and Dad and I had to sneak out the back door. These were not our premises. The women with children were to come aboard tomorrow.

September 3, 1946, and the thundering herd arrived on board and took over the ship. Two hundred or more curious, tired, and ornery children were milling about. Draw your own conclusions. There was not only bedlam, it was a long day! It was not until eight o'clock that evening that the Ship's Captain gave the orders that we were soon to be underway. Our long awaited departure had begun! Tired and hysterical women and children lined the railings on the starboard side of A, B, and C decks. A very bored, lackluster army band on the dock played *Over There*, and other music.

From out of the clamor came the *toot, toot,* of our sibling tug, signaling forward to the engines. Then, just before the moment of first movement, it was as if we had become a ghost ship. There was not a sound in that pause for breath as the passengers, and the ship herself, filled hesitant lungs for the future ahead. Then with screams, whistles, shrieks, and bells the last hawser dropped from the wharf and we moved!

Almost every emotion experienced in a lifetime was implanted

on the faces of the people around me. My own emotions were turbulent. It was the old question? Had I done the right thing? Nevertheless, as the pier dropped away and we headed into the narrows, I tossed such thoughts to the winds. Not only was it too late to turn back, but I was also experiencing the thrill of the adventurer. So I took a firm grip on the railing and watched the last tangible bit of America slowly fade in the coming night.

Down the narrows we went and into the ocean with the silver of the moonlight over the smooth water. Dimly we could see the skyline of New York behind us, while, on the left, the bright lights of Coney Island seemed to want to call us back. It was as though Coney Island represented all of the gaiety, independence, and freedom of America. The red lighted buoys on our course seemed to toll out the somber mood of the crippled country awaiting us ahead.

CHAPTER III

AT SEA

The S.S. Holbrook was formerly the U.S. Taft and had made passenger and cargo runs along the West Coast. What luxury she might have had was removed and she had been converted to a troop ship. The few staterooms left were on B deck and were allotted to the ranking military aboard, and to two generals' wives traveling with us. C deck was for pregnant women and mothers with small children. These rooms usually had six to eight bunks. D deck, where by the grace of lady luck I managed to be, was for the rest of the members. Luck, because any lower in the ship and we would have been under the water line. I was a bit phobic regarding living under water.

My compartment had thirty-six bunks. These bunks were attached from floor to ceiling, and consisted of a piece of canvas that supported a hard mattress. We had military issue blankets and sheets and there was a ladder for the upper bunk occupant. We also had three portholes that could be opened during calm weather. Someone always forgot to close them and more than once we had a shower and small flood. We had about seven young children and eight teenagers in our compartment. After getting into a routine, this situation was not so bad.

On the ship were two dining rooms or *mess halls*. We ate in the forward mess that was originally the officers' hall and it was quite pleasant. The aft (in the stern) mess hall was not as good. It was terribly crowded and always too warm. The people had to sit on benches and the service was poor. So, again Dad and I were lucky. Our food was decent although it seemed to come in lumps and meat

was usually pork, pork, and more pork. That may have been when I developed an allergic response to pork for the rest of my life. Topside consisted of a promenade deck, a boat deck, and a sun deck where we spent most of our time. We also had a very pleasant lounge on B deck with tables and comfortable chairs. In the evenings, they had movies in the dining rooms, and they were recent films. Nurseries and playrooms were also available for the children. Overall, there had been thoughtful planning for the convenience of the travelers. The Queen Mary it was not.

It was a lark, until we were clear of land and on the open ocean, to rock and roll with the erratic sea. Many passengers were seasick. Thank God I have never been seasick! There was no land in sight. Our world was all sky, and the water was like marble with foam and dark greens. At night the ship's lights illuminated the water and we could see flying fish skimming in all directions. I spent most of my time on the upper decks. Many friends were to be made. Games and movies were available. Dad always found liquor somewhere, so we had some great parties. This was good practice for what lay ahead—many grand parties in castles and palaces. We were invited to the captain's cabin one afternoon for tea and later he showed me the bridge. This was Captain Lutz, a Swedish fellow and very courteous. The Kincaids had sent me six huge mums as a farewell gift, and, since I had no place for them, I gave them to the captain.

One night we watched a movie in our dining room. We sat on wooden folding chairs in about five rows across the room. The ranking army Colonel (Dad was still a major then) sat alone in front of us. We were having a very rough sea when the movie started and it grew worse. Eventually, the ship began to rock sideways. We would slide to one wall and then back to the other. The Colonel, without others to brace him, began sliding the full length of the room, back and forth. We really had to bite our tongues not to laugh aloud, as that would not be *protocol.* The Colonel acted as though nothing was wrong, maintaining a composure we did not share. Finally, some officers in the front row hung onto his chair and he settled down to our short slide.

About three days out, a woman became ill and was transferred to a homebound ship that night. It was a dramatic scene with floodlights illuminating the water. The patient was strapped onto a stretcher in a life boat and then was lowered into fairly calm seas. The little boat seemed so small as it moved between the two ships.

We all let out a cheer when they arrived safely on the deck of the other ship. Secretly, we must all have felt relief that we could now continue on our course.

Dad had *encouraged* me to take a course on the German language, so I did! It was a good idea too, as I soon learned that Dad had no ear or tongue for foreign languages. I, on the other hand, could pick up a language quickly, although primarily by ear. They held the lessons in one of the ship's lounges. What a strange language, *grrrrs* and *achs*, etc. A few ladies that shared meals and parties joined me and we became, we thought, proficient in beginning Deutsch.

We were also allowed to shoot skeet off the stern of the ship. I had never done this, nor fired a shotgun. I just knew about BB guns and had used .22 rifles. It was very important to learn to tuck the shotgun well into the shoulder to avoid a painful bruise. Dad was a good teacher. This was also great practice for the hunting days that lay ahead. Dad took the first go and did well despite the pitching motion of the boat. I think he made eight out of twelve pulls. Of course, we never knew which direction the skeet would take, making it a challenging sport.

When it was my turn, I decided to really try to please the Colonel so I concentrated very hard. *Pull, hit it. Pull, hit it!* This went on as I racked up a perfect score of twelve. Suddenly, I ran out of concentration, and suggested I was through. However, old Dad liked the attention we were getting and pushed me on. I missed the next five and he, seeming embarrassed, finally told me to quit. This was the backlash of our relationship. If it was my idea, I would do well. If it was his, or if he pushed me, I usually quit.

We were thirteen days on the sea before the exciting cliffs of Dover loomed ghostly white in the moonlight as we eased past. They told us that this could be a dangerous time as mines were still floating in the channel. They also told us that an American ship had run aground the previous night. This was Friday the 13th! However, earlier in the day I had *inspected* the bridge and met our famous pilot, *Down Wind* Downy. He was English, surprise, and while he and Dad chatted, Captain Lutz showed me the many instruments of our ship. At least it was reassuring that the ship had an instrument called a *demagnetiser* that grounded us so that we did not attract mines! Feeling safer, it was a glorious sight to see these chalky cliffs and remember them in so many stories in history.

CHAPTER IV

GERMANY

We arrived at our first German port, Bremerhaven, on September 14, 1946, after steaming through the North Sea. All around us were awesome and grotesque signs of bombed ruins, rubble, and sunken ships still in the harbor. Ragged and hungry looking German laborers scurried aboard, more intent on picking up cigarette butts than the luggage. Cigarettes, in any form, were highly prized for trading. I remember how shocked I was to see these Germans as everyday people. War propaganda had indoctrinated me to believe they were all helmeted bullies. I slipped them a few cigarettes and practiced my German lessons with the then happy fellows. Later in the afternoon, little German children came to the dock to beg for candy and gum. They were ragamuffins with torn clothing and socks at half mast in shoes that looked ancient. We threw candy to them, and there was a mad scramble to get the *chocolade.*

On the 15th we were allowed to go ashore to our waiting train. Dad was the ranking officer with a female dependent, so he and I were to go down the gangplank first. I had the usual cold water shampoo, had dressed in my better black dress and heels, and was ready to step graciously onto German soil. A band played and Dad waved me ahead of him, and down I went, crash! Somehow I had developed a rolling pitch to my balance, and the high heels after *tennies* were not helping me. I was staggering like a drunk out of tune with the band. I could hear Dad barking and hissing at me to straighten up. I tried, but for the life of me I could not help but pitch and fall several more times. No one laughed and that told me

One cleared street

We lived amidst this destruction

Views of German cities, a chair on the third floor

I was not the only one with sea legs. Finally I gained a semblance of control and stood on the solid ground of Germany.

Our train was on the tracks in front of the debarking pier area. It had compartments so we had some privacy and a chance to catnap. My sea legs and equilibrium seemed better when the train was in motion. We went straight through horrifying scenes of bombed, leveled streets. Gray and shuffling people appeared purposeless. Their faces were emotionless. Even their clothes were depressingly grey, brown or black. The scenes from our train were of a ruined country with peasants and oxen plowing every available garden area for food. The whole mood was depressing and dismal. Until a person has seen such devastation, there does not seem adequate or graphic words to describe it. If one were to imagine one's own city leveled, with just mounds and no streets left, it is a vague description. A person would not know their location if the sun were not out. All direction is lost, as all familiar markers are gone!

The countryside in the rural areas seemed mostly untouched by the war, except for bombed bridges or an overturned tank or truck. Often we caught glimpses of beauty and color that seemed inappropriate for the time. Streets were mostly cobblestones, and oxen pulled large carts as they have done for centuries.

Only one scene added a comical twist to this devastation. In one part of Frankfurt, terribly bombed, the side of an apartment building was gone. On the third floor hung a precariously balanced bathtub. There was no floor under it. Just the water and drainpipes supported it. Later, when the American movie people came to produce pictures, they wanted to use this scene as an advertisement for their movies. The idea was to have one of the stars sitting in the tub as though bathing. The military government turned the idea down as the building was too unstable. What a tremendous task lay ahead for the Germans to rebuild their country. Depressing? Yes, but my mood was not down as I looked forward to my new life.

STUTTGART

It was late when we arrived at our home at Richard Wagner Strasse. The house seemed modern and fairly new for what I expected in Europe. A brick wall around its large perimeter guarded it. No lights were on and the streets were also dark, so it seemed a bit

overwhelming. However, inside was comfortable and Dad's usual Hollywood flair was present in the modern furniture and paneled walls with fluorescent lighting. A fireplace was central in the living room and parquet floors added warmth. He had found some oriental rugs that accented the parquet. We stepped out the French doors to a small patio area overlooking Stuttgart. A winding path went down the hill to terraced gardens and fruit trees. This was a lucky area as it had escaped the bombing that so obviously lay below us.

Dad had the master bedroom off the dining area and mine was upstairs. Besides my room, there was a guest bedroom, a bath, a large attic area, and a small closet that later became my photography darkroom. The windows were small in my room, but there still was a view of the hillside and it was private. Exhausted, we were unpacking when the telephone rang and we were invited for dinner at Colonel Dawson's, Dad's superior officer. This invitation was welcome as we could not just run to a store or to a restaurant. Dad had been away for over a month so the help had been on vacation, and there was no food in the house. The only clothes I had for the evening were the ones traveling with me. My trunk would be weeks in arriving. We could not go to a shop and purchase clothes as everything was either black market or parachute silk. Also, we were not supposed to buy from the Germans. Parachute material often came from parachuting fliers shot down by the Germans. Dad was friends with Angelo Hommelbacher, owner of a large shoe factory near Stuttgart. Angelo was a great party man, but his shoes were clogs, heavy massive things that were ugly. I was so glad that I had carried my best clothes with me, but it left me very formal or in slacks and *tennies*. I had very little selection in between.

Colonel Dawson's home was three blocks from us and he gave us a warm welcome. Other officers there were obviously delighted to see a young American woman. I was rapidly to learn that a Jane Wilson, her sister, and I were the only three single American ladies in the area. It was apparent that I was overdressed that evening, but the men appreciated it. The servants served a rather basic menu as the commissary was still military and did not offer much variety. Eggs were packed in isinglass in those days and might be two or three months old. Out of a dozen, two or three might be edible. They were mostly used for cooking. The black market was the source of fresh

eggs, paid for by American cigarettes.

I was not used to the strong liqueurs, nor the concentrated (thick) after-dinner coffee served in demitasse. Therefore, enjoying the attention I was receiving from the men, I was more than embarrassed as I took a drink of orange Curacao. I found it too strong and then tried to lessen it with a drink of coffee. The result, I quickly learned, was a terrible burning in my throat and a great loss of composure. However, everyone was very considerate and we all had a good laugh. I was to become friends with many of those men and to become one of the *group*.

Exhausted, I slept a little late the next day, until five o'clock in the evening. I was up just in time to greet Dad as he returned from his office and head over to Colonel Dawson's for dinner, or was it breakfast? This time I was better prepared from past experience. Thank heavens, as present that evening was the Consulate General Dana Hodgdon and his wife, and the former Governor of Maine, Sumner Sewall. Governor Sewall was to be our military governor for one and a half years. Also, a Mr. Meede was there. He was quite charming and we were having a good time together. I noticed several people watching us and later learned he was President Truman's top aide. I understand he died the next year and he is buried alongside General Patton. We enjoyed them all, but especially, Governor Sumner Sewall. He, and his wife Martha, were to be our good friends during their stay in Europe.

Dad had evidently had a talk with Colonel Dawson and learned that he must return his German car, an Opel, immediately. The Military Government had requisitioned it for return to the Germans. The American military were reassigned American cars or Volkswagens. Dad was very upset, for two reasons. First, he felt that the Americans were losing *face* by going to the lesser Volkswagen. Secondly, he had illegally driven the Opel to LeHavre, France, to catch his ship to New York when he came to meet me. Dad felt very pressured by this threat to his position. Before we could settle down from our journey, we were on our way the next evening, by train, to Paris.

Catching that train had not been easy. Somehow we missed the train at the depot in Stuttgart. We rushed back to the car, at least Herr Braun, our driver, had not yet left. We went at breakneck speed

Governor Sumner Sewall, Military Governor of Würtemberg/Baden

to catch the train at the next stop. I felt somehow swept along with little control. It was dusk and as we came around a corner in a small village there was a man ahead of us on a bicycle. Herr Braun honked but did not slow down. The man did not waver, and we hit him. Bicycle and man went flying. It looked as though we had really hurt him. However, Herr Braun helped him up, dusted him off, and de-

clared him all right. Dad gave the man twenty dollars for his wrecked
bike. It seems the man was deaf and, of course, did not hear us. He
seemed pleased by the money, we were relieved that he was all right,
and off we went now further behind our train. We did finally catch it,
and what a relief to settle back and enjoy a calmer ride.

PARIS-SEPTEMBER 1946

Arriving in Paris, by now bedraggled, tired, and a bit overwhelmed by all of the changes in my recent life, I was then plunged
farther into unfamiliar territory. My first impression of Paris was that
it was quite dirty. Things were still very grim from the war in that city.
However, as we drove past Notre Dame, the Tomb of the Unknown
Soldier, the Arc De Triomphe, and other beautiful sites, I mellowed.
What at first seemed ugly, gray, sooty, and too old, became a vision of
history and greatness. These were all symbols of beauty and romance
from the past. Ah, Paris' charm was there despite the ravages of war.
How we Americans love our clean new buildings, and seldom appreciate the beauty of age and history.

We took a taxi to see some French friends of Dad's, Roger and
Jackie Perron. Roger was the son of the owner of Pernod wines and
liqueurs of France. They were lovely young people and I felt at ease
with them immediately, although they did not speak English. Dad
had not previously explained to me, in his way, that he was leaving
me here until he could get to LeHavre and drive the car back. A matter of perhaps two days! At least Roger spoke some German and I
had taken the German classes on the ship.

I had many things to learn about the European culture and habi-
tat. In those days (and still in some situations today) the toilet was
usually downstairs in a small room with a sink. The bathroom was upstairs with a tub, sink, and a *bidet'*. This is a half toilet appearing thing
without the tank. It has a fountain like pipe that sprays the private
areas when the faucet is turned on. As time passed, after Dad had
left, Roger, Jackie and I were awkwardly trying to carry on a conversation that several two year olds would have easily understood. Finally, I made it known, politely, that I wished to *wash the hands*.

Now I had no idea that the toilet was separate from the bathroom. When Jackie took me upstairs and left me, I could not under-

stand where they had put it. I quietly opened the bathroom door and tried a few doors near by, without success. Finally, I began to study the *bidet* with some urgency and decided this was it. It was not until that evening that Jackie, who must have been becoming increasingly concerned, showed me the *closet* to the relief of both of us. I later learned, after telling my story to several mutual sufferers, that most of the American soldiers had taken for granted that the *bidet* was for washing sore feet.

Dinner was another lesson. Jackie served a plate of cold meats and the wonderful French breads and wine. I assumed that this was the meal and I had three helpings. Next came a wonderful salad and a cup of soup. By now stuffed, I made a polite effort to continue with the meal. A roast of beef, potatoes, vegetables, and a casserole then followed this! The wine was helping a bit, and youth, but it was a struggle not to insult my hosts. The main course was then followed by dessert, followed by cheese and fruit, followed by after dinner demitasse and liqueurs. One other thing, Dad had warned me not to drink the water, but had not told me what else to drink. I became quite thirsty despite the fruit juice and coffee for breakfast. As a result, I drank a good deal of wine, whisky, and liqueurs. This kept me in a quite happy, if not foggy, condition.

The next day Roger and Jackie took me to meet Maurice D'Okhuysen, the owner of many famous jumping horses. He was a friend of the Perron family and a very kind person. He took me to the place where they trained his horses. In one area was a very large circular track with jumps every fifty or so feet. They released a young horse, free of saddle or bridle, into this enclosed track. A trainer would crack a whip to get the youngster moving. If the young horse easily cleared the jumps and showed a talent for this, they put him into training. If he used avoidance or crashed, they put him up for sale. They wanted horses who were natural jumpers and those that would enjoy their work. We later attended a steeple chase that we viewed from the comfort of an elegant club room. I made several bets on Maurice's horses and, with his advice, won a few francs.

That evening we all went to Maurice's home for dinner. Dad had arrived from LeHavre with the car, so the pressure of trying to communicate was lessened. We finally (the French enjoy late meals) sat down to dinner, after cocktails, at nine o'clock that evening. Having

learned my lesson at Roger and Jackie's, I ate sparingly as they served
the courses. The cook's name was Daisey, and she decorated all en-
trees with the daisy flower. She was an enormous woman, and I remember the floors groaning as she moved about serving us. The
food was excellent and plentiful, so close to war-torn Germany. How
the French hated the Germans and were not interested in sharing
their fare with the former enemy. Despite my requests for small por-
tions, the cook heaped our plates with the delicacies and, at 11:00
p.m., we struggled from the table.

Dad, of course, remarked about my drinking when we left
Roger's and when I explained why, he did laugh. We stayed in the
Hotel George V (*Cinq*) that night. This was a lovely and grand place,
despite the war's deprivations. They treated us with charm and grace
and we relished it. Out on the town, many people approached us
wanting to buy my shoes or purse, etc. We spent the day shopping
for things that were not available to us in Germany. Obviously, there
were shortages in France too, but nothing like we had in Germany.

Dad thought a part of my education should be a trip to the Follies Bergere. This was a theater where nudity was considered art and
it was done quite tastefully, for the most part. It was like Erroll
Carol's club in Hollywood with lavish costumes and headdresses.
There was much dancing and there were plays set to music. Nudity
was unheard of in the United States, but was no stranger to France.
Dad spent more than usual for tickets, to get us *good seats. Hmmmm.*
We were pretty close to the stage and, before the show started, he
handed me his Leica camera and told me to get pictures of the
scenes. This did not seem much of a challenge at the time so, of
course, I practiced focusing to do a good job. I never questioned why
he was not going to take the pictures himself.

There was a good deal of fanfare and the dancers were at first
prancing about the stage in exotic gowns. Then there were some
lovely three-dimensional scenes as though staged in a gigantic picture frame. They so intrigued me that I forgot to take pictures and
Dad did not remind me. These were not what he was interested in,
per se. As the show progressed, the costumes became skimpier and
would eventually disappear entirely. However, the men were still in G
strings, sigh! About this time, as the women shed their outfits, I began to get an elbow in the ribs. *Take that one,* and *get that.* Each time

I had to take a picture I had to stand up to see over the heads in front. It became more embarrassing as the women became more scantily clothed. As usual, a heated, whispered argument arose between the two of us. My complaint of the attention drawn to me by standing up was overruled by his need for the *artwork*.

Now, years later, I look at these scenes and laugh. His more prurient needs obviously overshadowed Dad's artistic interests. I do remember that the whole show was done well, and I enjoyed the extraordinary physiques of the male dancers.

We left early the next morning and had a beautiful drive back to Stuttgart. However there was the usual confusion of finding one's way out of Paris. The city has many circular streets and many branches shooting off the avenues. With so much traffic and speed, we must have gone around eight or nine times before getting the right avenue. These trips were one of the few times that Dad and I seemed to enjoy each other's company. We bought good bread, wonderful cheese and wine, and munched as we drove or stopped for picnics along the rivers.

Occasionally the car would run low on gas and we had to stop and refill the tank from jerry cans of gas strapped to the car. Gasoline stations were not to be found and so we always carried our own.

A familiar scene, a jerry can and spare tire

We had to filter the gas through an old felt hat, as the gas usually had water added to increase the sale. It was also to hide the fact that someone had *borrowed* a gallon or more. This filtering process took precision or there was a loss of valuable gasoline, or the car stalled. I often wondered why we did not blow up from the fumes of that felt hat stored in the car trunk.

As we drove along, we passed centuries old castles and houses still decorated with geraniums. Along the little cobblestone roads and in the villages, we stopped to shop and little children would call out, *Americaner*. When we would get back in the car, they would shout *Good-bye* with a French accent. Very friendly people.

That night, on the way back to Stuttgart, we drove through the Black Forest. It was both beautiful and frightening. We had heard that there had been some instances of cars being stopped by thieves. They might kill or rob the occupants, or both. There was very little traffic, It was dark, and yet beautiful in that heavy forest. We were both glad when we reached the other side without the motor stalling or other breakdown. We were two tired travelers when we finally arrived back at Richard Wagner Strasse in Stuttgart. Later, Dad was allowed to return the Opel without consequences, Somehow, we acquired a charming Mercedes roadster in its place.

CHAPTER V

RICHARD WAGNER STRASSE

Dad awakened me the next morning, although I could have slept for a week, to introduce me to the servants. The house seemed alive with voices. Windows were being opened. (The habit of the European of hanging rugs and blankets out of windows in order to air them) The smell of something similar to coffee was coming from the kitchen. I was soon to learn that some so called ersatz (ground acorns usually) often extended the coffee. The grounds were used two or three times to get the most from the can. The truth was, the servants loved coffee and could drink it all day. It was only available through our commissary or on the black market. It was usual for the servants to attempt to cover up their drinking of the coffee, hoping we would not notice. I often went into the kitchen at night when the servants were gone and salted the pan of used coffee grounds hidden behind the window curtain. This would cause an uproar from Dad at his morning coffee and, then, fairly decent coffee for a while.

Two women were working around the house. Frau Wagner, who cooked and *managed* the house, and a little lady who seemed to do most of the work, ironing, etc. Frau Wagner met me head-on, and seemed to have laid claim to Dad and the house. This was not too much of a challenge at first, until I became more acquainted with things. Herr Braun, our driver, was there. He was a very serious man who was supposedly a communist. He had great respect for Dad and loyalty to us, to a point.

Once, Herr Braun was driving me home from a hunt in the country. We came through a small village and a gaggle of geese walked

Herr Braun, our German driver.

onto the road. Suddenly we picked up speed, drove right into the flock, and slammed to a stop. Before I could summon my lesser German to the tongue, Herr Braun was out of the car. He was grabbing dead or flailing geese, and throwing them in on top of me. He jumped back into the car and we sped off before anyone could complain.

I doubt that they would have anyway as this was a military car. It might have been reported it though. There I was in the backseat with three large geese, two dead and one starting to come alive. I used my English to berate Herr Braun. We thought he understood English, but he would not speak it. Whether he understood or not, we stopped a good way from the village where he dispatched the geese

and put them in the trunk. This was fresh meat for his family and overrode any concern for me. He did apologize, but I did not forget the incident.

On another occasion, the Countess Clary and I were traveling to a weekend at Babenhausen. Herr Braun was driving us in the army car. How Dad managed to use the car for private purposes amazed me, but I did not usually question it. Well, I did once on a trip into France. However, Paula and I were in the backseat of the car playing Backgammon, my favorite game. Her goal in life was to beat me at this game. It happened rarely. On this day a German truck was ahead of us and obviously slowing down and speeding up to irk us. He also would not let us pass. The German's revenge. Angered by this, I loaded my hunting rifle and gave it to Herr Braun to fire out the window. I thought the driver would think he had a flat and stop.

When Herr Braun fired the rifle, the truck slammed on its brakes while we were going about fifty and Herr Braun had to apply our brakes to avoid him. That threw me against the back door. Then car doors did not have safety handles and the door flew open. Out I went. I remember the look on Paula's face. Things seemed to move in slow motion for me. I saw the outer front door handle going by and grabbed that. I remember my legs dragging alongside the back wheel, and thought how easy it would be to stick my legs under it. I think by then I was in shock. Herr Braun was doing his best to slow the car and finally stopped it. He jumped out with a look of sheer fright. By then, I had released my death grip on the handle and was sitting there taking stock of my condition. Not a bruise, but ruined stockings-and thank God for my heavy tweed coat. It was in shreds where I had dragged on the pavement.

I am not sure what Herr Braun was saying in German, but I could catch something about a gun and an ass. I was never sure if he referred to my bright idea about the gun, or the truck driver.

Our Stuttgart house was really quite nice and surprisingly modern for Europe and this era. The grounds were about an acre and a half and terraced. A wall and fence surrounded the whole property. The front gate worked by ringing the house. The servants would identify the visitor or turn them away if no one was home. I cannot recall ever being worried about any harm coming from the Germans. However, once I was home alone and I heard a noise in the base-

ment in the area of the garage. I went to Dad's room and took his pistol from the drawer and loaded it. Then, taking my shoes off, I crept down the dark steps toward the garage where I could see a light coming from under the door. Calmly placing my hand on the doorknob, with the pistol ready, I threw open the door. I found myself pointing the gun at Herr Braun who had come to clean the car! He froze. As he stared at the gun with disbelief, I thought to myself this paid him back for the goose episode. I do not think Herr Braun had a sense of humor, nor did I, as I lectured him about not announcing himself.

The doorbell at our gate also came in handy when the German tutor or piano instructor would come to give me lessons. The idea of lessons was not mine, but Dad's. He never learned to accept my stubborn qualities as my mother had. I had refused to practice the piano as a teenager and Mother had quit prodding me. I did not want to take piano lessons and I did not like the German language teacher either. So, just before they were due, I would slip into the hallway and turn off the bell at the gate. That worked for a few times until Dad finally gave up. However, not without the usual, "you will be sorry someday!" Of course, *someday* covers many years and now I wish I had learned to play the piano. This was not a very mature way for a twenty-one year old to act, either.

One of the most skilled servants we had was Robert (I am unable to recall his last name) who had been the chef at one of the finer hotels in Hungary. He was married and we hired his wife as our housekeeper. They were housed in our basement apartment. They were a well educated and intelligent couple and not used to this station in life. The wife was perhaps ten years older than I, and tried her best to use this as an advantage. We just did not hit it off, but Dad was impressed with her appearance. Also, we did not want to lose Robert.

We were entertaining practically every night as his cooking was perfection. Our supplies from the commissary were abysmal but we could trade deer meat, etcetera, for needed foods. Robert was also a gentleman. Dad finally gave up trying to put up with the wife's attitude. The feuding was creating too many problems for all concerned. We reluctantly found Robert another place in the open arms of the general's wife. It was slim pickings again. Several months later I was having dinner with a German friend in a German restaurant

that served exceptionally good food despite the shortages. Suddenly a man rushed to our table took my hand and kissed it. It was Robert! He was the chef of the restaurant and had seen me at the table. I was happy that he was still my friend.

One episode that occurred with our servants was atypical of most of the people who worked for us. I do not recall where we found Molly. I was not really impressed with her, but she was hired as our housekeeper/cook and did a fair job. I often wondered about her fur coat as it covered quite worn-out clothing. She never tried to become friendly but went about her work never asking for *specials*. Most of our help would let us know what they needed, or wanted, in sometimes polite and sometimes demanding fashion. She never did either.

As time went on, I became rather suspicious of her but could not pin it down. Dad, as usual, felt I was just carping. However, when I began to miss my bobby pins (a doubled wire that held hair back or in place), I was finally able to get Dad's attention. It might have seemed a minor issue, but it fit into my suspicions. Dad admitted that he had also lost a favorite cigarette lighter and felt that Molly might have it. He worked out a plan with some men in his office and they set a trap for her. Dad left some cuff links on the floor by his bed. Just before she left, noting that the cuff links were gone, he gave a signal to the officer across the street. Molly was stopped outside the gate and searched. They found a deep pocket in the back of her fur coat and there were the cuff links.

The officers took Molly to the German police station and had her booked, despite her pleas that this was just one incidence. The next day the German police and I went to her apartment. She was brought from the police station. What a shock! The place practically looked like our home. There were yards of material that I recognized as some that Dad had bought on his last trip to France. We had not had time to have these made into clothes for us. She had been cutting one meter at a time off the material so we would not miss it.

I was missing some pearls my grandmother had given me. We found some of my lesser jewelry, but not the pearls. The police officer saw a covered place in the wall. There we found some of our kitchen and bathroom articles, but no jewelry. At the end the officer went to the cold stove and glanced inside, but did not open it. Molly seemed anxious, but for some reason I did not press for a further

search. The whole thing was pretty awful and I was glad when it and the trial was over. Molly was behind bars for two years. Nevertheless, I never saw the pearls again.

Ina and Eugene Dochman were our next live-in help. They were displaced people and came with a Schipperke doggy named Teddy, who was their *child*. They had been referred to us by Ella Neher, daughter of the Leuttichs. Eugene was a very serious man who had been a prisoner of war in Russia. Like us, they both had a great fear

Eugene and Ina Dochman, our family servants

of Russians. Ina, in German, would try to tell me of the terrible conditions to which Eugene had been subjected. Rumor had it that she, like Herr Braun, understood English but would not speak it. I never heard her speak English in the three years I knew them.

Ina was very friendly and settled easily into the *family*. She and I often had confrontations over her wearing of slippers when she answered the door, or when we had guests. It became a sign of trouble brewing when she would start wearing them. This happened about every three or four months. There would be a build up of tensions over various things. Then there would be loud words between us and Eugene would enter in if he thought I was too severe with Ina. I would end up firing them both over some minor thing. Then Dad would come along and calm everyone down, which we all wanted anyway. I think it was Ina's way of letting us know that she was not a servant by birth. I hated those slippers.

Eugene's nerves were pretty bad from his experiences during the war. If he were asked to do something and did not understand, he would get a stricken look and freeze. He was easily rattled under pressure. I do not think he was ever really happy with us, although there would be a rare smile. He was good at many things around the house and property. He really disliked being a butler though and I would try to encourage him with smiles and nods. He would usually end up getting Ina to butler for him.

I remember once when we were getting ready to go hunting and we had everything in the foyer. This entrance was slate floored with tiled walls. Eugene picked up one of the rifles and it, somehow, discharged in this tiny room. With luck the bullet went into a corner. I was there with him and can imagine what might have happened if it had ricocheted. We were deafened by the noise. He was so upset he left and Ina had to come and load the car. Despite the problems we did care for them and they were good and loyal to us.

With servants to take care of things, it often left me and many army wives with time on our hands. German nannies took care of the children and were usually quite dependable. Babysitters were unheard of in those days. Parents often found it impossible to understand their children's language of mixed German and English. It did not take the older children long to learn to use this to their advantage. Most of the youngsters picked the language up easily. They

were allowed to play with the German children, who languished over
the American toys and sweets. We had very few problems, and a German child never failed to show up when invited.

Having few home responsibilities led to much social life as we
searched for ways to stay busy and productive. We spent lazy time in
the beauty shops where one could have *the works* for one or two dollars. We had pedicures, manicures, greened hair, etc. One hair-
dresser was a forerunner of the hippy days who liked to surprise his
patrons with purple or green hair dyes. We quickly learned to avoid
his place. A permanent was one dollar and fifty cents. The beauti-
cians used old machines where the curlers were attached by electrical cords from the overhead hood. Once, 1948 I believe, I was having
acute anxiety attacks and had one while attached to one of these
machines. When a person has such an attack, they want to find a safe
haven, which is usually home. I contemplated jumping up and heading for the door but I managed to stay in my chair and weathered
the horrible attack. I still have a mental picture of myself running
away down the street with the machine clattering behind me.

I have always been very modest about my person, and really never
liked to even be seen in a bathing suit. However, one of my American
friends talked me into trying a steam bath with her. I think it is safe
to say I will try anything once! We entered the steamy building and
were met by a strong appearing German lady with a no-nonsense approach. I had reassured myself, in case we had to remove our
clothes, by vowing always to have a towel covering me. We did have
to undress and, covered by our towels, were escorted into a ten-by-
ten room where other ladies were steaming sans towels. My friend
dropped hers, but I tightened mine to the amusement of the experienced group. After wilting in the steam for what seemed a life time,
the husky German woman directed us to another room where we
were to be rubbed down.

I had to give up my towel while she worked on my back. However,
I quickly rearranged it when asked to turn over. Again, a knowing
half-veiled smile made me wonder what was next. Next, was another
room where there was a woman of greater girth and determination.
She stood with a hose to powerwash us with cold water. She told me
to drop my towel! Never! I condescended to drop it as she did my
back, but kept my front covered. The cold spray knocked the breath

out of me, but I did not lose my grip on the towel. When she asked me to turn and drop the towel, *Bitte*, I was fast losing ground. I again noticed there were amused looks all the way around. So, on the second *Bitte*, I dropped the towel. The spray was so cold and intense I just gasped and took it. Grabbing my soaking towel, we were marched back to the steam room. This cold water procedure was repeated three times. Admittedly, these steam baths leave you feeling quite clean and invigorated. However, once was enough for me.

One social group that I joined was comprised of the general's wife, Mrs Funk, and other officers' wives. We took it upon ourselves to try to better the lives of the displaced children in the refugee camps. There we found many displaced people who were from prisoner of war camps, horrible concentration camps, and people who had lost their homes. Former President Hoover had started a Care Package plan and we became a part of this program. As such, we went into these depressing places and searched out families to help. This was not a difficult task. On one such visit, we stumbled upon an army jeep and some U.S. soldiers dealing in the black market with members of the camp. Worse, they were trading in government guns. I still remember the looks on their faces as they saw us. Very poor timing. Of course, they were reported to the authorities. There was no doubt the soldiers were jailed, and possibly court-martialed.

There were many instances of violence, theft, shootings, and looting by these angry, homeless people. Our GIs were also angry because they had fought the war and wanted to go home. Morale was low, venereal disease was rampant. It was rather embarrassing to be at a lovely party, take out a cigarette, and receive a light from a packet of matches advertising VD (venereal disease) protection. This transition from war to peace was not an easy one for the soldiers.

By the end of 1946, there was concern for the safety of the dependents and the Germans. The United States Constabulary was established to control the problem. Major General Ernest N. Harmon was responsible for this organization. He was a flamboyant person who carried a riding crop and wore breeches and boots. His men wore colorful uniforms, a bit reminiscent of the Nazi. They wore helmets with the insignia of the Constabulary-blue and yellow with a big C. Their jeeps also bore this insignia. The Constabulary soldiers went in twos or more and drove around the cities and country sides in these

colorful jeeps. The effect was quite dramatic and caused an immediate reduction in crime. Life became much safer due to this group. The camps were more orderly and the morale of our troops improved. The Constabilary was a no-nonsense group.

Dad was the Assistant Military Governor of *Würtemberg-Baden*. He was in charge of approximately fifteen U.S. officers who were responsible for overseeing the German government in the smaller towns. The German officials were to follow strict guidelines set up by the occupying forces. Each officer had a geographically assigned area with, usually, a fair sized village government to oversee. These officers were housed in requisitioned German homes, as we were, and provided with servants. Dad would visit the branches and supervise the officers' work. He was well liked by his staff, and we would usually have parties with them at our house or theirs. Very often these officers arranged a good portion of our hunting jaunts.

As stated, trouble from the Germans was rare. However in November of 1946 a bomb went off near Dad's office in downtown Stuttgart. This put the army on alert until it was determined it was directed at a German politician. The Germans believed him to be a former Nazi and they wanted him hung. I do not have enough correct data to identify him, nor to comment on what became of him. Usually any such problems were taken care of by the German government officials.

Of course, the American military selected or approved any German in office until 1949. Then, the Allies began pulling back and allowing Germany to rule herself. In just four years, despite a horrible war, they had gained our trust and were allowed this freedom. Still, there was close supervision by our government. However, the Germans had proven they could manage their reconstruction better than the Allies. Also, in September of 1946, the Allies were broadcasting the trials. The prosecution trials of the Nazi officials had begun in November of 1945. These trials were a good reminder to all of the atrocities that had so recently occurred. Regardless, one town did give 70 percent of its vote to a politician who had been a well known Nazi. Actually the Allied powers had a problem in that the former Nazis were often the only experienced politicians, businessmen or tradesmen. This often led to a tendency to overlook or tone down information of the Nazi's background.

On one of our Care groups forays into the displaced persons camps, we found two families with very thin, depressed children. It was my suggestion to have these children come to a luncheon where we were trying to recruit volunteers for our program. I thought it would be better if we showed the condition of those youngsters we were trying to help. It was then my job to pick up the children and Herr Braun drove, of course. We had three little waifs who were obviously frightened, but dear Herr Braun tried to reassure them. At the hall where they were holding the luncheon, I ushered the children in and the ladies took over, some with tears.

The children maintained their depressed appearance though showered with attention, food, and dessert. I remember they did not know what an orange was, and did not seem to like it's taste. Still, the children enjoyed the hot chocolate, cake, and other sweets. They impressed the ladies with their need and we were quite successful in our recruiting efforts. However, on the ride back to the camp, all three children threw up all over themselves and the car. What a mess! Poor Herr Braun had the cleanup detail. These little waif's stomachs were just not used to what we thought all children should know and enjoy. Nevertheless, we had given the ladies the opportunity of seeing the children and this had given us many new volunteers. Our Care program did help many underfed youngsters and their parents.

Meanwhile back at Richard Wagner Strasse, as time went on, I began to take over and Dad seemed content to have me run the household. We had a gardener who spoke *Schwäbisch*, a regional German dialect. It usually seemed a language other than German to my inexperienced ear. I had a terrible time understanding him and would just end up nodding yes. There was such a shortage of decent food for the Germans that we were not able to get fresh vegetables with out paying very high prices. It seemed to me our commissary was not much better regarding fresh produce so we were dependent on our garden. One day the gardener approached me and asked a totally unintelligible question. It was something like *gobac* or *jabac* and *pflanzen*. I knew the latter meant plant. So, in great frustration, I nodded *yes* and we had our whole garden planted in his tobacco. Dad had a few words about that too.

As a result, we had to do just like the Germans. We would go out

Faces of
DISPLACED CHILDREN & WOMEN

into the farm areas and pay high prices for the fresh vegetables. Vegetables were potatoes, rutabagas, turnips, potatoes, carrots, potatoes, and cabbage. It seemed to me most everything had a potato base. Rarely did we ever have leafy or green vegetables. We missed corn on the cob, and the army's creamed corn was abominable. So we would often buy corn from the farmers. The Germans would not think of eating corn. They fed it to the pigs and cattle. Occasionally when we served it as a treat, we had to apologize to our German friends as they considered it an insult.

We did not have frozen foods then. Food from the commissary was tastelessly cooked and canned in huge tins. Ugh! It was no wonder Robert, our chef, was such a prize. Fruit was often a rarity although there were lots of apples, pears, and plums in season. I remember citrus fruit was rare. The grapes were wine grapes and not particularly sweet. The bread was wonderful, and I still enjoy their bakeries when I am there. I remember the German children with three or four loaves of bread, no sacks or wrappers, throwing them to the ground while they stopped to play. On the trams, the bare loaves stuck out of pockets or were carried under an arm.

I have a note from that time that lists the prices for some things at the commissary. Butter, 32 cents; "good steak", 40 cents; and it was eight cents for a pound of coffee. In 1947 the United States government and people provided 60 percent of the German food supply. It was a steadily dropping percentage rate though.

When German friends invited us for a weekend or overnight, we took gifts of food. Coffee, butter, mayonnaise, or things such as shoe polish, candy bars, cigarettes, and soaps were appreciated. Silk stockings, even the heavier nylon stockings we used during the war years, were in great demand. There were so many things they could not get. Also, we did not allow the Germans guns, so when they invited us to hunt, we took ammunition and guns. Of course, Americans were often invited hunting. Our hosts always offered us fresh meat from the hunt. We usually declined as we felt they needed it. We were also given our trophy horns. If we hunted on a farmer's land, we could often trade the deer meat for beef or pork. German beef was tough and not cut as we do. It seemed to lack flavor, possibly due to poor feed. However, it was fresh and appreciated.

CHAPTER VI

BABENHAUSEN

Castle Babenhausen; Photo credit: Rödle Kneuzer

We had been in Stuttgart about two weeks when Dad announced that we would spend the weekend at the Castle Babenhausen, with his friends, the Prince Friedrich Carl and Princess Gunilla Fugger-(pronounced *Fooger*)Babenhausen. This was the third ranking noble family of Germany. Their very colorful history dates from an entry in the city records of Augsburg in 1367. They pass the titles in these families, unlike the royal families, to the eldest son upon the death of the prince. If there are no sons, it can pass to a daughter. The Fuggers had been bankers and had helped many ruling families meet their financial obligations. In this time, they were also timber

owners and had a brewery at the castle.

With my still limited wardrobe, either slacks or party dress, I had to opt for a lovely suit that would normally be worn to a cocktail or dinner party. I was very nervous about meeting this family, and had no experience to tell me know what I would be getting into. Despite my grilling of Dad, I received little assurance about what to expect. He just kept telling me that they would like me. It was about a two-hour drive on the autobahn, which had no speed limit. The Allies and the Germans had bombed the bridges in this region so we had many detours. I was to come to know this road very well in the following years. It led on to Garmisch (the skiing mecca of Bavaria), to Austria, and to Switzerland. On this day, we stopped in Memmingen so Dad could show me where he had first been stationed. He had always liked this little town and had been its first military governor when the American forces captured it. It was while stationed here that he had received word that there might be stolen art in the Castle Babenhausen.

At that time, a great debate was going on regarding the art that Hitler had confiscated from countries he conquered. He had had his trusted officers stash these treasures in various monasteries, churches, castles etc. The Allies were finding and cataloging these collections. Some of our government officials felt they should send this art to the United States, and others felt they should return it to its rightful owners. I am not sure how Dad stood on this issue. He had discovered art treasures in a convent in Buxheim, near Memmingen. In this collection were some pieces that belonged to the Rothschild family, and others were from France. It was Hitler's friend, Rosenberg, who had hidden and stored this cache of tapestries, paintings, and other valuable pieces of art.

Dad was an artist himself and had watched the restoration of some of the pieces. In fact, he had a professional film made regarding his finding of this collection. It was in color and included a filming of the first Catholic religious celebration in Memmingen since the war. He had hired a professional movie producer and it was quite well done. He was never able to market it, however, and later it fell to ruin in the moist air of Mexico.

It took time to verify the real owners of this art collection at Buxheim. Various professionals tried, meanwhile, to restore some

damaged pieces. The rooms where the Germans had stored the art had been occupied by displaced families. Their children played in these rooms filled with the art objects. Some tapestries were dirty and soiled. Picture frames had taken a beating. But generally things were in fine shape, considering the wars effect on other settings.

One painting in particular was X-rayed as it was an average piece compared to the others.. Hitler had hired artists to paint over well-known works so he could hide them under lesser art. The X-rayed painting showed a picture underneath. Thinking it was a hidden masterpiece, the restorers destroyed the outer painting only to find an unknown, poorly done, piece underneath. It seems the artist of the time had used this canvas to paint his better-known work on.

Dad, in full uniform, had first arrived at Babenhausen with some of his staff to search the castle for stolen art. Very businesslike and stern, he was introduced to Princess Gunilla Fugger (fooger)-Babenhausen, the wife of Prince Friedrich Carl Fugger-Babenhausen. Friedrich Carl was in Northern Germany where he had been stationed during the war. He had not yet returned to the castle. Gunilla, a Swedish Countess nee Bielke before her marriage to Friedrich Carl, had been managing Babenhausen during his absence. She was in her early twenties at the time. After her marriage to the prince, they had settled at the Fugger's small and beautiful castle, Wellenburg, in 1942. It was near the city of Augsburg where the family had originated.

The Princess Gunilla Fugger, in 1944, moved to Babenhausen where she found the huge castle had been badly used and neglected. Gunilla worked quite hard to reorganize and return the castle to a more livable condition. This was quite an undertaking for a young woman during those years of war and shortages. At one point, diplomats of countries not at war with the Nazis were fleeing to the borders to avoid the bombing. She took in some Irish consulate officials who posted their flags and declared Babenhausen an Irish Consulate. This saved the castle from bombing.

Once, a Nazi general had come and demanded the castle for his troops. The princess refused him, and as he threatened her, the Irish Consul General came and talked the general out of the take over. Gunilla had also taken in other refugees. Some of these were the Countess Sigrid (Sigi) Welczeck, wife of Count Hansi Welczeck, and

Princess Gunilla Fugger-Babenhausen

her two sisters, the Baronesses Gundi and Reni Laffert. Their brother, Baron Pümi Laffert, was also there.

When Dad met her and the other beautiful ladies, he instantly dropped his stern demeanor and, as Gunilla recounts, they became friends almost immediately. No hidden art was found in the castle, although there was a search made. Often after that, Dad would help Gunilla obtain the necessary papers for travel or for needed repairs to the castle. He also helped with other important procedures needed to keep the castle in order.

One of these occasions was when Gunilla asked for help regarding their second castle, Markt Wald, not far from Babenhausen. Former Russian prisoners of war had taken over the castle, mostly Serbs. They had ransacked it and the building was deteriorating.

Prince Friedrich Carl Fugger-Babenhausen

Gunilla wished to reclaim it. Dad secured the official red tape for this without problems and Gunilla was most grateful. Later, I was to go there for a hunt with Friedrich Carl and a group of friends. It was a small, rather unimposing castle, if that is possible. Perhaps I was contrasting it with Babenhausen. We had the usual late night party, and then all adjourned to bed. My room, thank God, was on the second floor. I remember that it was sparsely furnished, but I just fell into bed exhausted. During the early morning hours, with little light,

Baron Pümi von Laffert   *Baroness Gundi von Laffert and author*

the servants awakened me to prepare for the hunt. Stumbling out of bed, I groped for the light switch and managed to stick my fingers into a live 220- volt socket in the wall.

My scream was heard throughout the castle, and I am sure my hair was standing straight up. I could remove my fingers, but not before receiving a very strong dose of electricity. I think that my being on the second floor might have saved me from a more serious situation. Everyone soon surrounded me. Naturally, it was a great laugh for all. It cured any semblance of a hangover and left me very wide awake.

While we were still in Memmingen, Dad talked about some of his earliest experiences in this little town. He said he quickly learned that when he called the *Burgermeister* (mayor) to have him clear the roads into town, he would give him a definite date and time limit. He said if he did not do this, it usually did not get done. Dad felt that this was due to the strict controls of Hitler's regime, where the German had forgotten how to think for himself. I had a different conclusion. It seemed to me that the personality of the German was to seek a leader, and to trust only those who acted as leaders. If a

person showed weakness by saying "will you" and "please," they did not do what they were asked. It was necessary, therefore, to assertively state what was wanted and when, and it did not hurt to add a consequence.

When our military government was first setting up its occupying forces, it was not unusual for a German farmer to come and ask for a gun and ammunition. Many hungry deer, stag, some wild boar (often imported), and rabbits were destroying their fields. A herd of boar would go into a potato field and root up whole rows of potatoes. They then just ate the last few in the row. Although some of these requests for arms were from legitimate farmers, some were not. Too often the guns were used against American soldiers and other Allies. In order to stop this, Dad ordered the *Burgermeister* to come to his office. He told the mayor to have every gun, antique or not, broken or functioning, brought to the center of town. This was to be on such and such a date and time.

This *Burgermeister* was having a very difficult time with his citizens. Many townspeople thought he was siding with the invaders and adding to their already difficult lives. The idea of giving up the family weapons was a bitter one. Nevertheless, the consequence was imprisonment, so the lines formed on the date set. Dad had a system set up where they would inventory each gun with the hope of possibly returning it to its rightful owner, *sometime*. This was to prevent later consequences regarding this unpopular operation.

The lines moved slowly and Dad stayed by the desk where the sergeant was taking the inventory of the weapons. He was intrigued with the many very old and different types of guns. Some of these were called *Drillings* which were double-barreled shotguns with a rifle underneath. Even the Germans found these guns dangerous because of the trigger system, which seemed to go off without any help. Among the guns being brought in were canon lighters. These were old powder pistols whose barrels would fly open and the black powder firing mechanism lighted a fuse. As time went on, Dad began to see less of the antique and exotic guns and began to wonder what was happening. Going outside, he found many GIs going up and down the lines *requisitioning* these valuable pieces for their own benefit. They were in deep trouble.

In this same time frame, some U.S. soldiers in Bremerhaven were

making a name for themselves too. In that town, a building housed
a wine vat of four hundred (or so) year old wine. For many years the
famous and the wealthy had traveled many miles to taste this wine.
Their names were placed in a book covered with a gold cloth that
rested on a lovely old piece of furniture. In it were such names as
Goethe, many emperors, kings, queens, Hitler, etc. Occasional *fresh-
ening* preserved the wine in color and taste. Only carefully appointed
experts were allowed to do this. It had survived many wars. It was an
important part of German culture and was quite a tourist attraction
for Germany. Well, thirsty American soldiers found the vat and, not
reading German, did what was normal. They drank the vat dry.
Friedrich Carl always delighted in telling this story and pointing out
the boorish ways of our soldiers. A bit of loser's snobbery I think.

Leaving our tour of memories and Memmingen, we drove to the
small town of Babenhausen, east of Memmingen. The castle dominated the terrain as it loomed over the town. It was surrounded by a
high, protective wall. Anton Fugger had purchased this castle in
1538. It was an imposing structure with sharp lines, many windows,
and high-pitched roofs. There were perhaps one hundred rooms in
the different wings and, of course, a ghost in one area. This ghost
was of a woman who had been murdered and could be seen haunt-
ing the halls on special nights. These were nights of heavy drinking
I think.

As we neared the castle, I was becoming increasingly nervous, my
mind racing from one movie to another in an attempt to remember
how *royalty* acted and appeared. As we entered the castle through an
arched opening in the wall, we passed a larger-than-life-sized statue
of a religious figure in a second wall. Then we continued across a
field and through a second wall's opening into a large field. To our
right was the Fugger Brewery. We often enjoyed this strong dark
beer. On we drove to a bridge over the moat and through a third
wall's opening, which led us into the courtyard with its circular drive
around the inner grounds.

We stopped in front of an ivied wall with a double door, which led
into the castle. The door was opened by Janni, Friedrich Carl's personal servant, announcing in German that the *Fürst* (Prince) Fugger
would be there promptly. I was so overcome by this whole scene that
my personality seemed to go into a dormant stage. I felt numb.

(Somewhere back in the beginning of this book I mentioned that I felt at ease with important people, but this was too much!) The Prince emerged looking as a prince should, tall, dark, thin, and aristocratic. He kissed my hand! Thank God I was so delayed in my responses. My hand was limp and he did not meet my knuckles. Very often I would forget and move to shake hands when the German gentleman was moving to kiss the hand and, collision.

Just behind Friedrich Carl, *Fürstin* (Princess) Gunilla was greeting Dad and had young Count Toni (Anton) her two-year-old, in her arms. She was very pleasant, attractive, and wore a smock as she was expecting her second son, Hubertus. Gunilla, although young, had (and has) a regal presence. She carried herself in an assured way, with elegant manners. Despite this bearing, I found myself relaxing a bit. Both were in comfortable clothes, so I stood out like some overdressed clod. However, fine clothes were very scarce so I think they just saw me as someone who was very lucky. As Dad chatted with Friedrich Carl, Gunilla took me into the castle.

The inside hall had a double staircase of very old wooden stairs with steps worn by feet through the ages. Between the two staircases an armored suit seemed to stand guard, and a metal gloved hand held a lance at ready. The walls were lined with age-darkened oil paintings of the Fugger's ancestors. At the landing where the stairs met to branch off again, a large stag mount, with an enormous rack, was displayed on a baroque plaque. Why did that gorgeous beast have a china carrot in its mouth? At the top of the stairs, we entered the grand room with lovely parquet floors. This large receiving room's walls were lined with ancient portraits. They had also filled the area with beautiful antique furniture and furnishings.

Ceilings were very high and these rooms were difficult to heat. A mammoth fireplace dominated one wall and would have helped a bit to ease this chilly day. Gunilla was kindly telling me about each area and I was beginning to feel comfortable with her. We headed down a long, dark hall with slate floors that clacked a bit, to the guest room where I was to stay. Beyond my room was a visiting room for tea and gossip, the dining room, the kitchen, then the nursery and bedrooms. My room was quite spacious, with a lovely tiled stove that the servants filled from the hallway. Damask drapes, belying the austerity of the times, covered the windows. A lovely, old carved bed stood

near the pretty stove. The ceiling was what I loved most. It had been done many years before by an Italian artist in work called *stucco*. The figures were three dimensional. They were of cupids and angels in play, and their foot or hand or head would hang down into the room. The room was in white with gold and gilt moldings. It was all, truly, a lovely work of art.

A maid brought me my suitcase and Gunilla left me to change. Into what? All I had was my slacks and a blouse. I decided to stay in my dressy suit. It was about two in the afternoon and Gunilla had told me to meet them in the visiting room, as we all had already had lunch. I freshened up a bit at a little, old wooden cabinet holding a basin and a pitcher of water. Lingering for what seemed like an appropriate amount of time, I managed to make my way to the meeting room.

There I found myself alone with Prince Friedrich Carl! He quickly made me feel at home with questions about my life in the United States. He seemed genuinely interested in my observations of Germany. We were chatting away like old friends, (which we became) when the Baroness Gundi von Laffert and her brother, Baron Pümi von Laffert came in. Gundi was a very easy person to talk with, while Pümi was a bit stiff and shy until he had a drink.

Gundi was a pretty, young woman but poorly dressed, and must have hated me at that moment. We were to become good friends. Pümi was tall, gentle, and good-looking in a warm way. He was often the life of the party, but suffered terrible hangovers. I think he just had a guilty conscience for having a good time. Also joining us were their sisters, Countess Sigi von Welczeck and Baroness Rene. All were Lafferts. Sigi, a very beautiful woman, had been a personal friend of Hitler. This was never discussed openly and I think we felt a little uncomfortable with her at first. It was rumored that Hitler was very angry with her for becoming engaged to Count Hansi Welchek. He (Hitler) had been enamored of her beauty, himself. Later, as I came to know Sigi, I found her to be a very open person-serious and friendly.

We all seemed to find a great deal to talk about and finally it was time for tea and champagne. I think I had done well to this point and had no trouble with the tea served with a beautiful sterling service. However, they served champagne after tea. All the ladies had ac-

companying little glass rods in the lovely crystal glasses. The rods were solid so they were not straws, perish the thought. I looked around to see what others were doing with theirs and noticed that the men did not have one. Gunilla, always the good hostess, noticed my dilemma and told me, quietly, that the ladies used this rod to tap out the bubbles in the champagne. Evidently this was to keep sneezes from embarrassing a person, and to cut down on the acidic effect of the wine. I put down the little rod and enjoyed the drink, with thanks to my hostess.

Gundi later took me to see the stables where they had a beautiful white stallion that Gunilla rode. We (Gundi and I) were both fair riders and she was able to outfit me with riding clothes. We had a marvelous ride out across the beautiful fields. The Germans mow their fields for silage so they have a green lawn effect. All of the forests in Germany seemed landscaped and trim because the people gathered every stick or low limb for firewood. Seeing through the trees was not difficult and they offered the deer little place to hide. We passed peasants working in the fields and these people appeared to be unaffected by the war. They reminded me of a statement made by such a person. "My family planted potatoes for the Kaiser, they planted them for Bismark, I planted for Hitler, and now I plant potatoes for the occupation."

After our ride, it was time to dress for cocktails and dinner. We always changed clothes a lot at this castle. The servants served the dinner. It consisted of soup and a main course of meat and potatoes. After the main course, we had either fruit, cheese and rolls, or a dessert. A good land wine was always an important part of the meal. The cook prepared one meat and potato dish by slicing a boneless roast and then completely covering it with mashed potatoes. I loved watching the Prince search through the potatoes for the meat. He did not have much patience for the dish.

At later such meals, he would threaten someone with a spoonful of mashed potatoes, and did let it fly once. I do not remember who the victim was, probably Pümi. Such behavior always upset Gunilla, who tried to maintain a genteel atmosphere. This was sometimes an impossible task with Friedrich Carl who loved a good time. We would always have drinks before dinner, the wine with, and cordials or liqueur afterwards. This usually created a very lively group and Gunilla

would then excuse herself from the party. She rarely joined in our parties at the castle. However, when she attended social affairs elsewhere, she was relaxed and joined in the festivities.

This was an early evening and they told me to dress casually the next day for a morning of tennis. I was at least prepared for this, as I had packed my slacks and *tennies*. Waking up in the morning was a delight. This family was devoutly Catholic, especially Gunilla. A lovely church was in the castle. It was decorated with much gilt, scrolls, religious figures, and stained glass windows. There were seating areas above the ground level where we could watch without being seen. On this Sunday morning, as always, the bells were ringing all over the town. They did so for about an hour (or so it seemed). A sinner would find it difficult to sleep in with this beautiful din, and the religious would be awakened in plenty of time for church. I had not heard the servant start the fire in my stove, but the bedroom was warm despite the chill of an October morn. It was good to get into my sport clothes and feel relaxed as I made my way to the dining room.

I was beginning to feel at home in this lovely old place. Baron Pümi was up and looking a bit uncomfortable from the past night's party. He was such an enjoyable fellow. Friedrich Carl joined us and soon he and Dad were telling some hunting stories. Friedrich Carl said he would like to take me hunting one day and would arrange for me to get a good buck. He explained that his foresters kept track of the bucks and knew their habits and when and where they would be at, at certain times. Dad provided the guns and ammunition, as Germans were not allowed firearms. I had learned to shoot with a .22 rifle when I was a teenager and felt I could at least try a regular rifle. It could not be much more powerful than the skeet guns on the ship. Hunting was the main way for this family and their employees to have meat, either deer or rabbit.

There were rivers and ponds on the lands of Friedrich Carl where we could fish. Once, Friedrich Carl took us to the river where he had a large wooden rowboat with a motor. In the boat were two long poles with metal plates on one end. These were put into the water and electricity from the boat's motor went down one pole and the other pole was the ground. This sent out a regulated shock that would determine the size of fish that they wanted. Large pike,

stunned by the shock, would float up and we would net them. They were then placed, alive, in a large holding tank. If the prince wanted trout, electricity was lowered and that seemed to affect the smaller fish. Later the fish would be taken back to the castle and put into a pool in the courtyard until the kitchen was ready for them. Not exactly sports fishing, but it put food on the table. In fact, it was more of a harvest.

Meanwhile, our tennis game started after Gunilla came from church. She was a very good player and kept Dad and I, also good players, on our guard. Gundi and Pümi also played and we had a work-out. The court had a crushed brick surface, was in good condition, and was obviously well used. We played several sets, doubles and singles, before stopping for some cool beer before lunch. This was their good beer (12%) brewed in the castle brewery. One rapidly realized that the Germans needed parties and diversions to put the war far behind them. We rarely addressed the war, as it might lead to bad feelings. We had quickly learned this.

Later, after lunch, we said our goodbyes with the promise of an early return for hunting. What a wonderful weekend and we looked forward to many good times together.

CHAPTER VII

GETTING SETTLED

Back in Stuttgart life was falling into a pleasant routine. Dad and I were invited to many parties, sometimes two or three a day. Wine, champagne, liqueurs, and beer were very cheap and good. The best champagne was one dollar and fifty cents. Good land wine was twenty-five cents. With servants to do the work, there was little else but to shop, plan parties or dinners, and enjoy oneself. Most American Officer's wives were not accustomed to having servants. It led to much spare time and the inevitable bridge parties and other ways of keeping ourselves occupied. There were maids who did the cleaning, washing, ironing, and cared for the children. Cooks cooked and gardeners tended the yards. We also had drivers who drove us wherever we needed to go. We often felt there was too much time on our hands.

One Saturday afternoon I was coming home from Ilse Flòters and saw smoke coming from our basement. It did not look friendly. Suddenly the sirens I had been hearing were very close. The German sirens were more of a *"bleep ah bleep ah bleep ah . . . "* An old decrepit fire truck came laboring up the hill and parked in front of the house. The fire fighters jumped down as an elaborately uniformed man drove up in a red sedan. He was obviously the fire chief. With smoke pouring out of the basement, they all stopped to shake hands. I was standing there amazed by this whole process and wondering where Dad was.

They finally allowed me in, to find the Colonel, in his trunks, blackened by greasy smoke and looking quite hysterical. He had

been on his way to take a bath when he first smelled the acrid smoke. It was later determined that the gas meter had caught fire. That was the warmest that meter had been in a long time. We were only able to run the heat in the early morning and late evening due to rationing. Germany had a great shortage of coal-one of many shortages.

Poor Dad was terribly shaken by this near tragedy, and seemed to need some consoling. I guess I heard this story repeated many times in the next few months. When he realized there was a fire, he had immediately gone to my room to save my scant jewelry. He had thrown compacts, mirrors, etcetera, into a pillow slip and thrown them out the upstairs window. Rushing downstairs, he started to push the huge living room sofa out onto the patio. It became stuck in the door. He then had to try to get the chairs and tables out over the sofa or through narrow windows. Frantic, he was finally rescued by the elaborately uniformed fire chief who told him they had contained the fire to the meter. The fire was now out. I bet he could have cried from relief. I did cry when I found my broken compact and mirrors.

My trunk had finally arrived and, to my and the maid's horror, almost everything in it was moldy black. Evidently a hole had been poked in it back in New York, three months before. The contents had become wet and were now almost solid. I was able to rescue a few pairs of shoes and some articles of clothing that I could wear, but very little else.

This was a crushing blow, especially with no shops or materials available. Dad had a very good secretary, Miss Trede, who was a font of information and spoke good English. She knew a sewing lady who would come to the house and make me some clothes. I had also fired off a letter to Mother asking her to send me shoes, dresses, blouses, skirts, etc. That concerned me a bit as I was sure that my mother would finally dress me in fussy clothes. However, that, thankfully, did not happen. I had put in a damage claim to the army and, optimistically, intended to pay for the clothes with the proceeds. At least the PX had stockings and sundries.

I wish I could remember the name of the lady who arrived to do the sewing. I must have been hoping for a Parisian designer, and had not prepared myself for the mountain of flesh that arrived. I am sure it was Ina, our housekeeper and cook, who was with us then. When

she announced the arrival of the sewing Frau, she had her hand over her mouth, hiding her grin. I also think her next thought was of our food supply. This sewing lady weighed at least four hundred pounds. Ina and I had to push on her posterior to get her up the groaning stairs and into the small room now designated the sewing room. Despite the bulk, however, this was a friendly woman and she was a fair dressmaker. Once ensconced, she left the room only to use the bathroom. The rest of the time she sewed and ate. She told us that somewhere in her voluminous left breast was a sewing needle. The doctors evidently did not want to search through all that mass for it.

Dad had brought me materials from a trip to Paris so I could have some dresses made. No dress patterns were available, and I had to explain to the Frau what I wanted. The language difficulty made things quite frustrating, and finally Ina assured me that she and the Frau could design a very lovely gown for me. This was one of my greater errors. The Frau did a decent job on a plain dress sewn from a German material made from wood. However, when the "lovely gown" was finished, it was Scarlett O' Hara's dress from *Gone with the Wind*. Bouffant sleeves and layers of pleats lent an air of days of yore. My mother would have loved it. When I tried it on, they could quickly see my stunned reaction and the Frau began to cry. She was going to leave immediately. I turned to Ina who waved me out of the room. Somehow, she managed to talk the Frau into staying, but we rarely spoke after that. I did not have her make any more clothes for me, just repairs or alterations.

Dad had known a very good dress designer in Karlsruhe, Liselotte Haüser. He arranged a trip to her small shop where she actually had clothes. Her husband was living in Switzerland and sending materials to her. Liselotte was a handsome, bright woman who had her original designs printed on the materials. She also made her own styles for her dresses and outfits. She once asked me to model for her in her next fashion show. I really did not want to do this and I started to gain weight. Remember my stubborn streak. Each time I tried on the clothes, I seemed to go up a size. We eventually agreed that modeling might not be my forte. Nevertheless, I did purchase some very nice outfits from her. With my mother's help from home and the good old Sears catalogue, I managed to stay well dressed.

The reverse happened later (regarding weight) when I was seeing

a very excitable little tailor for some skiing and riding clothes. We were using army material called "pinks." This was a good woolen gabardine used for officers' dress uniforms. When the tailor fitted me for the pants, he had me sit in a chair and measured from my waist to the chair. This was a very courteous way of measuring to the crotch. At this time in my life, I was having a nervous condition that was causing me to lose weight rapidly. It is a problem today called acute anxiety, but the doctors could not diagnose it then. Each time I went for a fitting, I had lost more weight.

I lost thirty pounds and two dress sizes. The poor man kept altering and measuring me every time I went for a fitting. He would wring his hands, ruffle his hair, and mumble under his breath. When he finally finished the clothes, I was down two sizes. By nature, I was a size sixteen. I think he thought I was trying to ruin his reputation and was never available to me after that. He would, however, still work for Dad. In fact, I believe he quit making any clothes for women.

We were lucky to have scarce materials for ourselves and would offer to bring them in from France or Switzerland for our friends. I remember one trip I made by train to Switzerland for shopping. I was to be the guest of Roland Stahill, Dad's friend. As I had not met him, and this was my first trip alone in Europe, I asked for a description of how I would recognize him at the station. He told me he was bald and would wear a brown coat. It seemed everyone was wearing a brown coat that day. I approached several bald men, no Stahill. Finally there were about five of us left standing there when Stahill finally took off his hat to introduce himself. I found out later that he was just being funny. He was a really enjoyable person. Also, anyone who did not recognize me as an American was blind.

German ladies were wearing very outdated clothes. Either the parachute silk or material made from wood was used in new dresses. The wooden material was what the Frau used to make one of my dresses. It was all right new, but once washed would lose its color and starch. Many German ladies, out of desperation, also wore really terrible coats made of red fox or rabbit fur. Foxes and rabbits were too abundant, so there was no shortage in that department. Of course, these coats did help keep the ladies warm. Their shoes were abysmal, heavy, and very old-fashioned. During the later war years they simply did not have newer items as everything went to keep the troops going.

German fashion model 1947

The parachute silk was also used for stage and opera costumes, curtains, and backdrops. One evening we attended an opera and sat in our box enjoying the beautiful voices and the music. At the intermission a ballet company performed and they were costumed in parachute silk. The Prima had slender straps holding up a pretty top like a bra. In one of her moves, a strap broke! She managed to continue with a few alterations to height of arm stretches. Now we knew her partner, Hans von Kusserov. Hans had told me how superb she was and that the finale was two male dancers swinging her, arms raised, out over the audience. Tension mounted, and as they swung her up and out, the other strap gave way. Bare breasted she completed her

dance without a falter. The applause was deafening. I am sure it was for her wonderful composure! Poor Hans was a perfectionist and was appalled at what had happened.

I asked Hans to come to the house and let me take pictures of him. He came in his bat outfit from his part in *Die Fledermaus*. At the time, I was learning photography from Hubs Flöter, a well-known German photographer. Hubs had suggested this photo session. I was using a Leica camera; thirty-six photos, and a Rolleiflex; twelve photos. I decided the Leica would be the faster camera for the action shots. I was nervous and did not want my shaking hands to blur the pictures. Hans was not only a perfectionist, but did not seem to have much of a sense of humor. He dressed in the outfit, parachute silk, and pade' dewed to our patio. Although I was a rank beginner at photography, I did know a bit about ballet.

We went into the yard where I asked for jumps and leaps, which Hans did with great poise and agility. I had him leap the thirty-six times until he was sweating. Both he and Hubs remarked on my good timing in catching the moves at just the right moment. The lawn dropped off to the hillside and a view of Stuttgart in the distance was a good backdrop. Everything went to their satisfaction and

Ballet artist Hans von Kusserov

mine. Hans left when I had finished and I assured him he could choose the best photos. I had my darkroom midway up the stairs in a small lavoratory closet. Opening the camera to remove the film, I found none. I had not loaded the camera. Well, there was only one thing to do. I called him to come back. Surprisingly, he was all right about it and I did get some good shots that time.

I met an attractive German man, Ivar Lissner, who had been the editor of a large German magazine before the war destroyed it. He was working for Dad's office and would help me with translations. He was free lancing as a journalist for several magazines and a newspaper. Ivar was a brilliant man who could encourage a stone to move. He suggested I write some stories about my life at college and about the American ways. He actually convinced me to do it. I wrote about life in my sorority house, the serenades by the Greeks, picnics, and dances, etc. I also wrote a story about "babysitting," which was not yet popular in the German household.

When I finished my writing I felt very proud of my endeavors and imagined myself quite an author. The stories were accepted for publishing in *Der Spiegel*, a German magazine, and my name was in print! However, Ivar had to first translate them to German and, I am sure, put the finish on them that made them acceptable. The magazine even paid me for them, which helped my dwindling finances a bit.

One thing that truly struck me as odd was the fact that there were no Nazis in our circle of friends or acquaintances. Dad, of course, had access to the military records of many people whom we knew. He did not share this information with me. I know that he would not have fraternized with a Nazi. Yet no one claimed to have been a member of any of the Nazi or gestapo groups. Instead we heard more about those who had been a part of groups that tried to kill Hitler. As mentioned, we rarely talked about the war so perhaps the subject of Nazi members just never was discussed. Most Germans were quite defensive about Germany's war crimes and many felt ashamed of things that were emerging from the war crimes trials. Many of the horrible facts, they had not known about. Again a subject that was better not discussed.

CHAPTER VIII

COUNTESS PAULA CLARY-ALDRINGEN

Shortly after visiting Babenhausen, Dad planned a trip to the Castle Bronnbach to visit Prince Karl Löwenstein and his family. Also living there was a young Countess Paula Clary-Aldringen, nee Schaffgotsch. A friend had introduced Dad to her at a party some months before. I feel he had fallen in love with her before we made this trip. Paula was married to Count Marcus Clary-Aldringen, who was still a prisoner of war. She had been engaged to the very popu-

Countess Paula Clary-Aldringen and children, Ronni and Resi.

lar brother of Marcus, Count Ronni Clary-Aldringen. Count Ronni
was killed in the war and so the families had arranged a marriage between Paula and Marcus. This was not a good marriage, and later
ended in divorce or annulment.

Paula had two very beautiful children, four-year-old Ronni and
two-year-old Resi. Her third child, Christian, was born just before I
left Germany. She had a very strict children's nanny who wore long
uniforms and a nurse-like cap. I never received more than a polite
greeting from this nanny, although she often stayed at our house.
Paula also had a maid named Hedi, who is still with Paula fifty years
later and is really more like family.

The Russians destroyed Paula's family castle, and their property
was confiscated during the war in Silesia. Many years later, the family received a settlement from Russia, and the Russians returned
their real estate. However, the family fortune was lost and never really recovered. This had happened to many aristocracies. Paula and
I were close friends, being just five years apart. We often traveled
together, hunted, rode horseback, and enjoyed each other. She and
Dad remained friends through her divorce from Marcus, and then
went their own ways during Dad's marriage to Bebe Jorgensen. They
were later to start their relationship again in approximately 1957 or
1958. She often visited me at my home in Montesano, Washington,
and stayed at the resort in Mexico. We really considered her family.

Arriving at Bronnbach, a much smaller castle than Babenhausen,
we were greeted by the Prince Karl and Princess Carolina
Löwenstein. They were expecting us for lunch. This was sometimes
quite a hardship for these families, as the food was so difficult to
find. So we were always mindful of this and tried to help when it was
acceptable. The Löwensteins were in their sixties, very pleasant and
friendly people. Their castle had survived the bombing and they had
taken in friends and relatives who were homeless. Countess Paula
Clary-Aldringen, the Prince Alfons Clary-Aldringen and Princess
Ludwine Clary-Aldringen, Paula's in-laws, were there as such guests.

Paula seemed very shy at this time, perhaps because everyone was
aware of Dad's interest in her. Although they treated us politely, we
were never sure we were accepted by some Germans. Whether they
were still angry over losing the war, I do not know. The Löwensteins,
I believe, were not a part of the Hitler movement. However, we were

still the conquering Americans with powers to create difficulties for problem Germans. This would create a distance that sometimes disappeared over time, or not at all. Often there was a question of, were we being used or were we accepted? Everyone was quite polite on this occasion and we were invited to return.

Paula was having a struggle finding housing, food, clothing, and income. This provided an opening for my infatuated father. We invited her for weekends as often as she could come. Usually the children came with her, but as time went on she felt comfortable enough to come by herself. I often felt that my father was using me as an unwilling chaperone. She would also come when Dad was away and be company for me. She was fun to be with and she and I often set Dad up in some funny, but difficult, situations. It was a shadowy line that defined where the boundaries of our friendship and their relationship merged.

More than once, Dad forgot the consequences of his actions in favor of pleasing Paula. Once it was by taking her into Strasbourg, France. This was to give her an opportunity to buy clothes for herself and the children. The Allies did not allow Germans out of the country. What frightened me most was if we were caught trying to get her back in. I mention "we" because they took me along as Dad intended to stay overnight.

Again, I was the very reluctant chaperone and acted accordingly. My anger at this breach of regulations was obvious, and I was not a pleasant partner in this crime. Especially after all the lectures I had received regarding my black market forays. Worse, we took the army car as Dad believed it would keep the border patrols from searching it. This was did not work. We had stopped before reaching the border and put Paula in the trunk, just in case. Dad put a blanket over her. I cannot say she was not game, despite the problems she faced if caught. The guard came and inspected our papers and asked for the car pass. Dad asked to go into the little office where there was "better light." This drew the man away from the car. It worked, and when we stopped to let Paula out, Dad crowed about how easy it had been. I relaxed a bit after that and we did have a good time.

Strasbourg is a very old town. The buildings are brick and mortar with pretty pastel paintings on some of them. It was a dirty city, but teeming with business and stores. Many old cars and pedestrians

crowded the narrow streets, and police officers directed traffic. We saw the famous, huge cathedral with golden spires that age and dirt had dulled. The people were brusk and serious, seemingly still feeling the war years. Even the old buildings were such a welcome change from the stark, ruined cities of Germany.

✓ We stayed in a small hotel and had a decent dinner and an excellent breakfast. It was a pleasant treat from our rations in Stuttgart. We spent the day enjoying the shops and picking out materials for clothes, mostly for Paula. I had difficulty with this as Dad rarely asked what I might need. Many years later Paula told me that I used to frighten her at these times. I explained to her that I was quite jealous of Dad's buying for her and not for me. For Paula this trip was really wonderful and reminded her of what life was like before the war. The bombing did not affect this area, but how they hated the Germans. We spoke no German and Paula stayed quiet. I think it was an eye-opener for her to see such hatred. We could buy wonderful cheese and some excellent wine and bread, which we enjoyed on the way back.

As we approached the border, again at night, Dad saw no reason to put Paula back in the trunk. This brought my feathers up again, without success. She got in the back seat, onto the floor, and Dad put a blanket over her. When they stopped us, the guard asked us to get out and to open the trunk. This time I knew they had caught us. Dad paled, I am sure, and kept the guard talking as the man searched the trunk. Then he came to look inside the car. He asked what was under the blanket in the back seat. I blurted out, "dirty clothes" in halting German. I must have looked embarrassed to him because he started to look and then decided against it. Dad and I tried not to hurry as we entered the car and drove off. What a relief to be on our way, and what a lecture I gave them!

Dad and I were invited to a grand party at Regensburg in January of 1947. It was to celebrate Paula's sister, Ushi's, birthday. We were to be guests of Prince Johan Thurn-und Taxis. Paula arranged this for us. It was snowing and cold as we arrived at the castle, but the lights of the rooms beckoned warmly. We were a bit late, having driven on bad roads from Stuttgart. The party was in full swing and members of Paula's family welcomed us. Somehow, I had missed the name of our host. When a tall, rather pompous fellow introduced himself to

me, I could not fathom his name. Torn the taxes? I kept asking and getting more confused. Eventually, he walked off haughtily. Although, not before telling me that his was the second ranking family in Germany. I hurried over to Paula to learn, with chagrin, that this was our host.

The list of guests that night read as follows: Countess Ursula (Ushi) Arco-Zinneberg, Countess Mädy Arco-Zinneberg, Count Engelbert (Engel) Arco-Zinneberg, Count Ferdinand Arco-Zinneberg, Count Constantin (Tin) Berckheim, Count Geisbert Boch, Baroness Gabrielle Fürstenberg, Count Toni Saurma, Countess Maria Saurma, Countess Sophi Schaffgotsch (Paula's mother), and her sister, Countess Gabriella (Riella) Schaffgotsch, Count Friedrich Carl Schaffgotsch (Paula's brother), Prince Johannes Thurn undTaxis, Princess Mafalda Thurn und Taxis, Baron Alexander Loudon, Countess Eda Tohun, and Count Karl Josef Henckel.

We were treated quite well, and the party went on into the night with dancing and games. We did not just talk and drink at these parties. There was always some organized activity. The guests usually played games of a sort that required thinking, like the solving of mysteries or riddles.

Some months later we would party with Count Engel Arco-Zinneberg, who could become quite out of control at a certain point in his drinking. He would act a wild man. This occasion was at Babenhausen where we were having the usual after-the-hunt party. Friedrich Carl had a lovely screen of old maps made for Gunilla's birthday. She was not attending this party, having gone to bed early. Engel became increasingly out of control and eventually stuck his head through Gunilla's new birthday screen. I do not believe she had seen it yet. Dad and I, wanting to avoid trouble, immediately left and had a late drive home.

Shortly after this, Freidrich Carl purposely went to Engel's home for a "visit." Engel was known for his very old, lovely crystal collection. Somehow, Friedrich enticed Engel to serve them drinks in some of these glasses. When Friedrich Carl finished his glass, he stood up and smashed it into the fireplace. Engel blinked, did not say a word, finished his drink, and smashed his also. They finished the glasses, all smashed, and Engel had not said a word.

Sometime later, Engel came to see Friedrich Carl and insisted they have drinks from Friedrich's best crystal. Friedrich Carl complied. There was no fireplace in the room where they were drinking. So they sat on the balcony that night, throwing each glass out the window as they finished. When he left the next morning, Engel was looking quite self-satisfied. What he did not know was that Friedrich Carl had chosen that room especially, as there was no fireplace. He had Janni, his valet, downstairs catching the glasses as they were thrown out the window. One glass was chipped, but none were broken. My very bright friend, the Prince.

CHAPTER IX

HUNTING

My first hunting experience was with Captain Bill Wright. Bill was one of Dad's assistant military directors for the area around the town of *Buchen*. This is near *Heidelberg*. Bill arranged the hunt about three weeks after I arrived in Germany. The kill would provide fresh meat for the local families and the hospital. Bill was to be a good friend for the rest of my stay. Herr Braun drove Dad and me. We were loaded down with warm clothes, guns and ammunition, and some whiskey for "warmth." This was on a cold, clear, bright day in October. I was really excited about this hunt. I did not know that I could kill and do not think it really mattered at the time. It was all just very invigorating.

We were to have beaters, local men and boys who would rattle pots and pans or sticks as they moved through the woods. This would frighten the animals and drive them toward the hunters. It also protected the beaters as we knew where they were. Hopefully, we were going to see wild boar, deer, possibly *hirsche* (like elk), rabbits, badger, and red fox. The wild boar were vicious things and I have seen experienced forest- meisters freeze when they come by. They may weigh up to six hundred pounds and have huge, sharp tusks.

I was given a small Army carbine, which was no match for a wild boar. I knew they did not expect much of me. We climbed into Bill's jeep and headed for the hunt. We must have looked like the gestapo going through the village with guns pointing up and bundled in military winter garb. We no doubt cut quite an image for the Germans. The forests were hand planted and clean, and laid out in

German Forestmeisters at the hunt

about six square block sections. Our foresters and beaters all shook hands with us (part of the German ritual) as we arrived. They had already had a long walk as few had cars.

Many Germans had hidden their good cars so the Americans would not requisition them. Perpetrators faced a serious penalty if these cars were found. Friedrich Carl had hinted about an Opel. This was an excellent German auto. However, we never saw it until late 1949. Then, cars were no longer requisitioned. He would never tell me where it had been hidden. Years later I asked Gunilla and she said it had been in a forester's barn. Guess who would have been in trouble?

Meanwhile, at the hunt, they assigned us our positions. They also reminded us to look for something to climb if they wounded a boar. Great! That did not do much for my already nervous feelings. My station was along the road. This gave me a good opportunity to see clearly what I might shoot. I looked around to be sure I knew where the other hunters were so that I would not hit anyone. I hoped they were doing the same. Off to my right was a stacked pile of wood that would hold me if necessary.

The beaters left and headed to positions far in front of us to drive the animals toward us. They were very quiet until the drive began. While I was crouched waiting by a big tree, a motion on the road to my left caught my eye. Coming right by me was a red fox intent on where he was going. He was no more than a foot away. I froze! Lucky fox, caught me off guard. I wanted to reach out and touch him but did not want to move. It was not until he passed me that he caught my scent. He leaped into the air and came down running, and was gone in a flash.

Suddenly, a horn blew and the beaters began with a deafening din of pounded metal pieces and yelling. As they moved toward us, I tensed and prayed not to get "buck fever." (The latter refers to a sudden case of nerves and shaking that renders the hunter useless. Shooting when one has the fever is dangerous as there is little control over one's aim). There was a sudden movement, again to the left, and three small red deer bounded across the road. They too caught me by surprise with their speed and size. They were about forty or fifty pounds-the size of a large dog. These deer were not at all near the size of ours in the United States.

I realized that I should become serious about this hunting and shoot something. A forester had moved in about fifty feet behind me. He had whistled to alert me of his presence. As I stared down the road again, the forester behind me suddenly fired several shots. I turned to see what was happening and a red fox bounded toward me. My little gun was at my hip. I pulled the trigger automatically and that fox dropped. I had shot from the hip! The forester was dumbfounded. I was not about to let him know that I was also! He had missed two shots while this American Fräulein shot the fox from her hip! He picked up the very dead fox and went back to his position, shaking his head.

Now I was shaking with excitement, thoroughly involved in the hunting sense. The beaters were getting near when the grunts and smell announced wild boar. They came crashing through the woods toward me, looking like determined mounds of hell. My whole instinct was to run, and I did, up that woodpile scattering wood as I clawed my way to the top. Those boar could have cared less as they ran for their lives. Shots rang out and two boar went down. Another was still running, but wounded. The call went out, "wounded boar." I refused to come down from the woodpile until I heard shots and they sent the word that the boar was dead. Thankfully, this dramatic scene of my frantic race up the woodpile did not alter my image as a hip shooting hunter. Everyone understood the caution one must have about these animals. At the end of the hunt, Dad had two deer and I had my poor, mangy fox. Nevertheless, what an exciting day! I was now a hunter.

Sometimes, when driving to Babenhausen, I would have Herr Braun stop in a forested area and I would look for deer in amongst the trees. More than once I would develop "buck fever." I would shake so badly I could not, dared not, pull the trigger. This seems to happen to the best of hunters and is an unexpected thing. Sometimes I was calm and quite relaxed at the hunt.

Once while hunting with a group at Bill Wright's, I became lost during a heavy snowfall. That was also a very frightening feeling, losing your sense of direction. The snow muted sound, so I could not hear the others. Also, it quickly obliterated my footprints. I knew that Bill would give me a difficult time when he found out I had been lost. If he found out! I had been hunting downhill, so I started

climbing back uphill, praying it would stop snowing. It finally did lessen a bit. It was just enough to let me see about twenty feet ahead. I could just make out the top of the hill, or the rim. I thought someone might call out if I fired my gun. Aiming up at the snowy sky, I pulled the trigger. Just after the shot, I heard Bill yelling, "did you get it?" "No," I quickly said, "missed." Complaining about the poor visibility, I made my way to the cars. "You were lost weren't you?" Bill asked. I denied it, but Bill just shook his head. He later admitted that he had been lost and by luck had found the cars. I still would not admit it. It was a lucky day for the deer.

Often Bill and I would hunt at night for wild boar. I rarely shot at one, as I was usually being bounced about at fifty miles an hour over the fields. I was the official searchlight operator. Bill would stop the jeep when we had spotted the boar. He would whisper his plan of action, "approach from the right and get in the middle of the herd." Then we would take off as fast as he could go, while I trained the light on the boar.

Slamming to a stop, he would start shooting. Even when he stood beside a dead one, I would not get out of the jeep. These were very dangerous animals and I had great respect for them. We would leave them in the field and Bill would have them picked up the next day. The farmer whose fields we were driving over was always pleased to see another dead boar and forgave the tire marks. These farmers were often attacked by the beasts while working their fields. The tusks of the boar are razor sharp. A mother boar was especially dangerous when she had babies.

I hunted in many areas in Germany, such as: Buchenwald, Brombach, Babenhausen, Waiblingen, Lauder, Bartenstein, Niederstetten, Wellenburg, Ludwigsberg, and some not remembered. Today, many people consider hunting is a merciless "killing" and not a sport. I can only say that back then it was a way of providing meat for the Germans and for us. It protected the farmers' crops, and was a way of culling a rapidly overgrowing population of deer, hiersch, fox, rabbit, and boar.

This German style of hunting was all a learning experience for me, and I would often find myself in some peculiar circumstances. Once at Babenhausen when it was the buck season, I saw and shot a good rack. (This is the term used when a buck has good or excep-

tional horns.) It was late in the season, but meat was scarce. When the forester came, we walked to the spot where the buck had gone down. There lay a doe, no horns. The forester turned and looked questioningly at me. I looked again at the deer and wondered how I could have made such a mistake. Then I saw that my shot had hit the buck high enough to knock the horns off. After scouting around, we found the two pieces of horn. It made a good story that evening at dinner.

We gathered for another hunt at *Buchenwald* in what is called the *rutting* season. This was the deer's breeding time. The bucks were clashing horns and being driven by one urge-find the doe. I was given a whistle that could be tuned to sound like a buck, doe, fawn, or rabbit. I was not always too sure which animal would respond as I did not recognize the different calls. On this occasion, I had decided to take advantage of the high grass growing around us. Remember, the deer were small and about forty to sixty pounds. I knelt in the grass, completely covered, and blew the whistle, hoping it was the doe sound. After some minutes, I heard a rustling and a snort. Clever me, the buck had taken the bait and I was downwind. I thought I could call him in quite close and get a good shot.

I called again. Again he moved warily toward me. The buck seemed a bit hesitant, but then he began to move seriously in my direction. The snorting became bawling and panting and it suddenly dawned on me that this buck might not appreciate this "doe." Despite their size, they were strong and their horns were sharp. How could I get out of this one? There seemed little else to do than resort to firing my gun in the air. This sent him flying. I have often wondered what might have happened if I had waited him out.

Hunting at Babenhausen was always a pleasure because Friedrich Carl was at his happiest in his forests with a gun. At these times, he really was a jovial companion. We went duck hunting once when we were first getting to know each other. Before getting into the boat, he suggested I try shooting the shotgun to get some practice. We walked down a road and found a flock of pigeons on some overhead wires. He whispered to shoot and just then they flew. I knelt down on one knee and shot into the flock. Next thing I knew I was flat on my back and Friedrich Carl was laughing unmercifully. As he helped me to my feet, he reminded me, as Dad had on the ship, always to tuck

the gun into the shoulder and never shoot at the flock. The hunter must pick out one bird and follow it before shooting. Red faced and hurting, I decided to get back at him somehow. I wanted his respect, and that was not an easy thing with Friedrich Carl.

The dogs were all excited by the shot and eager to start the hunt. We climbed into the boats and shoved off. A strong wind was blowing, so Friedrich Carl said we might not have luck as the birds would be restless. The ducks would come in, but not land. They also stayed up high. Several hunters in other boats took long shots but hit nothing. Every time I would follow a bird, Friedrich Carl would whisper not to waste my shot.

Time went on and we were not having any luck. The Prince's patience was wearing thin so I was trying not to bother him, but still thinking I could get a bird. A hiss warned me that a flock was coming our direction, but it was high. I could not wait any longer, stood up, and aimed my gun at the lead bird. I tucked the gun well into my shoulder and followed the bird. "Too high, damn it." Not paying attention to Friedrich Carl, I pulled the trigger and watched the bird fly into the shot. I more than redeemed myself as the near dog carefully picked up the dead duck in the water. Friedrich Carl was more than impressed. He could not get over such a shot and told everyone about it. I had surprised myself. Besides, it was also the only bird shot that day.

Once when the Prince and I were hunting early in the morning, he offered me a drink of schnapps from the bottle. It was a cold, damp day so I lifted the bottle to my lips and took a sip. Something in the bottom of the bottle caught my eye. A frog-a very dead, tiny frog. Friedrich Carl tried to convince me that this was how they cured the schnapps. I knew it consisted of different distilled fruits or potatoes, not frogs. About then, I saw some movement on the road and there were hundreds of tiny frogs all over the place. It was some kind of migration and he had scooped one up and put it in the bottle to play a trick on me.

Friedrich Carl wanted a hunting dog and for some reason bought a Dalmatian. Despite our trying to tell him these were coach dogs, he sent the dog off for training. He did not take advice willingly, like me, and must have also talked the trainer into working with such a breed. Of course, they could never train the dog. It preferred run-

ning with the horses and wagon, or after an occasional deer.

At Babenhausen we would go out to hunt in a horse drawn wagon. We sat in the open wagon with legs hanging over the side, ready to drop off when we saw a deer. This, like the beaters, did not seem fair to me. When the huntmeister spotted a deer in the forest, a person on the opposite side of the wagon would slip off. The deer would watch the wagon and the hunter had a perfect shot. Friedrich Carl's Dalmation just trotted right along with the wagon.

Later, I was so pleased when Gunilla presented me with a Bavarian suit of boiled, hard, wool material. The buttons were deer horn. Then Friedrich Carl gave me a hunting hat of felt with the *bart* (beard) of a mountain goat sticking up at the band. This was held by a silver pin from Babenhausen decorated with the family crest. Now, they had truly outfitted me in Bavarian style. When with the Fuggers we often had a barbecue at a forest cabin following our hunts. Foresters would prepare everything and we would have the fresh tenderloin of the day's kill, over an open fire. Topped with the wonderful land wines, we would end a perfect day. Sometimes the wine went to champagne, then beer, and a night of bowling in the castle's bowling alley. The lanes were warped and the balls were not very round and they were made of wood. Still, we had a great time despite these irregularities. I remember an early morning following one of these late night parties when I shot a tractor that looked just like a deer. I still recall the resultant "ping."

At times Gunilla and Gundi would be our beaters, which I always considered the ultimate sacrifice on their part. We all tried to be especially sober and careful on those days. Dad and I had provided the ammunition and the guns at first. Later, Friedrich Carl came up with some rusty ammunition and began to bring out some of his favorite weapons. I remember one was a "drilling," a combination shotgun and rifle. It could be quite dangerous, as it had three triggers. Even more dangerous was the ammunition Friedrich Carl was using. He had, during the end of the war, put many rounds of ammunition in the lake so they would not be confiscated. He was now bringing them up from the water and the rusted bullets would often late fire. If they did not fire when the trigger was pulled, it was necessary to keep the gun pointed away from targets until it did, or did not, fire. This was nerve wracking. However, Friedrich Carl seemed pleased to

be using his own ammunition.

Naturally, with all our hunting, we had deer meat in every possible form. Most of us who hunted were forever trying to find a new recipe. Other than the tenderloin or the filet after the hunt, I soon tired of the flavor no matter how it was disguised.

CHAPTER X

PARTIES

I felt some pangs of homesickness around our first Christmas in Germany. However, there were so many parties and festivities that thoughts of home did not last long. This was a time to be with friends and forget that some of our German hosts and hostesses had recently been our enemy. We always had many parties at the house. Dad would give me the list of guests and I would plan the event. I often hired musicians to come and play for us. Once, at one of my first parties, when we were having over forty guests, I decided to make a punch. I really had no experience, so I relied on the taste of the mix. To this day I remember the ingredients. I mixed three batches of: three bottles of champagne, two of white wine, and one bottle of vodka. It was a bit dry so I added four cups of sugar. Maybe it was the sugar that did it. About one hour into the party, people began to get quite high. I was so busy checking the servants, the empty glasses, and trays that I had not been drinking. So, I did not realize how strong the punch was. The pianist and violinist I had hired, had been given drinks and were changing from classical to modern music. The party was getting very noisy.

Little Angelo Hommelbacher, a charmingly funny man, had been doing the *hopak*, the Russian dance with "bent knees." At one point, he came over to me and said he had broken his thumb. He was holding the thumb, and I thought he was joking, as he usually did, and grabbed it. Giving it a twist, I said, "see it isn't broken." He dropped to the floor in agony, so someone took him off to the doctor as it *was* broken! I felt terrible.

92

Meanwhile, the party was thinning out. Some guests were walking up and down the street trying to sober up. Someone had gone off with the violinist. The pianist was no longer able to play well nor keep his mind on what he was playing. By now most of the high-ranking officers and their wives were beating hasty retreats to their cars after quick, "Thank yous." Some stayed and later wished they had not, as they dropped their ranks and had a rather raucous time. I was thinking that this was happening because it was a very warm day.

Some cool head figured out it was the mixture of liquors in the punch. We quickly made coffee and sandwiches as we attempted to subdue those remaining. Thank God Dad was also mellow as he did not give me the usual "talk" in front of the guests. I heard him telling guests that "these German liquors are quite potent". He also made a mental note never to let the musicians we hired drink. Some people were still having a great time, while others were eating the sandwiches and getting sober. Actually, it all ended well enough and those who managed to stay on their feet felt it was a great party.

However, Dad received a call the next day from the general suggesting more prudence with the punch ingredients. Dad did let me know that this had, "put me on the spot." Nevertheless, he also recognized that I had no knowledge about liquor, and dismissed the matter with the suggestion that I never use that mixture again. About two weeks later, the general's wife called and asked for the punch recipe!

With practice, my attempts at giving great parties improved, especially with Dad's guidance. He was always a great host. I always liked to add a little spice to our parties to make them different than just drinking or talking. I might hire singers, or musicians, or like the Germans organize games. We were soon in great demand socially and gave many parties ourselves. Again, it was our way of filling some very depressing times. Teas and bridge were the ladies' ways of socializing during the day. Protocol required returning these invitations. The army rank determined the seating and place in the welcoming, or greeting, and introduction process. In those days, protocol was everything, and an error was devastating. Perhaps one of the worse things that could happen was to appear at a party or gathering in the same outfit someone else was wearing. This was not a problem in our German groups, but occasionally happened among the Americans.

Wearing the wrong outfit was about as bad as wearing the same, or having a slip showing. We seemed, in those days, to try very hard to be perfect. Men had, and still have, their pants zipper to be concerned about. We were having some important guests at a party and Dad was late arriving home. He hurried in to change and came out in his usual charismatic way. He greeted the ladies in a charming manner. Never afraid of a center stage, he walked to the focal point (the fireplace) and rested his back against the mantle. It was then I saw that his fly was unzipped. He was telling the guests about some dignitary he had just met, and appearing quite handsome in his dress uniform. Handsome, except for this one huge social blunder. I quickly went behind the guests and frantically waved to him. He dismissed me with a "do not bother me now," look. I then apologized for interrupting him and said we had an emergency in the kitchen.

He excused himself and, with a grim face, followed me into the kitchen. Ina saw him and put her hand over her mouth so he would not see her laugh. When I told him what was wrong, I saw him blush for the first time I could remember. He zipped up and said that from now on we would have a password to let him know if this ever happened again. I do not remember the password, but I do remember having a great time telling this one on the colonel at more intimate parties.

I put on a tea once to introduce a new lady to the regulars. I was usually fairly good at introducing many people to each other and did so on this occasion. However, the general's wife was late. When she arrived and Ina ushered her in, I was "horrified" to see that she had come in a formal gown. We were all in our short party dresses. Protocol would make it my error in not informing my guest about the proper dress. I thought I had!

Struggling through my shock, I was trying to get everyone's name pronounced correctly. Although Mrs Funk knew most of the ladies, it was polite to give the name of each person just to be sure. I did, until I reached Ruth Semaschko. I could not possibly recall her name and gave up, saying after a pause, "This is Ruth 'Smith'." Mrs Funk, the general's wife, was a good sport and everyone laughed. The afternoon went well after that. When I asked Mrs Funk, privately, about the confusion regarding the dress, she told me she had

asked me what to wear. She thought I had said, "It is in a formal." She had thought it odd. I told her I had said, "It is informal." Thank heavens she was such a brick.

Dad took a course from a Toastmaster's group to learn to improve his speeches. He always seemed cool and unruffled, but his mind raced under pressure and he would wander from the subject. One thing he learned was to have an opening, a middle, and an ending. He also learned that opening with a joke helped warm up the audience. On the night of a large formal dinner and dance, he was picked as the moderator for the dinner speakers. This was his chance to use his new skills from Toastmasters. We ladies were all turned out in jewels and formal gowns, and the officers were in full-dress uniforms. I had a little trouble dressing after having lost so many clothes in that trunk. I did not have a long slip. I had hastily made one by cutting a satin nightgown in half and adding hooks at the waist.

We all took our places at our tables and Dad stood up to begin the speeches. I learned later that he had forgotten to rehearse a joke and had to come up with the last one he could remember. He was doing quite well, seemed composed, and introducing members at the head table. Then he started his opening speech. Horrors! I recognized the joke. It was a long one about a subject requiring the use of the word "urine" at the very end. I watched him start to squirm as he realized where he was going in front of this illustrious crowd. It seemed he was stalling, because people began to lose interest. He was also rambling and pausing in what I knew was agony. Eventually, it had to be said. Perhaps there was some reprieve as he substituted "number one."

That had to be one of our most embarrassing moments, most certainly his. No one laughed. Well, maybe a few good friends tried. He was devastated, but did manage to carry on and complete his speech. Later, the general and the military governor reprimanded him for his "poor taste." I do not remember any requests after that to give speeches. Later though, much later, we all had a good laugh. At this time, it was a difficult evening for us both. After dinner, a major had asked me to dance. He led me to the dance floor and we were in the midst of a waltz when my improvised slip cascaded to the floor. Worse, it was white and my dress was black! I gathered the slip

up like a train and headed to the ladies' room. Red faced, I stuffed
the slip into a garbage can and went back to my partner, sans slip. We
completed the dance. He never said a word about the incident.
There is something to be said about a gentleman.

I remember attending a party at an arty German's house. Many
artists, movie stars, and producers were there in this colorful crowd.
The daughter of the well-known woman psychiatrist, Karen Horney,
was there. This was Brigitte Horney. She told me that Freud, the famous psychiatrist, had bounced her on his knee when she was a
child. I was with a fellow who loved this Bohemian life. He was the
one who found me a bit part in the German movie, *Die Vern Luft*.
This evening it was an exciting group and I was loving it, but tiring
as I had just returned from a trip somewhere. At 1:00 in the morning, I told my escort that I just could not go on and asked him to
take me home. Instead, he produced a small pill and told me to take
it. I was reluctant, having never tried drugs.

Still, this was a great party and I was young, so I swallowed it. In
about twenty minutes I began to wake up and in another ten was sailing. I went nonstop until we closed the party at 11:00 that morning.
Earlier, I had looked at myself in the mirror when adding lipstick
and my eyes' pupils were pin-pointed. It was some kind of stimulant,
but to this day I do not know what it was. Now, by this time of the
morning, I was wearing down rapidly. When I looked at myself in the
mirror at home, I knew how I would look when I was old. My skin
was gray and dry and my eyes were two red orbs. I slept for two days.
I have never tried such a drug since.

Dad, myself and our guests often made up excuses to have a party
and then we would organize some kind of game. One time I had
Paula and Gundi staying with me in Stuttgart. We decided to invite
George, a fellow I had been seeing, over for drinks. We had already
had a few drinks and were feeling devilish. The ladies had been trying on my clothes and both looked like college girls. The Germans
loved our materials, especially the wools and cottons.. They had few
decent clothes of their own and this was a luxury. In the spirit of the
evening we decided to trick George. We set up a bucket of water over
the front door to douse him when he rang the bell. Poor George!

Meanwhile, unbeknownst to them, I called George and warned
him of what they were doing. I told him to park above the house and

walk on the opposite side of the street where it was unlighted. I would then meet him at the garden gate below the house. We would then come around the side of the house and scare the wits out of them. They were both hiding on the porch waiting to pull the rope attached to the bucket of water. So George (it was really quite dark) walked down the far side of the street. The ladies saw what to them appeared to be a furtive man sneaking along. This scared Paula and Gundi, as they were now convinced he was a robber or worse.

George and I met at the gate and sneaked around the house. We could hear the two crouching ladies asking each other in whispers if the other could see where the "criminal" had gone. Was he about to get them? George and I let out shrieks and ran toward them. Paula and Gundi jumped up, the bucket of water fell on them and they slipped and fell to the porch, screaming. Well, it was a while before the ladies found anything funny about what had happened. They accused me, rightfully, of the double cross. Still, George and I were in hysterics at how both looked. Later, I dealt with the fact that they had my clothes on!

Besides many teas and parties, we were once invited to a wine tasting at Count Johann Neipperg's castle at *Schwaigern.* Johann was a very handsome fellow, but I could not seem to get his attention. I did try. On this occasion a group of officers and their wives, joined Dad and me at the castle. Jof, as he was called, had invited us to a private party later that evening, so we had driven our own car as we planned to stay overnight. We were to taste the wine, have dinner, and then there would be dancing. The wine here was considered one of the finest in Germany. It was all processed and stored underground in the cool cellars of the castle. The weather that day was quite warm. We were told that they would offer us small sips of various wines and that we should eat the bread provided to reduce the effect of the wine.

I remember Dad's warning to take it slowly. Who listens to fathers anyway? The wine was marvelous and we guests savored, as amateurs, the delicate flavors and scents. One sip followed another, and the bread was eaten sparingly. The wine keeper and Jof described each wine for its qualities and its year. Between trying certain vintages, we went upstairs to walk around a bit in the sunshine. It seemed a long day and people increasingly were having trouble with their speech

and walking. I do not know if many in the group had ever been to a
wine tasting before. I certainly had not. We heard giggles from the
general's wife, and we all seemed to be having a great time. The
stairs became more difficult as time went on. Our group began to
thin out. Just we beginners and the experienced sippers seemed
game to keep on.

We heard rumors about someone who was having trouble walking. Someone else was sick. People were making their excuses and
going home. Thank heavens they had drivers. Somehow it had now
become a contest of who could last to the end of the tasting, or so it
seemed to my now fuzzy mind. Others thought the hot day was getting to us when we went upstairs. Whatever, I was now eating as much
bread as I could manage, and the wines all tasted the same. Hic.

Finally, we were finished and I literally staggered upstairs. I wonder if this was when Jof decided I was not for him? Although why had
he allowed so many people to over drink? My guess would be he was
too polite to stop them. Or, food was scarce and perhaps he saw this
as a way to cut down on the number of guests for dinner? At least
Dad and I were present. I know I did not touch my dinner wine.
However, I was dancing at 10:00 that evening, and feeling fine. It
pays to practice, and we Americans were certainly having many parties. I believe this was the castle where knights could ride a horse up
the stairs to the ballroom. That is one thing I did not try.

Paula, the children, and the old nurse nanny joined us for that
first German Christmas. The commissary did not have turkeys but we
could get a ham, cranberry sauce, and some pineapple. I spent time
decorating a small tree with some decorations Mother and Gram
had sent. We wrapped the packages and the place looked festive.
The children, Ronni and Resi, were very excited by the tree and
packages. The Germans did not decorate at Christmas as we did.
They just put their presents for the children on a table, without their
being wrapped.

Paula's children were very polite youngsters and we always enjoyed their presence. After a really decent dinner, we went to the
general's for a Christmas party. While there, I was told I had a telephone call. It was my mother, my grandmother, my brother, and his
wife, Toddy, wishing me a Merry Christmas. It really helped my
homesickness and I especially liked the fact that Dad had arranged

it for me. These moments when he was considerate of me were very important. I can remember few of these times, unfortunately. My mother and grandparents–Haines, were my best supporters. I believe this helped offset Dad's familiar complaints and lectures about my behavior.

CHAPTER XI

SCENES OF DESTRUCTION

This is 1946-see the crosses

I think it is important to note that all of us, in this war torn country, had our individual struggles to keep the postwar situation from depressing us. A drive to the store, a neighboring town, or to a party, took us through the streets where death and ruin were still very obvious. One could still smell death in the town of Pfortzheim. This had been the jewelry capital of Germany. Hitler's Generals had converted the jewelry industry into factories that made small parts for bombs and aircraft. This made the town a target for the Allied bombers when Allied espionage learned about the manufacturing going on there.

It was the English who decided to bomb the town. They had sent a warning to the civilians to get out on a certain night. This was humane, but it also warned the German antiaircraft and German air

force. For some reason, the English flew on over that night and they dropped no bombs. The flak from the antiaircraft guns might have deterred them. Several nights later they again warned the towns-people to leave, and again they flew over without dropping their bombs.

It happened a third time. So when the fourth warning came, only a few people left and the air force and ground forces were also slow to action. On that night the bombs fell, and in twenty-three minutes . . . they killed twenty- four thousand people. Horrible. The whole town was leveled. That means practically no building was left standing in the town itself. Direction was lost as all familiar landmarks were gone. The streets were littered with bricks and debris and were useless. All that could be done was simply to clear the streets by making huge mounds of the debris, without removing the bodies. Just covering them up! When I arrived in 1946, a year after the war ended, the thirty-foot piles of rubble still existed. Our minds had to wonder what stories were under those bricks. The people had stuck crosses into the piles to represent someone's loved ones still there.

At a crossroad to one of Dad's governing officer's territory, we would pass a familiar scene. Off the road, in a field, and turned up-side down, was a blown-up German army tank. The twisted tracks and crumpled body showed the force of the bomb, or shell, that hit it. Alongside, someone had built a large, crude cross. The soldiers'

German tank and helmets of eight dead boy soldiers ages 14 to 17.

Block after block of devastation

eight dented helmets were placed in a row. On the cross were the names of the soldiers and their ages. They were ages fourteen to seventeen! No one had removed the helmets for souvenirs. The message of this place to me was of the futility, stupidity, and death of innocence in war.

The people on the streets of Germany walked with their heads down. Their expressions were dull, yet, they seemed to be moving forward with more determination. Clothes were dark brown, black, or blue. The lagers (camps) were full of displaced people without homes, and many would never find their loved ones. Certain countries, America included, were allowing many of these people to immigrate entire families. The paperwork involved took considerable time but eventually the camps would be empty. The children were depressed and poorly fed in these camps and in the poorer homes. At one point, I went with Dad to see some prisoners of war coming back from Russia. They were a ghastly white, seemed well fed, but looked absolutely broken. I expected them to be happy or smiling to see their home again. Instead, they cried, or just stared at the crowd that met them in hopes of recognizing someone.

One man was fortunate in finding his wife and two children. I learned later that these released people were all taken to the army

hospital for check-ups. They were found to be severely malnour-ished. The "fat" I thought I saw was from fluid in their bodies and joints. Two young women I had seen had been used as prostitutes by the Russians from the time they were twelve and thirteen years old. No one came to meet them. They would all bear these scars as long as they lived.

The Germans feared and hated the Russians. The Americans were also very concerned about the behavior of Russia and could we trust them? We were always worried that the Russians might try to take the rest of the country by force. Gunilla warned Paula and me that if the Russians attacked, we should paint our lips and nails be-cause the Russians did not like "painted" ladies. She also told us to put a pillow under our dresses to look as though we were pregnant. She said the Russians had some respect for pregnant women. I do not know whether this was true or not.

We American dependents felt they were a bit sub-human. When we saw Russian soldiers, we crossed the street or avoided eye contact. No one seemed positive that Russia had finished the war and rumors were flying. At one point, a military government official delegated me as a "block warden". We had practice tests for the women and children. We would meet at a designated street in our cars. We were to drive toward the west. The day that I scheduled our first practice, we learned that the road where we were to meet was a "dead end." I can imagine what a mess this could have been if this were a real emergency.

A great deal of spying was going on between the Allies and Rus-sia. There was a tremendous amount of tension between these two groups. It is a wonder nothing terrible happened. I traveled a great deal while in Europe, but never to Berlin because of the Russian oc-cupying forces.

In June of 1948 Russia blockaded Berlin and attempted to take control of the city. This frightened us all. An airlift began, very well organized, to get food and needed products in to the Berliners. Eventually, the other Allies, England, France, and the United States began military maneuvers in the area to send a message to the Rus-sians to cooperate. Russia then exploded an atomic bomb. Obvi-ously, it appeared this military display on our part was not working, and the Allies then took a more diplomatic approach.

In May of 1949 there appeared to be a general consensus that Russia really was a threat. Countries began working together to protect, not only Germany, but themselves. This was when we returned a good deal of control to Germany. The capital was in the city of Bonn, Germany, despite the people's wish that it be in Berlin. Also, at this time, our War Department turned its governing units over to the State Department. John J. McCloy became our High Commissioner for Germany. I had the opportunity of meeting this serious man and photographed him and his family in Stuttgart. He was touring the area and Dad was the official greeter. We had them for lunch at our home.

Dad often traveled to Berlin on official business. He dreaded these trips due to the problems encountered going through the Russian control points. The Russian soldiers seemed anxious for situations in which they could dominate and shoot. They made everyone wait long periods of time while they seemed to check papers. Dad knew they could not read or speak English, so it was just their need to exert their power.

Once, when he and his driver had cleared one control post, they continued on the icy roads. Around the corner they suddenly came to a second guard post, and had trouble stopping the car on the slippery roads. Isolated as these places were, there was no one to call for help. As they slid past the guard Dad said he felt the hair rise on the back of his neck as he anticipated being shot. Luckily, the Russian did not fire. While this man was checking their papers, a GI who had been driving an ambulance came to speak to Dad. He said the Russians had held him there for eight hours and he was afraid they were not going to accept his papers. Dad knew of such situations where the Russians had impounded American vehicles and they had held our soldiers for no reason.

He suggested that the soldier walk into the woods as though he needed to relieve himself. He was then to meet them around the next corner. This was quite a risk for all of them, but it worked. Dad expected trouble regarding abandoning the ambulance, but none came. Eventually, he could fly to Berlin when the Allies had opened the airport, thus avoiding these problems. I never saw Berlin as I was too cowardly to take these risks.

SKIING

Germany had many skiing areas. These were often used by our military as R&R sites (rest and relaxation) for the forces and their dependents. Even before the end of the war, we occupied and held certain ski resorts for this purpose. They were also for the recovering wounded. Officers had their usual separate quarters, which were the better hotels and resorts. Nevertheless, one of the largest hotels in Garmisch was designated to the enlisted personnel. It was on the beautiful Eibsee Lake with fishing, skiing, boating, etc. It was really a lovely place and I spent many good times there as one of my friends was the manager.

I most enjoyed Garmisch-Partenkirchen, south of Munich, usually in the winter, but also in the summer. It was a lovely little town, without bomb destruction. The hotels were, as usual, painted with murals, and had lovely plaster and wood siding over plaster and brick. The streets were cobblestone and narrow. The homeowners covered the buildings' window boxes and porches with their favorite geraniums, in the summer. We often saw oxen in these small villages, hauling their loads to or from the farms. These oxen and giant draft horses pulled the wagons and sleds in the winter.

I do not recall the name of the hotel where we usually stayed, but I came to know the American manager, Lou Montford, of San Francisco, California. His buddy, Al, ran the Eibsee, so we spent summers mostly at the lake and winters in Garmisch. Lou and I dated for the three years I was in Europe. He proposed to me two months after we met, but I was not to be tied down. Lou was well liked and he was a perfect hotel manager, getting along with all. He came to visit me in 1954 when I was living in Seattle, and I visited him in California. I hope that he is today the charming fellow he was then and in Garmisch.

Driving into Garmisch in the winter was a thrill as the roads were narrow, crowned, and covered with compact snow and ice. The approach to the town was a straight, down the hill road. It was like a ski slope for cars. I cannot remember the number of times we spun out of control. We had no cross-country or snow tires in those days, and the Germans never seemed to use sand on the roads. We would end up going backwards, hopelessly sliding into the snow banks, or miraculously correcting our motion. It really stirred up one's blood and

Lou Montford

the anticipation was a killer for me. I have always had a great fear of ice and snow. I dread that feeling of being out-of-control. I was in sixteen accidents in those three years, most of them in the winter. However, it never stopped me from going to Garmisch or anywhere else whenever I could.

Never a coordinated person, I found skiing was too much of a challenge. Lou, a great fluid skier, would try to adjust my genetic makeup with lessons, but without success. Eventually exasperated, he took me to the beginner's "hole." This was to teach me to relax my stick-like behavior in a "safe" place. The "hole" was just that. It was probably about forty feet down and forty feet up the other side. No place to go, so nothing to be nervous about. I could handle this. A bit embarrassed by the children who were also using this area, I perched on the brink and taking a big breath, shushed down the hill. Later, Lou said he had to push me.

I made it to the bottom and put on the brakes, but I was not good at that either. I found myself now shushing up the other side, but slowing rapidly. Among my other problems, I did not like to fall down. I had, by now, come to a complete stop about halfway up. Vi-

sions of becoming a perpetual motion skier came to mind as I wondered what to do. I began now to slide backwards down the hill in my own tracks. It did not take long before my tips dug in and I lost my balance in this backward angle. Lou gracefully flew to my rescue, lifted me up, and set me down facing forward. Off I went again, and not so far up the other side before repeating the procedure. By now a crowd had gathered, the children were gleeful, and I was near tears. Disengaging my skis, I plodded up the hill and headed for the bar. Lou was gliding quietly alongside and we never skied together after that.

Once I skied well! We had driven, perilously, through deep snow to the Fugger ski hut somewhere near Austria. Our friends were piled on each other's laps, and I think I was on Friedrich Carl's. Gundi, Pümi, Dad, myself and several Fugger friends were just skiing for the day. We could not have been too far from Babenhausen. We parked the car and had been driven to the ski hut in a snow vehicle. Gunilla had cleverly stayed home, although she did usually ski with us. We had a packed lunch and the usual schnapps. I tried once or twice to keep up with the others on my skis, but quickly gave up. Dad was quite good and of course had no fear. After a few hours of their skiing up the hills and down, and my watching, we stopped for lunch. A cosy fire warmed us and soon the schnapps turned us into a carefree group. It looked like skiing was over for the day. Like horseback riding, liquor and skiing do not mix.

While we were enjoying ourselves, we heard a shout and looked out the window. A fellow was telling Friedrich Carl that a big snowstorm was coming and they did not have time to get the snow vehicle to us. We decided that we should leave at once and would have to ski out. Dad and Friedrich Carl were concerned about my ability to keep up with them. I was also concerned, but as we started, and the skies were darkening, I felt a sudden rush of excitement. Perhaps it was the schnapps? Whatever, with dear Pümi staying behind me to be sure I stayed up, we took off.

It amazed me to feel fluid and relaxed and to let the skis go as fast as they wanted. The snow was three or four feet thick and at one point a fence was sticking up about a foot above the snow. They all jumped it. However, I had visions of catching my skis under the board, never to walk again. Nevertheless. it was too late to stop as we

were going downhill. As usual, I did not give myself the option of falling. I was rushing up to the obstacle. With a mighty push on my poles, and a leap, I made it over. Continuing, I even passed one of the other skiers. It was a great thrill, never to be repeated.

We were fortunate to be able to watch the 1948 Olympic ski jumping in Garmisch. That was a thrill as we perched on the side of the jumping slopes-a risky business. More than once a skier went off the course and crashed into the onlookers. It was amazing to see those jumpers go over our heads in perfect form, landing sometimes not too gracefully. The workers would repair the course by having fifty or more skiers move sideways up and down the slopes. As they moved, they stamped their skis to cover holes and even up the area. We were also able to attend the Ice Follies and the bobsledding. The bobsledding was as dangerous then as it is today. We saw some very bad accidents. I am so glad to be a rooted person!

One summer we attended a horse show in Garmisch. I was introduced to one of our American riders who had been an Olympic medalist in jumping. I am sorry not to remember his name. He was a Captain in the army. His horse was nineteen and he and that horse were one. He put on a demonstration that left us all rather teary-

Paula and Dad in Garmisch

eyed, considering the longtime relationship he had with the horse. The horse was to be retired following this show. I do not believe I have ever seen man and horse so much as one as they were.

About this same time, Lou was trying to get me to learn to water ski. Some people never learn. For one thing, I rarely appeared in a bathing suit, even if there were just women present. So he had to overcome this and all of my other excuses. We were at the Eibsee Hotel and using one of their boats. Maybe this was when Lou stopped proposing to me. He was so good at all of these sports. I could, at least, beat him easily at horseback riding.

After a few false starts, I arrived at the dock, in my suit, and covered by the usual towel. A large one! Unfortunately, Lou was waiting for me, the boat's motor was running, and the skis were in place. Damn things! He had briefed me about the simple procedure of sitting on a dry dock, skis in the water, tips pointed up. Hands poised waiting for the "gentle" pull on the line and then, the take off. Of course, he also described the bent knees and the forward position. I already knew what was going to happen, but he would not hear of it. So, he patted me and jumped into the boat. When he was occupied with driving the boat, I finally dropped my towel. With a reassuring wave, he started the boat and I waited for the "gentle" pull. Panic set in as the rope tightened, and when it started to jerk me off the dock, I dropped it.

Patiently, Lou came back and we went through the debriefing again. This time I was really going to try, especially if this would end the session. He waved again and I felt determined. The slack ran out and again I dropped the rope. On the third try, I hung on and made it off the dock to plunge face first in the water with quite a whack. I had gotten my skis behind me, he said. Of course! The next try was better and I managed to keep the skis under me. Under the water! Whether he had slowed, or I had gained weight, I do not know. He towed me for about two blocks as I continued to sink, still upright, and still on the skis. I let go as we neared the dock and only my head was above water. When I arrived on the the dock, skis in hand, Lou said nothing and we quietly headed for the bar. My towel was securely around me.

CHAPTER XII

PHOTOGRAPHY

I had never thought of my living expenses in Europe before the trip. As Dad was tight regarding money with his family members, this was beginning to be a problem for me. I did not like to have to ask him for needed expenses. He always gave me a lengthy lecture about the shortage of money. Yet, he would spend whatever it took to entertain his friends and dignitaries. I took this personally, rather than seeing the diplomacy in it. So, I was hard pressed to come up with cash as needed. Later, Dad added the suggestion that I should find a job to support myself. The thought of working was actually a shock to my system. By then I was too spoiled by the travels and parties to want to be tied down to "work." I did have the settlement I had received from the damage to my trunk. That carried me for a while. My mother and grandmother were wonderful about sending me what I needed, and enclosing a bill for Dad. However, he began to highly resent this, as he was duty bound to pay it.

Early in 1947, I came up with the thought of becoming a professional photographer. This would pay for my expenses and give me further opportunity to travel. Also it would be a great delay in having to face going to work eight hours a day. Dad fell for it and helped me buy a wonderful Rolleiflex camera and get setup with a darkroom. We knew a family that had a fabrik (factory) where they made photographic lenses, developers, etc. As such items were scarce, we were lucky to be able to get what I would need from these pleasant people. These were the Von Bergs. They were a very fine couple and she was an excellent artist and sculptor. She later did a very good clay

bust of me. It was awarded a ribbon at an art show.

We also knew Hubs and Ilse Flöter, both well-known photographers. I had been traveling with them on their various photographic projects learning all I could about taking artistic photos. Ilse, an attractive and shy person, was the photography fashion expert who was known for her dramatic pictures of models and outfits. She and I often traveled to fashion shows, or just enjoyed each other's company. I remember during the worst years for the Germans that she had come and asked for some food, "for a friend." I had, stupidly, assured her that it was all right to ask because we wanted to help. She had burst into tears at this embarrassment and I felt quite miserable. Pride was quite important when so little else was available.

Hubs did more news and celebrity shots, and portraits with excellent use of black and white shadow technique. There was no decent color film available at that time. We shot photos of trees and shadows and the structure of bridges, anything to accentuate the contrast of black and white. I loved photography and really studied and listened to whatever the two of them taught me. I would help repay them with cigarettes, film, silk stockings, etc., to compensate for their time. They did not have a car so I was also their transportation.

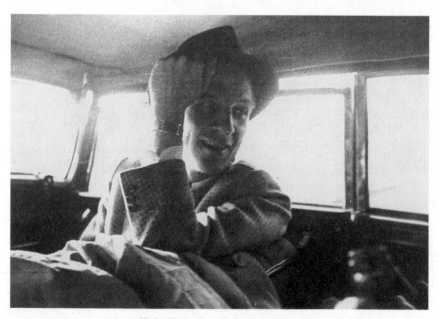

Hubs Flöter German photographer.

Ilse Flöter German photographer (photo credit Hubs Flöter)

As time went on, I gravitated to Hub's style, enjoying the more artistic qualities of his subjects. Ilse and I continued to be friends. She also had a crush on Dad. Hers was not a very happy marriage. These references to "unhappy" marriages should not excuse my father's or the ladies' behavior. However, it seemed a rather common practice in Europe. These *liaisons* were not to be openly pointed out, nor was it polite to confront someone. It was gossiped about by all, but never

recognized by the participants. This seemed to make it all right.

Ilse was rumored to have an old love in Austria. In her struggle to survive in these difficult times, she developed a strong need to see this man. She had tried to get Dad to help her get a pass to Austria, but he could not do this. Although he tried. She also was afraid that the authorities might find out that she was a quarter Jewish, if she had to make out papers. This was an old fear that they would discover her "secret," hidden during the terrible anti-Semitic war years. Ilse could have been ostracized as a photographer if her Jewish background was known. She also feared if she were to get to Austria, the Germans would not let her back and she might not see her child, Renatus, again. How this must have weighed on her mind—such a conflict.

We learned, after the fact, that Ilse had finally managed to get a ticket to Vienna. How she did it, we never found out. Both Dad and I feared for her safety, as the Russians would not be kind if they caught her. After a long time, Hubs told us that they had indeed apprehended her. Dad did his very best to contact Austrian and Russian authorities, without success. She was gone. No one could believe that she would have abandoned Renatus, whom she had left with a family member near where she had taken the train. We never knew what, if any, was Hub's role in all of this. It was a great loss to us all, especially the way it happened. I often wonder what her fate was.

A Countess Sigi von Diergart, a friend of the Flöter's, would often join us on our photo excursions. I really liked Sigi. She and her brother had escaped the Russians, but the soldiers had killed her parents and burned their palatial castle. Sigi and her brother had both witnessed this and she told harrowing tales of their escape. The parents had hurriedly packed a few mementos, some money and clothes for them and sent them down the back road toward the west. These few mementos were all they had of their former life. She was an intelligent, proud person and very well raised. We became friends and she was often at the house.

One day she presented me with a lovely crystal and sterling decanter that was from her family estate. I tried to refuse it as I knew it must be terribly important to her. However, she was so appreciative of my help and friendship that she insisted I keep it. She was also helping me with my halting German and I was getting better at

Countess Sigi von Diergart, a friend

speaking more freely. I always dreaded making mistakes. Shortly after receiving the decanter, we were having lunch at the house. When
we were finished, I jokingly said, *"hast du gut gefrisst."* This is a statement made to your pets after you feed them. It means, "have you
eaten well?" It was my intent to be funny and show her that I knew
how to say this. Unfortunately, to my great dismay, it was a terrible
insult to her and she left immediately. I was mortified, very upset by
this innocent but stupid error of mine. She would never accept an
apology and that was the end of our friendship.

I have often thought about that blunder and wonder whatever
happened to Sigi. I do hope she found a comfortable life. The decanter is still with me, but I have never felt that it is really mine. It
had been an article from the castle of King Frederick the Great. One
of the king's relatives gave it to her family. Recently, I saw a similar
piece in an auction catalogue of a sale to be held in Denver, Colo-
rado. I bid on it by telephone, hoping to have a set if I got it. When
the bid was five hundred dollars, I gave up. I did write the auction
company to give them the history of the piece so that the new owner
might know where it had come from.

Hubs and I often traveled around Germany taking pictures of
various subjects of interest to the papers and magazines. Usually
Herr Braun drove us, and later when we had the Packard convert-

German Port Officials, not too friendly

ible, I drove to our assignments. We went to Bremerhaven to do a series on the shipments of aid from the United States It was maddening to see the pillage of the foodstuffs by the laborers. It was hard enough to learn that the sacks marked from the United States were emptied into German marked containers so the American tax payer received little credit for their gift. We were very careful in this area not to be seen taking pictures of the theft going on by the laborers, in case of reprisal. There seemed to be no one minding the store.

Another time, we drove to the movie studios in Munich for portrait sessions with some German stars. I remember a very dramatic Sybille Schmitz, who posed with great skill for me. I was told she had tried to commit suicide several times, and I believe she might have finally ended her life that way. She was one of Germany's greatest stars. Another rumor about her was her "partial exile" by Hitler because she would not sleep with Goebbels. On this day, the studio was filming a very good movie and we could photograph some of the best stars of Germany. Otto Wernicke, Willi Birgel, Viktor De Kowa, Hildegard Kneff, and Sybille. Hildegard later became a star in the United States. She spent time with me, asking about Hollywood, our stars, and life in our country. At that time, she spoke very little English.

Hildegard Knef German movie star

Later, I went to the same studio alone to do a bit part in a movie called, *"Die Ferne Luft."* A rather bohemian, American officer had arranged this for me. The same one who had me try the "pill" at the "arty" party. I was to answer a statement in German by asking, "What is in the air?" Try it. It does not come out easily, and it did not. Also, I was a nervous wreck in front of all of the cameras and stars. There was no one there to coach me, or to explain what was happening. They just told me to speak my "English" when they pointed at me.

To calm myself, I asked for a beer and was surprised to get one. They were also unhappy with my dress as it did not afford enough "contrast." I remember the long drive home from Munich that night as I felt a perfect failure. This was later verified at a party by the young star, Betsy von Fürstenberg. She could not wait to loudly announce that my portion of the movie had been left on the cutting room floor.

I began to do a series of pictures without Hubs as I was trying to get published in the United States. One such was a program I had helped develop. A group of our lady welfare workers had managed to help the town of Worthington, Minnesota, adopt the town of Sinsheim, Germany, and ship clothing and food to them. A whole

train carload came into the station at Sinsheim painted with signs of "Welcome Sinsheim From Your Sister City, Worthington, Minnesota." Newspaper reporters were there as were dignitaries from the German and United States governments.

I was snapping pictures and running from group to group when I saw officials unloading boxes of pretty white dress pumps. Shoes. Now, besides cobblestones, there was mud from the oxen and cattle that were driven through these streets. Most of the children were from farm families and were in mud caked boots. The opportunity to wear such fashionable shoes would probably be limited to a quick change after they arrived at church. I had a man arrange the shoes in a semicircle and had the children line up behind them for the picture. It was a stark contrast in footwear to say the least. Most important to me, though, was the look of wonderment and awe on the girls' faces. My pictures were published in *American* magazine. They were also published in the Army magazine, *Stars and Stripes* and in German magazines as well. Dad was pleased this time and I made

A gift to Sinsheim, white pumps for muddy boots.

some money.

I decided to do a series on the four military governors of the American Occupied Zone. They were all quite cooperative until I called General Mueller of the Bavarian Zone. I was not aware of this man's arrogance at first. We worked out a schedule where his driver would pick Hubs and me up in Stuttgart on his way back from Frankfurt. We were driven to Munich and finally ushered into the general's office after a long wait. I was not pleased by that time as I have never learned to be kept waiting. However, I took many pictures of this man who seemed to me like the Nazi prototype of a general. He was cold and aloof, and rushed me along.

When I had finished, I asked when the car would take us back. I was coolly informed that they had made no such plan and we would have to find our own way back to Stuttgart! This was about a five-hour drive. We had not come prepared to stay the night. Before I could gather my wits, he dismissed us. Probably a good thing that it all happened so fast, or I might have overdone my reaction to this pompous fellow.

I had about three dollars and Hubs had a few marks. We walked to the American occupied hotel where they told me I would have to pay in advance for my room. Despite my attempts to have them call Dad, there was no cooperation. I knew no one in Munich. Hubs came to the rescue by saying we would see an artist friend he knew, and perhaps she could help. I was feeling very whipped about this time and felt that the Americans were letting me down. It made me appreciate the Germans more. We walked, by now quite hungry, to his friend's. This was a typical artist's attic in the back streets of Munich. She was a very arty lady, dressed like a gypsy, and a bit too friendly. However, she was willing to lend Hubs some marks so we could eat and buy tickets on the next train to Stuttgart. After chatting with her, and seeing many sketches and paintings of her in the nude, we left to find a meal.

The streets of Munich were still in ruins from the bombings. Buildings were leveled and we were again walking past piles of rubble and crosses. This did not help my mental state at the time. My mind kept dwelling on what I would one day do to the general. There was no doubt by the Germans in the streets that I was an American. Nevertheless, there was no trouble. Bless them, as I was by now ex-

hausted. Hubs said we were going to the Continental Hotel for dinner. I wondered how far we would have to go, as there were no standing hotel-type buildings in sight. We came around a corner to a flattened pile of bricks with stairs leading down to the basement. This was what was left of the hotel. We went down to the cellar where they had restored some rooms into dining, bar, and dance areas. There we had a simple, but good, meal and some excellent wine.

Hubs and I finished dinner and off we went again walking to the train station. It was now about 10:00 p.m. as we neared the train depot where I thought we would have an early seat on the train. Again, I had a complete lack of knowledge of the real situation. We entered the station where there were hundreds of peasants with empty sacks, and hundreds of civilians with full sacks. It was the end of market day. There must have been a thousand people milling around the station. Hubs and I stood in line for our tickets for a frantic half hour. I was afraid we would not catch the train. We did not have enough money for rooms for the night. We finally made our way to the track, only to find hundreds of people waiting for our train.

It seemed hopeless, but Hubs gave me a strict command to follow him. We went down the track for several hundred yards until the crowd began to thin. The train was coming slowly in and Hubs told me to be sure to do as he did. As the train passed us, he suddenly swung aboard and I grabbed the handle and did the same. The jerk of the train was unnerving. To this day, I have nightmares about that scene. As I swung onto the train, I felt myself losing my grip and I looked down to see the rails speeding by.

Somehow I managed to pull myself aboard and I clung to Hubs as he made his way to a seat. Others were already doing the same and the train was filling rapidly. Our seats held six comfortably, but we were soon seven, with sacks and bags everywhere. When the train finally stopped, people were banging on the window, which was already broken, to be let in. Someone opened it further and we began letting them in. Others would offer schnapps or food for a seat. It was chaos with a purpose.

We were soon like packed sardines enjoying a bottle of very strong, horrible tasting schnapps. However, it was a camaraderie that included this American. After exchanging small talk, the long day had eventually caught up with us and we slept. I had sleeping heads

on both shoulders. They did not smell so good, but who cared. It was a long night in that we were restless, but short in that we arrived at five-thirty in the morning. By now we were all strangers again and went our separate ways. Hubs and I called a taxi, knowing that we could pay when I arrived home. I slept for two days.

Sometime after that I was in Munich with Herr Braun, our driver. I was hungry and remembered the Continental Hotel and directed him to find it. He had a puzzled look on his face and said he did not know such a hotel. It seemed to me everyone in Germany knew the Continental Hotel as we knew the Stork Club in New York. We were speaking in German of course, but I was pronouncing Continental in English. How many ways can it be said? The more I repeated myself, the more he became bewildered and the angrier I became. What was his problem? After seemingly endless tests of patience, and stupidity in my mind, a light seemed to dawn on his face. Proudly he announced, "*Ach so! Die Hotel ContinenTAL!*" The stress was on the "TAL." I burst into laughter over that one, and we went directly to the Hotel *ContinenTAL*. More than once we were to struggle with pronunciation of seemingly simple words.

My pictures of the four governors were accepted for the Army newspaper, Stars and Stripes, and I chose the worst one of General Mueller It was one where he looked as arrogant as Hitler, maybe worse. Later, at a party, I was the guest of honor of Governor Sumner Sewall, the governor of our area. General Mueller was also present. When Governor Sewall introduced us, I reminded the general of the pictures I had taken of him in Munich. He became quite flustered at remembering me and seeing me in this company. I made no bones about telling Sumner of my trip home from Munich and the general turned crimson. He apologized profusely, but he remained, I am so glad, embarrassed by the situation.

In 1948 Eleanor Roosevelt came to Stuttgart to speak to the German people in a gesture of friendship. Our military governor then was Charles LaFollette. His wife, Frances, and I were good friends. Mrs Roosevelt was to stay with them and Frances told me she would, somehow, arrange for me to be there so that I could get some pictures. Eleanor was making it well known that this trip was for the Germans, not the Americans. Governor LaFollette was following her instructions regarding this, and so was opposed to any efforts of the

Eleanor Roosevelt

American or German media to interrupt her plans. Still, Mrs. LaFollette was a bit of a rebel and let me in on the schedule. She told me that Mrs. Roosevelt would come from the airport to a meeting at their house. Eleanor was to discuss social issues with a group of German dignitaries. Frances had me come to their house just before Eleanor was to arrive. She showed me where the entourage would enter and told me just to stay out of the governor's way!

I was very excited about seeing Mrs. Roosevelt and made every effort to follow Frances' advice. We were not certain if Eleanor would permit me to take pictures of her. So, I risked a big rejection, but I also had the opportunity to scoop the press. I arrived ahead of schedule, already quite nervous. Frances let me in and we were like two kids afraid of being caught. She took me to the meeting room and introduced me to the German dignitaries, so they would know me. Then we went to the hallway to watch Mrs. Roosevelt come in. I think Frances was as excited as I. Soon the car arrived, and Governor LaFollette stepped out and held out his hand to Eleanor. I was so surprised at how tall and buxom she was. She stood straight and had

a lovely smile, despite being quite tired. Eleanor was not a pretty person, but obviously a very bright one. My photos of her walking toward the house reflected my nerves as they were not sharp and clear.

Eleanor and Governor LaFollette went by us and up to his office on the floor above. Charles, busily talking to Eleanor, did not seem to notice Frances or me. A soldier brought in her one suitcase and another brought in her case of bottled *Vichy* water. (a mineral water from the French town of *Vichy*) The soldiers told me that she always traveled with her own bottled water. While I was trying to compose myself, one of the men servants came over and asked if I would get his picture with Mrs. Roosevelt. I told him I would do the best I could, and he did end up posing behind her every time he saw me point the camera toward Eleanor. When I later developed the film. there he was. He was thrilled.

Time dragged on and no Eleanor. Finally, Frances must have run out of patience because she told me to go upstairs and ask the governor if I could take a picture of them. Not too bright, but I went upstairs and could hear them talking. Governor LaFollette saw me (Eleanor had her back to me) and he waved me away. Eleanor turned and smiled and asked me what I wanted. I am sure I mumbled something about taking a picture of her. She kindly told me she would be down in a short time. When Mrs Roosevelt came downstairs, I was again impressed with her height. She was dressed in a plain black crepe dress, and on the front were stains from her meals. She appeared to be a casual person, not at all fashionably turned out. Her shoes were "sturdy." Nevertheless, she was very, very bright.

I was allowed to move about the room while Eleanor talked with the Germans in impeccable German. The butler kept serving anyone who was in my camera focus. Bless him. Later, I gave him a picture of himself and Mrs. Roosevelt. He was very grateful. Following this small gathering, I attended Eleanore's meeting at a conference hall with about five hundred Germans. They seemed to have great respect for this lady. Eleanor spoke for one hour in perfect German without one error. She was extremely well received. Later, that evening, there was a dinner for her, given by the LaFolletes. They included me and there were other American ladies who were working on charities for the Germans. I had rushed home, developed,

Eleanor and author (photo credit Eitel Lange)

and enlarged an excellent picture of her. Slipping from my good behavior a bit, I intended to get Eleanor's autograph on the photo with a message to my grandmother, Edith Haines. Grandmother was a staunch Republican and thought Eleanor belonged in the home and not running around the country. I thought it would be quite a joke on Gram.

I stood in the receiving line and watched Mrs. Roosevelt being quite diplomatic and not showing signs of being tired from the long day. The woman ahead of me kept talking to Mrs. Roosevelt and was making us all wait. Eleanor looked a little short but constrained. Finally, I could not put up with it any longer and moved gently forward to tell the lady that I had an urgent message for Mrs. Roosevelt. She reluctantly gave up her hold. When the woman could no longer hear us, Eleanor thanked me gratefully for "rescuing" her. She liked the picture I had taken of her and gladly signed it, "To Mrs. Haines with best wishes from Eleanor Roosevelt." We chatted briefly. I was a bit ashamed of myself about the picture, but very happy to have met this lovely woman. Later, Grandmother was to finally accept Eleanor as "a good person" because she had said pleasant things about me. Not quite a concession, but close enough.

Dad somehow managed to get papers for Hubs to accompany me to the French Riviera for some photo work. Germans were not al-

lowed out of the country without special passes and these were very difficult to get. I was to drive as Hubs did not know how. He was to be the navigator. Poor planning, as he also could not read maps. When we stopped for the picnic lunch Ina had packed, I asked him to clean the windshield of the car. Although this Packard was all electric, they did not yet have windshield washer jets. So, when we packed up to get under way, I faced a smeared glass. Puzzled, I asked Hubs what he had used to wash the windshield. He said, "canned milk!" He really was of little help in such matters on the trip.

We reached Marseilles on May 1, communist day. This town reminded me of Strasbourg. It was very old and very dirty. The ancient buildings had a stately appearance for the most part, but seemed almost unfriendly. A huge parade was marching on the next street, and I thought I could pass in front of them. However, the car stalled and stopped right in the middle of the parade. The cultural conflict of a young American capitalist lady, in a brand-new Packard convertible, and the workers of labor and communism in the parade was an epic. I do not know who was more startled. Nevertheless, they gave us a push and I finally managed to get the car going and we were on our way. It was really rather frightening, for both of us.

To avoid the main street, and further contact with the paraders, I chose a street that ran parallel to it, I thought. The car was wide and the street narrow. Cement steps were jutting out from recessed doorways and we were narrowly missing them. Slowly the street narrowed even more, until I was inching along. We were also turning corners. Hubs was no help at all. In fact he looked about ready to panic and leave me there. We were so close to the buildings we could not have opened the doors. There was no way I could have backed the car out of there! My only choice seemed to be to continue. My mind's eye pictured a dented, scratched car and a more than furious colonel. I also had visions of having to abandon it altogether. A monument to American capitalism imbedded between two buildings on a street in Marseilles. Ahead was a slight bend and daylight, could we make it? I know there was only a half inch to spare on each side of the car as we came out onto the main road again, behind the parade. What a relief! I looked at Hubs who was absolutely white. At least, he had not offered directions during this ordeal.

After recovering from Marseille, arriving on the Riviera was excit-

ing and it was hot. We stayed in a small hotel in Monte Carlo and made our plans from there. I was anxious to try the casinos. Hubs was enjoying the world outside Germany. We went our separate ways for a while. They would not allow pictures in the casinos, so I just enjoyed spending and losing a few dollars. Old gentlemen and ladies, with their secretaries alongside keeping records, played all day and all night. One evening, Rita Hayworth, the American movie star, and Ali Khan, her then boyfriend, were playing the tables. He had a large roll of money and would bet hundreds at a time. They finally began verbally fighting and she left.

The interiors of the casinos were very grand and Victorian. They were pompous and ornate, and had a richness that reflected the money that flowed back and forth at these tables. After losing the grand sum of three dollars, I headed for the beach. The beaches were beautiful and the water a clear blue. I was a bit unnerved by people undressing under the sidewalk. However, suffering from the heat, I soon joined them and changed into my bathing suit. Quickly, very quickly. I even abandoned my cover-up towel! Here there was a certain feeling of freedom. Something similar to what I had seen at the *Follies Bergere* in Paris. But I was not going that far. I hoped Hubs was enjoying himself because I wanted time in this atmosphere.

Eventually, I returned to the shade and changed back to my street clothes, by now completely comfortable. I joined Hubs, who was sitting at the sidewalk cafe in front of our hotel. We enjoyed an afternoon drink and then drove up the hill to look at the Prince of Monaco's castle. We waited in hopes of someone driving out, but no luck. It was all very grand.

Getting back into a work ethic the next day, we drove to an area famous for its perfumes. It was a quaint little town with the nicest aromas. The town was very picturesque with its old buildings. Not seeing much in the way of public interest here, Hubs remembered that Maurice Chevalier, the French movie star, lived a short distance away. With a little sleuthing and a telephone call, we found ourselves greeting this charming man in his beautiful villa. Hubs was not much with autos but clever in finding good photo subjects.

Chevalier was dressed casually in slacks, an open shirt, and sandals. He was quite handsome. He showed us through his lovely home and its gardens. He was very happy to have us take his picture.

I had become a bit shy, and somehow must not have taken a single picture of him. I think I did not want to appear as "just a photographer," as I was quite intrigued with this Frenchman. It was a grand visit and not one to be easily forgotten. Maurice was outstanding and a gentleman! We would have been great together on the beach!

Hubs and I also found the studio of Picasso, the very popular painter. Luckily, it was open to the public. Picasso was very well known and it was his period for "cubism." Unfortunately he was not in his studio when we were there and we could not locate him. We had really hoped to be able to do some photos of him. However, I was most impressed with the studio. One easel was slightly off center in this smallish room. On it was an example of his classical style of painting, which I admired much more than his more recent work. I believe they arranged the studio in such a way that we became a part of his picture! The room was without anything else, except a few baskets lying around. Nothing like the clutter that usually surrounded him and no example of his cubism.

We worked most of the way back home, stopping at movie studios, art colonies, and just getting studies of local characters. It had done Hubs a world of good getting away from the destruction and struggles in Germany. I did not tell Dad how close we came to leaving the car in Marseilles.

The movie, *I Was a Male War Bride* was being filmed in Heidelberg. Dad had known the director, Howard Hawks, and the chief photographer, Russ Harlin in Hollywood. Howard had asked Dad, some years before, to be technical director for the movie, *Sergeant York*. As a result of their friendship, Dad arranged for me to be an "extra" so that I could "earn some money." We also arranged some hunts for Howard and Russ, which I will discuss later. This was a wonderful opportunity to use my photography, and I was able to get many good shots of the actors. Cary Grant and Ann Sheridan were the stars. We came to know other actresses such as, Marian Marshall and Betsy Drake. Betsy later became Cary's wife.

It was a lot of fun being in the movie and learning about film making. Having seen some of my photography, Russ Harlan asked me if I would like to be a photographer with him in Hollywood. I told him I would think about it and stupidly asked if an "apartment" came with it. This was, as Hollywood goes, a very pleasant man who

Cary Grant star of Male War Bride

Ann Sheridan star of Male War Bride

was surprised by my remark and not too happy. Perhaps I was being too cynical? I had lived long enough in Hollywood to know most offers for movie roles had to be *earned!* There went another opportunity for a new and exciting life. Also, I was not ready to leave the fascinating life I was already living for the unknown.

For this movie I was a WAC (women's army corp) and a private. Obviously I did not pull rank. All I had to do was cross a few streets

and walk down the sidewalk. We extras were scenery behind the stars. At one point, I actually came within twenty feet of the cameras. I really tensed up at that point. Trying to upstage (attracting attention to yourself) anyone around you was not unusual. They had paired me with a short, wiry lady who was an old hand at this extra business. She told me when to address the camera and how to get them to look at or notice you. Because of her shortness and my height, she had a hard time upstaging me. But she tried.

Today many of these scenes have been left on the cutting room floor. Seems to be a habit of mine, but I think I looked quite good in uniform back then. As extras, we would go on location with the crew and this gave me a chance to take pictures of the stars. Ann and Cary usually stayed away from the others so I made separate appointments with them. Cary was friendly and loved posing. He knew just the stance to take and was an ideal subject. Ann was more genuine, interested in others, and a very hardworking actress. If anyone thinks these movie people do not earn their fame and money, then they are wrong. They are usually up and on the set by 6:00 a.m. and work until the end of daylight. They spend time being coached, in makeup, learning their lines, and in endless repeats of scenes.

We had several parties with the cast and crew. I had invited Captain Dean Bressler, a boyfriend, to a fancy party given by General Eisenhower for the stars, other actors and actresses, and some of the head technicians. Dean was a handsome fellow, and I did my share of chasing after him to keep reminding him that he was with me. All the starlets seemed attracted to him and he was enjoying every moment of it. Even Cary invited him to lunch the following day. At least I was able to chat with Ann Sheridan. However, she had to leave early as she had an early morning scene. The party really gathered momentum and as I was dancing with someone else, I noticed Dean was missing. Well, he was a big boy and I gave up worrying about him.

Dad had been spending the evening talking to General Eisenhower. I found the General interesting, but he seemed a bit too serious for the party atmosphere. Many years later, at Dad's resort in Baja, Mexico, General Eisenhower arrived at the resort's landing strip. There was no advance reservation so Dad did not expect him. He had been president by then and was now retired. Dad made it a habit to greet all planes coming into the resort. On that day upon

hearing the plane arriving, he climbed into the jeep and tore off to the landing strip. The general, now a civilian and in sport clothes, was getting out of the plane with friends. Dad approached Ike and introduced himself. "How do you do, I am Colonel Walters, owner of Rancho Buena Vista, and I do not believe I know you." The general replied, "How do you do, I am President Eisenhower, and I do not believe I know you either."

Meanwhile, at the party, Dad wanted to return to Stuttgart and had a ride home with friends. He left me the Packard and suggestions about an early evening. Dean came up, about that time, looking a bit flustered. He said that Marian Marshall would like to ride to Stuttgart with us and see the city. "Yes, of course" I said. However, the implications of his request made me quite angry. Still, I kept my wits about me. We piled into the car, Dean driving, and me, guess where, in the backseat by myself. I was wondering where Marian expected to stay the night, when Dean suggested that perhaps both of them could stay at my place. This would save them a late night trip to his place. Why was I here? This woman was interesting as far as Hollywood chatter went, but this seemed too much for me. Arriving at the house, we had a few more drinks and then all went to bed. All night I heard the patter of feet up and down the hall. In the morning they were both gone, and so was my relationship with Dean.

Paul Lukas and Merle Oberon came to Stuttgart to make the movie, *Berlin Express*. This time I called and arranged to get pictures of them, on my own rather than through Hubs. I was feeling more comfortable working by myself, without him. I actually could get through directly to Paul, but had to go through Merle's secretary for an appointment. We were able to arrange for me to be there the same morning to do them both, but separately. They did not like each other. This is the life of the stars, very competitive. When I arrived at the hotel, I was to call Paul's room and he would meet me in the lobby. I noticed a familiar looking man sitting by the desk when I arrived, but did not pay attention to him in my preoccupation with meeting Lukas. I stepped up to the desk and asked the clerk to call Mr. Lukas' room.

The man sitting in the chair said, "I am Paul Lukas." I was so embarrassed. He was a very well-known star and one just did not do this to them. A star is a star to be seen. Despite this poor start, we hit it off

Paul Lucas star of Berlin Express

quite well and went to his room for the sittings. He told me about
the movie and how he and Oberon had difficulty working together.
This was fascinating conversation to me. I told him about my life in
Germany and he was genuinely interested. I had no difficulty getting
good pictures. These actors are well aware of their "best side" and
how to pose. All I had to do was place him where the light was correct.

After finishing with Paul, I went to a totally different situation
with Merle Oberon. Her secretary announced me, and after a short
wait, I was ushered into her room. She was quite heavily made-up but
I could see that she had heavy pitting on her face, especially around
the chin. She went on at great length about how horrible she found

Merle Oberon star of Berlin Express

the German situation, her shock at some scenes, and especially that,
"I weep for the children." It was not, I was sure, that she was not sin-
cere, but she seemed to be acting. Or perhaps she was just an extremely sensitive person. She was very theatrical or dramatic and it
was difficult for me to believe she meant what she said. Staged,

might be a better way of describing the moment.

I also found it quite difficult to get her attention and to position her for the proper light. I tried to get her to say something about Paul, but she did not even want to mention his name. When I was finished, they quickly ushered me out. I felt she was a very spoiled person, but a great actress. I loved her in the movie, *Wuthering Heights*. It was necessary to have Ilse Flöter retouch Oberon's pictures for me due to the pitting. The photos of Oberon and Lucas were published, along with an article I wrote, in the German papers.

I tried never to miss a chance to get a good photograph, and often did studies in shadow and light of interesting faces. One such was surely the Countess Brita Bielke, mother of Princess Gunilla

Countess Brita Bielke of Sturefors Slott

Fugger. A very handsome, proud, and austere lady, who seemed the last of her kind. She spoke many languages and rarely completed one sentence in one language. She wore exquisite clothes and was always immaculately turned out. The Countess had been widowed at a young age. She had reared her five children and governed the family palace, Sturefors in Sweden. Brita had a strong personality and usually directed most activities of her surrounding group. However, she loved parties and enjoyed the opportunity of letting her hair down. She was really quite relaxed and most enjoyable after a few drinks.

On this occasion, Brita was visiting us at our house in Stuttgart. She was such an interesting study and I decided to try some portraits. I was able to get her to settle down for a few minutes. I then tried to get a flattering image that would not need to be retouched due to her age. Brita made a good subject and posed well and confidently for me.

As much as I enjoyed my camera work, I also enjoyed my darkroom. It seemed a mysterious place where you found success or failure in your work. On this day, I carefully developed and dried the film. Good. Then I laboriously positioned the negative reflection on the back side of the developer paper to be sure I would get the right a balance on this profile shot. All in order, I developed the picture. What came out was a shock. There was a one-eyed cyclops with gold shell earrings and wrinkles on both sides of the eye. I had transformed this handsome lady into an ogre of hypnotic appearance. It was the kind of freak accident that makes money in its weirdness. It would have won any photo contest because it was perfectly balanced and developed. Obviously the image had developed from having centered it on the back of the developing paper.

I showed it to Dad who was struck by its grotesque nature. Nevertheless, he appreciated the originality of it. However, we both knew it would be an insult to the Countess to think of publishing it. For once, he left it up to me to decide what I would do about it. I kept the picture for a week and then destroyed it. I often tried to reproduce that image, but could never get it balanced nor evenly developed. I never told Brita. However, she did like the profile that I had done and I gave her several copies.

Dad decided to fly to the United States for a meeting and so

Paula came to stay with me. We rode horseback every day and had friends in for parties. Gundi joined us and we drove the Packard to Heidelberg for a party. For fun, Gundi and Paula were wearing my American clothing as they loved the cottons and colors. We were headed to the Counts Tin and Moppi (brothers) Berckheim's castle.

As I flew down the road, top down, a German motorcycle police officer passed us. This was rather amazing as I never drove less than eighty miles per hour. As he came alongside, he winked, and then drove in front of the car. He began swerving back and forth. He was obviously showing off. I was angry about this and motioned for him to pull off the road. I think now I was quite arrogant. Americans were not subject to any control of the German police, but my passengers were. I had forgotten this in my youthful indignation at his behavior. When we stopped, he pulled up beside us. I am sure he was expecting anything but my tongue-lashing. I lectured him abruptly for weaving in front of my car. I did not hear a peep out of him or the girls. A little time passed as he struggled with his damaged ego. He then straightened, nodded his head to me, and tore off. What a lecture I heard from Paula. If he had recognized they were Germans, there could have been a good deal of trouble for them. Thank heavens they were wearing my clothing.

Gundi stayed on at Berckheim's after the party to see some relatives. When Paula and I returned to Stuttgart, we decided to decorate Dad's bedroom for his arrival home. Laboriously, we cut out nude pictures of women from the magazines. We pasted them on the backs of some of my photos. We hung them in his room, along with a sign intimating that we hoped he had a "good time." He was not too happy with either of us as we had not met him at the airport on his arrival home. So, the decorations did not go over very well.

When I eventually returned to the United States, I made an appointment with a portrait photographer in Everett, Washington, regarding employment. I took samples of my photography to show this older lady. Imagine my horror as she turned one of the portraits over and asked if the nude was a sample of my work! Nudes were not photo subjects for the American photographer then. They were certainly not allowed in our magazines. I stumbled through the story about how it happened to be there. Needless to say, that was the end of another turning of the road.

CHAPTER XIII

MORE HUNTING-RIOTS & DACHAU

When Howard Hawks and Russ Harlan of Hollywood were filming, *I was a Male War Bride,* we arranged a hunt for them with Prince
Fugger. Dad also invited some of his officers and a group of French
dignitaries who were visiting our zone. The French never seemed to
go at anything half-heartedly so we were all a bit worried about them
shooting someone. Evidently this was based on experience, but no
one told me about it. All I knew was that when I had seen them ride
horses, they rode with careless abandon to win at any cost. On this
day, we were to hunt a draw and I was to go down into the draw and
climb into a *hochstand.* These were the rickety, fourteen foot high
platforms that we climbed. They were made by lashing poles and
limbs together. I often found these more frightening than the wild
boar! This was supposed to be where I would be safe and have a
good shot at anything, except Frenchmen, of course.

By this time, I was hunting with a German Mauser rifle that was a
very powerful weapon of German manufacture. It had been presented to me by one of my hunting friends. Unfortunately, or so I
thought, it had a carving of a rabbit on the stock. I took this as de-
meaning. I had tried to carve a pair of horns on the rabbit to make
it appear like a stag. It did not work. However, the gun did, and was
a very sought after rifle for its excellent firing mechanism.

The beaters were already in position when I started down the hill
to the highstand. The French gentlemen and others were in place
on the rim of the draw. I must have been two-thirds of the way down
the hill when the beaters began to yell, *wildes schwein, or* "wild boar."

Hochstand

People, the French I am sure, suddenly began shooting all around me. All hell broke loose and I froze in my tracks. Not only were the bullets hitting all around me, but now I could hear and smell the boar. I was rooted. No woodpile in sight, and I could not have moved anyway.

As the boar charged past me, around me, and near me, I do not know who was more terrified. Those animals dodged me at breakneck speed and kept on going. They were grunting and squealing. I was struck dumb. As my brain began to try to function again, it seemed the bullets were now following the boar and no longer around me. I began to scramble up the hill. Dad met me at the top just livid that I had not gone on to the *hochstand*, or at least tried to shoot a boar. I just looked at him and tried not to cry. I locked myself in the car for the rest of the hunt. That was the last time I ever hunted boar from the ground, and I never hunted with the French again.

Russ Harlan was also disappointed in me, but did not tell me this.

I wish one of these brave men had been in my position with the boar.
He had wanted to have some pictures of the wild boar hunt. I did
promise to try to take some for him later. So it seemed a good idea
when I thought of renting a stuffed boar and staging a shoot. I
found a huge stuffed boar at a taxidermist's shop and arranged to
pick it up in the Packard. So smart! When I arrived at the shop, I
found that the thing was so heavy, as it was on a stand, that I had to
have the taxidermist come along. That worked out well because I
posed him as the hunter. What a picture we made driving through
Stuttgart with that hideous beast in the backseat. My dog, Alex, also
in the backseat, was not at all happy with the situation. He kept
threatening to jump out. By nature, most dogs are afraid of the

Russ Harlan and Howard Hawks, Russ' hirsch

musty odor of the boar. Some people too!

When we arrived at the forest outside Stuttgart, I put my hunting hat on the taxidermist. We positioned the stuffed boar in some bushes to look as though he was charging. The effect was not good as there was no action or motion. I asked the man to fire the gun, thinking I might somehow catch that action and it would look real. Well, catching an image of a bullet being fired is impossible with a Rolleiflex. The gun going off did scare me so that the picture was a bit blurred. Next, we tried to get Alex to look like he was attacking the boar, or at least chasing it. He would not pose facing the animal and always looked as though he was running away from it, which he was. The shot had also cowed him. At least the taxidermist was having a great time with all of this posing. I was paying him for this and he had not shot a gun for a long time.

I also tried having the boar on its side as though it had been shot. However, the base showed. So my final effort was the best. I had sent Alex behind the boar and had the man fire the gun as I called the dog. When Alex drew alongside the boar, I signaled the man to fire. Again I startled at the shot and so I knew I had blurred the picture. Pleased with myself, we took the stuffed boar back to the shop where I paid the happy man some of my hard-earned money. Later, I showed the pictures to Russ in high hopes he would not notice they not real. But he knew immediately that I had staged it. It was not just

Alex and the stuffed boar.

the boar that had blurred when I reacted to the shots. The pictures themselves were fuzzy. All was for nothing, but we had some good laughs about the whole episode.

I continued to send pictures to magazines in the United States. One editor of a hunting magazine also recognized the boar picture as staged (no one can say I give up easily), but he was interested in the German's use of dogs in hunting. I am sure he recognized that Alex was not a happy hunter. I told him of the *Drathare* hound who hunted by instinct and had a different voice for each type of animal he hunted. This was a large dog with shaggy, curly hair. Their owners prized them. Another dog was the Weimaraner, who had to be a natural hunter. They killed the pups if they did not hunt by six months. The Americans, who could not stand to kill the puppies, quickly ruined this long line of careful breeding and culling.

Fox Terriers and Dachshunds were used to worry prey or drive out the burrowing animals. In my letter to him, I explained that we used these dogs for rabbit and fox. He wrote back that it was his understanding that the Dachshund was used for badger hunting. "Oh no," says I, "the badger is too ferocious for these small dogs." After all, I lived here and hunted with these dogs so I should know. By now I was enjoying our correspondence, but not selling pictures. He wrote back to say that he understood *dachs* meant *badger*. He had me. Of course, they named these dogs after the animal they hunted. My mistake. I also sold no pictures to him.

By the end of 1947, Germany was making dramatic gains on her recovery. Many buildings were razed and being rebuilt. Tons and tons of brick, concrete, and bombed material had been hauled away. Certain areas were now looking prewar. There were still many shortages and the black market was flourishing. The U.S. army had returned the requisitioned cars to the German owners and we were now in staff cars. Some unfortunates were left to drive Volkswagens. This had upset dad, but we were never subjected to that "embarrassment." It was also at this time that Dad purchased the Packard, as a precaution to not having a decent private car.. To him, driving in a Volkswagen was a low rank and an insult. They were very tinny vehicles in his mind.

Some elements of the German population remained very discontent with losing the war and with the occupation. On a quiet

evening, when I was dressing for a party at Colonel Dawson's, Dad received a call that there was a riot down at the *Bahnhof.* (Train depot) He had no reason to be there but I had never seen a confrontation like this and wanted to go. Dad refused to let me drive the Packard for fear of some reprisal, so Herr Braun came to pick me up in the staff car. Speaking of a reprisal object! A United States army staff car with a well-dressed American young woman inside! It was times like this when I thought Dad valued that car more than his daughter.

We parked some distance from the large mass of people swarming about the station. I left a not reluctant Herr Braun at the car and walked into the crowd. There was much yelling and some screams. However, it was impossible to tell who was causing the riot and who was just innocently there. Nevertheless, as I pushed my way toward the station, there began to be some separation between the groups. A small cluster of perhaps forty people had taken over the station to protest no jobs and general conditions, especially the constraints of the occupation forces. Some of them were up on the roof. A speaker was making his demands as the soldiers moved in and arrested him and some others alongside. At this display of power from our military, the crowd on the roof began throwing bricks and whatever else they could get their hands on.

Most of the crowds of onlookers began to run back from the area. Naturally, I stood my ground, curious to see the resolution of this riot. Several warning gunshots rang out from the soldiers and that began to alarm me, especially as I was now alone on the corner. At that point, the bricks began to come in my direction. I rapidly turned to get away deciding I had enough excitement. I had gone about four steps when a brick hit exactly where I had been standing. It exploded with the force of contact, pelting me with its pieces and ruining my hose. Not bad, considering. Shaken, I returned to Herr Braun and we drove back to the house for me to bathe and change. When I arrived at the party, the German mayor of Stuttgart was there and knew nothing of what had happened. He was immediately on the telephone to learn that the situation was under control, but not before a "falling" brick had killed one man and others were hurt.

This was the only riot or "uprising" that I can recall during my stay. For the most part, the Germans seemed content with the leadership of our appointed German government. There were extensive

checks of the backgrounds of these officials. It was important to see that no ex-Nazis gained power. Of course, the trials to prosecute war criminals were already on in Nürenburg. The CIA and officers in Dad's position were scrutinizing the official documents of Hitler and his officers. The Germans were moving forward, although the die-hard Hitler people were bemoaning their losses.

Dad brought home some of the documents labeled top secret by the Nazis. They were from Goebbels's office and bore his and Hitler's signatures. They were discussing who was to be destroyed among the Jewish population. Children who appeared Aryan, Caucasian, and were one-half, or less, Jewish would be spared. If they were a quarter Jewish, and appeared as such, they would spend their lives in the camps. If they were one half Jewish, or more, and appeared as such, they marked them for death. They also discussed castration and hysterectomies. I understand these surgeries occurred. These papers read as though they were discussing beef, not humans. These Nazi individuals gave no human quality to the children in this discussion. They outlined elaborate testing to decide who lived or died. Children! Dad and I were both sickened by the fact that these people were totally ruthless.

We did go to see the concentration camp of Dachau. I was quite nervous about what we would be seeing, having heard grotesque stories of these camps. As we neared the town of Dachau, one could not help but wonder what the citizens thought, and how they lived next door to such a heinous place. Later, a woman who lived there told me that the town's people at first did not know what was happening in the camp. They would see the trainloads and truckloads of people coming in and assumed they were also shipping them out to other locations. Slowly, they put two and two together as they began to hear the rumors of what was happening there.

They were so afraid for their own lives and for their families that they could do nothing. The woman mentioned being at the train station to meet a friend who was arriving. While she waited, she watched a group of Jews working on the tracks. A young man was near the point of collapse and asked for water. She went into the station and managed to get a cup of water for him. As she walked toward him, a German soldier stopped her and asked her what she was doing. The woman explained her concern for the youth. The guard

knocked the cup from her hand. He took his rifle and prodded her into the station with it. He told her she was lucky that he was not going to report her as she would also be in a detention camp. She was terrified. When she could arrange it, the lady moved from Dachau.

We drove through barbed wire gates into what might have been a large army barracks. The American government had arranged tours of the death camp, often led by former inmates. The man who took us through had survived this camp. He became very upset when he showed us the different killing sites, and I wondered if this wasn't an extension of the torture he had already suffered. He showed us the trees where prisoners were tied and shot. We saw the bullet holes, still in the wood. We saw pits where the camp guards turned dogs loose on them. Then he took us to the shower rooms. Here they told the prisoners they could have showers and were to disrobe. These were groups of male and female, children and adults, fathers and mothers, and siblings.

The early groups had not yet heard this was a death room. Although apprehensive, they looked forward to a chance to bathe. Later groups knew this was their death sentence and went like the helpless victims that they were. When they entered the shower room, the doors were locked. The overhead shower heads then emitted the gas that killed these poor people. The guards then cremated some of the bodies in stoves that we saw. They buried other bodies in pits that these prisoners had dug before their trip to the showers.

We all heard about other terrible atrocities in this concentration camp. If anyone doubts these things, he is a fool. The records of the Nüremburg trials brought out these terrible things verified by many witnesses. Some of these witnesses were guilt ridden as they had been forced to do horrible things.. Others were survivors of the death camps. Some that were Nazis seemed to believe this had to be. For a long time, one of the closest kept secrets of the trials was the disposition of the bodies of the criminals that were put to death for their deeds. The governing countries were afraid that if they returned the body of the criminal to its family, they might regard the individual as a hero. To avoid this, they incinerated the bodies and dumped the ashes in the nearby rivers. A small group of Allied soldiers did this, and were sworn to secrecy.

This whole scene at Dachau just verified in my mind how far the

human can go if put in such a situation. Hitler detested Jews in a very paranoid fashion and his loyal followers went along with this philosophy.

The ovens where bodies were burned

The hanging tree where Jews were hung

CHAPTER XIV

STUREFORS SLOTT

In the summer of 1947 Gunilla, with Dad's help, received permission to visit her home, Sturefors Slott (palace), in Sweden. I believe this was her first trip home since the war. She invited Dad and me to accompany her and we readily accepted. Gunilla and young son Toni came to Stuttgart to stay with us overnight. The next morning we all drove to Frankfurt for our flight. By this time, things were beginning to improve in Germany. The airports were mostly back in service, food was more readily available, clothing was reappearing, and the rubble was rapidly being cleared away. They were already rebuilding damaged buildings and life was again becoming industrious and

Sturefors Slott

more normal for the Germans.

Whether it was from the excitement, or a fear of flying, Gunilla was not a happy flyer. We tried to cheer her up. I believe we were in a DC3 passenger plane, a very safe way to fly. It was a direct flight and it seemed short. The airport in Stockholm showed no hint of war and was very busy. We took a cab to our hotel where Gunilla's mother, the Countess Brita Bielke joined us. I do not remember if this was the first time we met Brita, but I believe so. She took every-thing in hand and issued instructions for our stay in Stockholm. This was one of the rare times my father remained subdued, as this lady really overwhelmed him. Countess Bielke was a tall person, perhaps about five-foot-eight or nine. She stood straight and there was a stud-ied, reserved quality about her. She was quite attractive in a strong way, and always well dressed and manicured. She was very "en-chanted" by the Colonel, and made this fact well-known by her atten-tion to him. She was very much the lady. .

We stayed several days in Stockholm. It was a lovely, clean city. I could not help but notice the numbers of ships at the docks, cer-tainly indicating a good market. While shopping for clothes with Dad, I found a much needed formal gown. He had difficulty with the price, but recognized our need to appear well-turned-out. Of course, I was strongly pointing this out to him. The dress was a beau-tiful gold lame' and close fitting. The attractive material reached to the floor. I felt like a queen. We were able to find shoes and a match-ing bag in black. The purse seemed fine, but the shoes were again heavy and not stylish, but functional.

The four of us attended several parties with families who were friends of the Bielkes and we went on tours of Stockholm. While at the hotel, I had the good fortune to meet Yousuf Karsh. He was a fa-mous photographer, who was in Stockholm to take pictures of King Gustav V. Karsh had a wonderful way of posing his subjects so faces and hands were dominant. He asked me to stay and go with him to the King's palace. However, once again I ignored that turn in the road and continued with Countess Brita's schedule.

We met a Count Gustav Mörner who had built a large sailing ship. This wealthy fellow had launched it, only to have it sink in a storm on its maiden voyage. We enjoyed a good deal of social life in the two days we were there. The long hours of daylight of the season,

Yousuf Karsh

gave us false energy. Getting dressed for a party in the daylight was difficult. Finishing the party in daylight, and trying to go to sleep at two or three in the morning in bright light, was equally difficult.

We caught the train for Linköping on the way to Sturefors, all of us needing a little rest. We were traveling through beautiful gorges and along waterways and lakes. However, it was not too long before Brita had us playing bridge. The game became quite animated as Dad and I battled Gunilla and Brita. Dad and I were ahead, and the pressure was on, when Brita leaned over and took a quick look at

Dad's hand. It seems she could not stand losing and would "cheat a bit" to get an advantage. We had a good laugh about it. We won, nevertheless. This was a short trip of about four hours, and we enjoyed each other's company despite the quick "peek." When we arrived in Linköping, Brita's car and chauffeur met us and we drove for about an hour to the palace. This was English style driving on the opposite side of the road. The corners were breath-taking!

It was late afternoon by the time we arrived at Sturefors. Gunilla was so glad to see her home again. It was a newer building than Babenhausen and more modern. The owners had started it in the early 1700's and they built it with a certain French architectural style. For example, a large pond mirrored the palace as at Versailles. This was due to the architect, Nicodemus Tessin, who had designed architecture for the king of Sweden. French styles highly impressed King Gustav III and he had passed this on to Tessin. In fact, Tessin used the same decorators and painters at Sturefors, as he had for King Gustav. To this day, professors of art and antiquities visit the palace to study its fine collections of books, china, and oil paintings. The palace and grounds were beautiful and faced a small lake called *Erlangen*. A river feeds the lake and there is a gated channel for boat traffic. For years boats have carried tourists on the lake to see and hear about Sturefors. The palace is one of the prettiest spots in Sweden.

The inside of the palace was very impressive, as well. On the walls were ancestral paintings in gorgeous frames. There were rooms of beautiful ancient furnishings, huge floor-to-ceiling tapestries, and massive fireplaces. Our bedrooms and bath were quite modern and very comfortable with a view of the pond and gardens. By the lake was the handsome stable where the Countess Brita kept her horse. The tennis courts were near the mirror pool. It was on these courts that we played some hard fought games. The lake was where we spent lazy time, boating and swimming.

It was here, at the palace, that a neighbor first introduced Gunilla to a young, handsome German officer, Prince Friedrich Carl Fugger. He supposedly wanted to view the palace collections. Gunilla was an eligible young lady of impeccable breeding. She was also Catholic and a beauty. She learned later that this meeting had been arranged for her and Friedrich Carl. When he later proposed, Friedrich Carl told Gunilla that he had very much admired Greta Garbo, also a

great beauty. However, he had chosen Gunilla. She was very flattered by this. There was no doubt that Friedrich Carl had an eye for the beautiful ladies.

Gunilla's younger sisters, Katherina and Mariann, were introduced. They were lovely young people. They seemed to enjoy our company, perhaps any company, as their home was rather isolated. At any rate, we were welcomed and treated, pardon the expression, royally. Our days were filled with tennis, boating, and parties at the homes of neighbors. We also had the opportunity of seeing Brita ride her handsome and spirited horse. She was an excellent equestrienne.

Countesses Katherina, Brita, and Mariann Bielke

The Bielke family celebrated the Midsummer Festival at the Slott. Brita and the younger daughters were dressed in their native costumes. The neighbors and local residents were there to participate with a dance around the pole. This pole was festooned with ribbons, much like our Maypole. Later in the evening, the adults gathered at a raised platform for the dancing. Dad was chosen as Brita's partner to open the dance, a waltz. Waltzing was not Dad's forte and it was obvious that he was quite uncomfortable. Brita carried him through with a strong lead. The other ladies were very attracted to this handsome gentleman, my father. However, Brita kept a close eye on him and kept him occupied with her program. She did this without much help from Dad, who followed along at a distance. After all, he was very much in love with Paula. Dad really preferred younger women who would follow his lead. Brita seemed to over-power him.

One day Brita was not feeling well and stayed in bed. I think we were all a little relieved although concerned for her. It gave us a chance to do the things we wanted, rather than what she planned. We all had a few drinks and were in quite good mood when we went to her room to pay a call. As we neared the room, we were pantomiming our improved behavior. We were acting quite silly, and trying not to get hysterical. This included Dad. By the time we entered the room, we had transformed ourselves into polite, quiet, sober souls.

Brita seemed better and asked if we were enjoying ourselves and what had we been doing? We were not very truthful, telling her, "Just walking around and chatting." She seemed a little reluctant to believe us, but dismissed us with a smile. As we turned to leave, I noticed a large mirror on the wall placed in a way that reflected anyone approaching her room. Nothing more was said, but we goaded Gunilla a bit for not warning us. She had forgotten!

The Countess Brita Bielke was a very popular person in her area and was involved in many activities. People came great distances to have the opportunity for tea and a chat with her. We used these visits as a time to get away for boating or tennis. Dad had been having some intestinal problems. Brita had dosed him with some "prune syrup" and he could not join us. The rest of us took the boat out for a row around the lake, though Dad asked us not to leave him alone. When we returned, Dad met us, looking much better. The prune mixture had been successful.

When I went upstairs to my room, next to his, our shared bathroom was a bit overwhelming. Just as I returned to my room, Brita came along with some very well-dressed ladies in tow. She was showing them her modernized bathrooms. Not wanting the blame for this delicate situation, I pointedly said, "The colonel just left." I left also, but not without some devilish thoughts about how Brita and her guests handled the situation. Nothing was ever mentioned about it, of course. I never told Dad that I had laid the blame where it belonged.

While we were at Sturefors, Count Nils Bielke, Gunilla's brother, arrived from some business function. Nils was serious, rather reserved, tall and nice looking. He was a bit stiff until he had a few cocktails and then he was quite the opposite. He also seemed in awe of his mother's controlling ways, but he would join in our escapades when we would act like truant children. Nils and I enjoyed each other's company and we had some good times together. He never proposed, but I never encouraged it either. We were just good friends. Yet another turn in the road that I did not take.

Katherina and Mariann were too young to and did not share our need for occasional independence from their mother. Most of our partying was at the palace as the Swedish government had very strong rules about drinking and driving. One infraction and the officials took away your driving license. They also levied a heavy fine. Also, the servants had just unionized, to the horror of the gentility. They now only worked an eight-or-nine hour day instead of the live-in, around-the-clock availability. As a result, none of us wanted to drive if we were to drink and no driver was available.

We spent a week of fun and good times with Brita becoming increasingly friendly with us. We planned future trips and visits for her to Stuttgart as our guest. I am not sure if Dad had to get her papers or how she managed to come into Germany. She did visit us on four or five occasions either on her way to Babenhausen to see Gunilla and the children or on her way home from there. She remained a friend and wrote to me after I left Germany. She died, in her nineties, blind and totally dependent on others.

We were having such a wonderful time at Sturefors and were reluctant to leave these friends, but it was soon time to return home. Gunilla and Toni stayed on at Sturefors. After fond farewells and

promises to meet again, Dad and I returned by train through this lovely country. It was a beautiful trip and we caught a ferry from Sweden to Denmark and then to Germany. Dad was glad to get back under his own roof, but we missed our days at Sturefors. Even though he felt a bit overwhelmed by Brita's attention, neither Dad nor I would ever see the Countess as other than a charming, regal, last-of-her kind, lady.

CHAPTER XV

BLACK MARKET

Black market was a way of life in Germany after the war. Despite warnings from the War Department, we all did a certain amount of "illegal" trading. Dad gave me a long lecture when I was first being shown the "closet" at the top of the paneled stairs leading to the upper floor of the house. This well stocked little cabinet reminded me of my great uncle's cigar and cigarette store in Portland, Oregon. Dad had cached cartons of cigarettes, boxes of candy bars, coffee, sugar, and other articles scarce to the Germans and Americans. It was necessary to keep these things under lock and key to avoid temptation. Mostly mine! The cigarettes, candy, and coffee were rationed. Now that I was also able to purchase these supplies, we would have even more reason to lock the closet. There was much buying and bargaining power in that little space.

Our black market activities could result in possible arrest, possible demotion for Dad, or "worse" if we were ever caught doing it. Yet, despite his lecture to me, Dad obviously traded for certain items. I had also been present when other high ranking officers were "bargaining." Dad explained that this was necessary to acquire "essential" items. Yes, good liquor, crystal, and silver items. Of course, I could play this game of "essential," and did throughout my stay. It surprised me, after the lecture, that he gave me the extra key to the closet. He suggested that I keep the key in a hidden place so that the servants would not be tempted. More than once this was the "possibility" when he would find some supplies low. As we could not confirm it, we were just more cautious about the keys. I knew Ina and

Eugene would not steal from us, so did Dad. Dad was never sure of the inventory as we were constantly taking things to friends. Also, I used this as a convenient excuse for some of my escapades.

There seemed a humane side to this practice of bartering. The staples such as sugar, coffee, tea, flour, etc., were not available to our German friends and it was a diplomatic way of helping them. The United States script that we used instead of dollars was really useless to most Germans. They could not get inside the army commissary or PX. So trading in needed items or saleable items seemed fair. If a friend needed stockings, we made a trade for something in like value. We also, politely, gave needed or scarce goods as gifts when we visited.

American cigarettes were the most popular trade exchange, especially in the early years following the end of the war. There were no German cigarettes of any quantity or quality. Of course, we were restricted in the U.S. during the war and tobacco in any form was rationed. This was so our troops had plenty. Even later, as Germany rebuilt, the American tobacco was popular. We often felt that a single cigarette should be wrapped in cellophane (our "plastic" then) and simply used as money. Very few of these cigarettes were smoked. They were traded again and again. The value of a carton of cigarettes on the black market was approximately equal to forty or fifty dollars. A lot of money in those days. I believe we paid $2.50 a carton at the PX.

In 1948 the German mark was devaluated with devastating affect on some of our friends. If a person had 10,000 marks before the devaluation, they had 1,000 after. Prices did not change and people found themselves, at first, unable to afford necessities. This, to me, was the time of the most black market activity. People would show up at our gate, knowing Americans lived there, with valuable, and not so valuable, linens, porcelain, silver, crystal, etc. These were usually their cherished belongings that they were sacrificing for essentials. Often the pieces were cracked, chipped or damaged in some way. I felt this meant these were survivors of bombing raids

Many people who had to flee their homes during the war, had taken the best or most important items, or whatever they could carry, with them. As many had just a suitcase, or less, these were the only mementos of their former lives. Not empathizing with them was

hard. I know Dad and I often gave too much and then had to listen to the clucking of Ina. It was sometimes just as difficult when a friend asked for something. We could see what they needed, offer it, and be met with proud refusal. I still have a card from Princess Gunilla suggesting that if we did not bring some black shoe polish for Friedrich Carl, he would "kill" her. In other words, "please."

Things rapidly improved following the devaluation of the mark. Germany was rising above the rubble and making tremendous strides toward recovery. Yet the black market still existed but on a smaller scale. The lower value of the mark brought sudden and plentiful products, long awaited and much needed. Stores opened and it was no longer necessary to travel outside the country to find what we needed. Black market dealings were fewer and the offerings, usually, more valuable. Variety shops sprang up and lovely antiques were available. Some other stores offered newer "Occupied Germany" porcelains for sale. The pawnshops were still good sources for precious treasures that the owners could not redeem. Here we did our trading openly. One shop, however, would not accept anything but the German mark. Always short of money, I found it pure torture to try to dicker about prices with the owner. I think this was his way of getting back at the Americans for winning the war.

One day I saw a beautiful pair of sterling candelabra in the window. They cost much more than I could ever pay, but I had to have them. I must have looked particularly beaten that day, or he was having financial problems, because he accepted cigarettes, chocolate, and a promise for a certain amount of marks. This was in early 1949 when things were not going at all well for me with Dad. Dad obviously felt a great deal of pressure regarding our war department's changes. He felt that I was becoming an increasing burden for him. It was also true that if he moved from the house he no longer needed a dependent! Things were building to where we were not getting along. I was also becoming increasingly homesick for the United States and my family. Obviously Dad was in no mood to help me with the candelabra, or much else. I could not come up with the remaining marks and eventually had to leave Germany without the candelabra.

Through the following years, after I had returned home, I kept putting pressure on Dad to pay for the silver pair. Eventually he did.

The German shopkeeper was an honest man to have held them for so long. My father, on the other hand, kept one and sent me the other. He felt this was just because he had paid the balance owing. My attempts to pay him (I was working by then) were not accepted. He had the one candelabra until his death. I never saw it during my visits with him, and he would never talk about its location. Since he had been so angry with me in Germany, things never really seemed the same afterwards. I know this was some of my "punishment." Some, because there was worse to come.

However, after the Colonel died in 1977, I returned to his resort in 1981 to help my brother who was dying of cancer. I had not been there since Dad's death. One day I walked up to the old house on the hill, above the resort, where Dad had lived. It had been empty for six or seven years after they had moved the Colonel to better quarters on the beach.

I felt Dad's presence in the deserted rooms, crumbling and open to the elements. I was concerned when I went into his old storeroom and found ancient books from Europe, decaying and infested. Old letters of his had been chewed by the rats and insects. The kitchen and porch were littered with things even the Mexicans had not wanted. It was accepted that if you left anything lying around a Mexican would pick it up. Evidently they had already picked through these left overs. Nothing had been done to preserve them. There was an old tin of 16 millimeter film he had produced when we were in Stuttgart. It was almost colorless. I went out to the backyard for a breath of fresh air, saddened by the lack of respect for these objects.

There, on a pile of sand and old mortar, was an old candelabra. It was black from the salt air and sun. It had a familiar look to it, but I could not believe it could be the mate to my old piece. Why hadn't it been stolen? Obviously, because of its blackened condition and some bending, no one had valued it. When I returned to the United States, I carried an old, worn leather bound book and the candelabra in a plastic bag through customs. The customs officer glanced at the blackened, dirty items and waved me through. I really did not feel there was anything to be declared. I was still not positive this was the matching candelabra, or if there was any silver on it.

When I arrived home, the first thing I did was compare the two and they were a match! A long wait for these lovely pieces. I could

not believe it! It was almost as if I had been guided to it. After all, my father's last words to me before he died were "I have made a mistake." That statement in itself is another story. However, I believe it was an admission or an apology for what he had put me through in the years following Germany. This was not about the candelabra, but about many thoughtless things between us. Therefore, to me the finding of the partner to my pretty piece closed a chapter of the book on my relationship with my father. Perhaps, as for his need to apologize, I owed him a few, also.

Dad had obtained some very expensive articles through the black market. He would never call it black market and I would agree. What he did was help a family of jewelers who lost their fortune when the devaluation of the mark occurred. With much less money and the same high bills, the family could not afford the basics to survive. The daughter was a handsome widow and, although about the colonel's age, attracted his attention. Dad always seemed drawn to younger women for romance. This family and Dad had known each other long before the German mark was unexpectedly lowered.

I do not know how much Dad gave to help them out. In exchange, he received a large diamond ring, which he later lost while skiing. He also received some watercolors and a lovely oil painting by an unknown artist. I believe they were all destroyed by the elements in that back room in Baja.

In the early days just about anything was available through the black market. We found my two German Shepherds that way. I also managed to get pedigree papers for one of them by giving the official cigarettes. The Gestapo had not papered Alex because his dam was cowardly and his sire was overly aggressive. Was this part of Hitler's need to build a super race of animals too? We also found rabbits for Eugene, our butler, to rear, and a cat for me. I named that cat *Elska*, as I had just come from Sweden and Sturefors.

Elska was as close as I could get to the word meaning "love" in Swedish, I think. What a time I had calling that cat when she was in the garden. "Here *Elska*, here *Elska*." The cat disappeared one day. Several days later, I saw her hide tacked to the shed wall of a house below us. I think poor *Elska* ended up in the soup pot. I know there was grumbling about the good food we fed our pets. I do not remember seeing many cats in German households, and I am not sure

Alex, our German shepherd

if they were considered a civilized pet. There were always many to be seen in the wild, in the cities, and on the farms.

Dad had always wanted some very good silverware for the table. He had found a man who professed to be a maker of such ware. A large brick of silver appeared from somewhere so we drove to the man's shop in a town about twenty miles from Stuttgart. I watched while Dad showed the man the pattern for the silver and discussed how many pieces of each he wanted. He also ordered large serving spoons, cake servers, carving knives, etc. I helped with the bargaining about the cost, and they finally agreed on a rather large amount of cigarettes. Dad could hardly wait for his new silverware.

Typically, the craftsman took much longer than stated, but finally the day arrived and we went to get the silver. Why Dad did not examine it before purchase, I do not know. When we arrived home, he had the unveiling. It was the saddest set of silver one could imagine. They had a plain detail and sharp edges on the handles. There was also a minimum of silver. Not a pretty sight greeted him. We had no doubt that most of the silver had gone elsewhere. Dad could do nothing about it, as he had illegally purchased it. I think the crafts-

man knew this too. Poor Dad, we never used the silver and I have no idea whatever happened to it.

Tipping a sentry, usher, or waiter with a cigarette to get what we wanted was accepted practice. Most garage mechanics would accept cigarettes and chocolate as pay. I really think it was a beneficial way of life and should not have been considered illegal. Both sides benefitted. In 1949 a well-known general's wife was just short of being arrested for her dealings in the black market. It had something to do with some landscaping and purchases for her home. The word went out that any dealings in these exchanges would be punishable by arrest and fines. That stopped many of us, and I was about to lose my key to the "closet" anyway.

CHAPTER XVI

THE PACKARD

In the fall of 1947 Dad had taken one of his trips to the United States. Upon return, he announced that we had a new car! He was tired of the exchanges of vehicles in the motor pool. He also wanted to avoid the threat of being placed in a Volkswagen. He had been trying to arrange for a car for me from the Germans, but it was not legal. I had not the least idea about Dad's income, only his lectures about conserving money. I now know this was to encourage me, by hints, to get a job. Hints never did work with me, never will. He would not tell me about the car until it arrived. He was certainly pleased with himself. Well, he should have been, as a brand new, last-of-its-kind, 1948 Packard convertible arrived at the door.

It was a beauty, a beautiful blue with electric controls for the windows, top, etc. I was as excited as he and was eager to try it out. Dad rarely restricted my use of the Packard. Perhaps it enabled him to be home alone more often. Whatever, I was very much on the road after its arrival.

Once while driving to Babenhausen with the convertible top down, I was cruising about eighty on the no speed limit autobahn. In the rearview mirror I could see a Mercedes sedan creeping up on me. I was not going to let this German get ahead of me, and so I speeded up. The faster I went, the faster he went, until we were both flying. My hair was long and streaming out behind me and I was clutching things on the seat to keep them from sailing out. I was not ready to quit and, sensing the chase, put the accelerator to the floor. The speedometer's top reading was 120, and it reached that. For a

short while I was ahead.

However, the Mercedes inched up, and up, and drew alongside. I was leaning forward, as if to propel the car faster, when I heard someone call my name. I glanced at the Mercedes and there was Princess Clarissa and Prince Carlo Hohenlohe-Bartenstein. I turned a bright red as it was obvious what I was trying to do. Prince Carlo raced cars as a hobby and here I was trying to outrace an expert. Well, I had given it my best effort. The most embarrassing part for me, however, was that they yelled they were also on their way to Babenhausen. We had a good laugh when we arrived at the castle, they before me.

On this particular visit, Carlo and Friedrich Carl took me with them to see a well-known phrenologist in the village. They thoroughly believed this man could diagnose a person's medical problems by the bumps on their head. I had a terrible time keeping myself from laughing hysterically as I watched these two seemingly intelligent men mesmerized by the doctor as his hands groped their heads. They were not satisfied with their own findings of gallstones, stomach ulcers, etc. They insisted I let the man diagnose me. I was able to control myself until he told me I had a "kidney bump" on my head. I then burst out laughing. No one was amused, and I guess I was a little embarrassed. The phrenologist was furious and we were ushered out. Friedrich Carl never let me forget about these times.

The German roads were crowned and the German cars had their rear wheels tipped in to hold the crown better. Driving was hazardous at anytime as the Germans did not seem to concentrate on driving and we had many accidents. I had sixteen, to be exact, and caused only one. That time I was on the crown of an icy road and a German driver coming toward me chose to stay on the top also. We approached each other as though we were in a game of bluff. It was only at the last moment that either of us gave way. We glanced off each other and I knew from the impact that I had a dent in the side of the Packard. It turned out to be only a small scratch, but the metal protection strip was gone. I received quite a lecture from Dad, especially as it usually took three or four months to get parts from the United States.

There were times when it was snowing that we did not know if we were on a road or in the field. The Germans and her conquerors had

also bombed most of the bridges to halt each others progress or retreat. This left us driving on improvised roads and bridges on the sides of sheer cliffs with usually steep inclines. Also the American cars were larger and wider than the European's. I still remember people in towns with very narrow roads, leaping into available doorways to avoid being squashed as we drove by. The autobahn, other than the detours due to blown up bridges, was in fairly good repair when I arrived in 1946. But other roads were miserably potholed or knee deep in mud from streams or cattle. Sometimes we would see American drivers being rescued from muddy ditches or holes by the local oxen.

When we drove to Paris to meet my cousin Bob and family for Thanksgiving, we were very popular in every village and in Paris. Wherever we stopped, a crowd gathered to admire our beautiful car. The young children were especially interested and they touched and patted the "Americaner" auto. Unfortunately, on the way back home from Paris the roads were again icy and our German driver lost control on a corner. The impact threw me out of the car and the driver landed on top of me. Dad had been asleep in the backseat and had a rude awakening. Luckily, none of us were hurt, but *my* car was pretty banged up. We were given a ride back to our cousin's apartment in Paris and then took the train home. It took about six months to get the Packard repaired. We sorely missed it.

I found a letter I had written dated October 3, 1946, to my grandmother, Edith Haines. In it I stated, evidently to reassure her, that we were safer here than in the United States. This did not mean we were not terrified of the Russians. Though I never worried about harm coming from the Germans, they did have some ways of reprisal. I was driving to a meeting of the ladies in our Care package and welfare group and had a flat tire! I had no idea where the spare was, and looked quite helpless in hopes someone would stop. The little wood burning three wheelers chugged on past, and the trucks occasionally honked. I would obviously have to do this myself. I found the spare tire under the floor of the trunk and managed to get it out. It was quite heavy and unwieldy, and after wrestling it to the ground, I noticed a man on a bike had stopped. I smiled at him and he smiled back and settled down to watch this American lady change the tire. Not once, as I struggled to get the jack in place and the lugs off, did

he offer a hand. He enjoyed every minute of it. Damn! I tried to act unconcerned, like any American woman could do this. When I finished, dirty and sweaty, he doffed his hat and went on his way. It was probably a good story for his family table.

A new army doctor arrived in Stuttgart, Captain Leroy Bates. My American friends could hardly wait to give him a party and introduce us. He was tall and good-looking and I found him interesting. Leroy really never seemed to get involved, but remained rather aloof. He was into psychological studies, one of my favorite subjects, and liked to diagnose my behavior. This did not win him points with me, but entertained my friends. Dad often agreed with him too, which caused me further problems. However, we did have some very good times together. We probably saw each other for a year before he was transferred to the States. We often went to Babenhausen for hunting, where he got along well with the Fuggers. He drove a Lincoln car that was made the same year as our Packard. I was told that at a party one lady asked another who Jean Walters was dating. The other lady answered, "Captain Bates." "Well," said the first lady, "the two best looking cars in Stuttgart going together."

DIARY 1948

As I was looking through mementos and photos of that time in Europe, I came across a short diary of days in 1948. I think this gives a good description of our and our German friend's social life.

FEBRUARY 28 Gunilla, Dad, and I drove to Karlsruhe to meet the Countess Brita Bielke and Count Nils, her son. This is Gunilla's mother and brother from Sturefors Slott, (palace), Sweden. Her mother has a fondness for Dad. She is a strong, very attractive, multilingual lady. We were all going to board the train and go to Switzerland for a holiday. Dad had bronchitis and did not feel well and wanted to get off the train near Baden Baden. However, Brita was very insistent and, reluctantly, Dad stayed with us. However, he rapidly worsened and the minute we arrived in Basel, we took him to the hospital where he stayed until we left. The rest of us shopped and enjoyed the sights of this clean and peaceful city. Seeing no signs of our depressing war scenes in Germany was wonderful. There were so many things available here and we thoroughly enjoyed ourselves.

Gunilla, Brita and Nils in Switzerland. Note the bottle in Nils pocket!

The last night of our stay, a friend of Dad's, Roland Stahel, came from Zurich and Nils invited a young male doctor friend of his. We were staying at the Drei Kònigen Hotel. In a festive mood, we had a party that lasted until about 4:00 a.m. I know Gunilla went to bed early. We all became a bit inebriated and Brita was enjoying the company of the two Swiss fellows. Nils felt duty bound to protect his mother who was more than capable of taking care of herself. I dragged him away and had him escort me to my room. We were having so many laughs and being quite silly. My shoes were hurting my feet and I removed them. Nils then removed his. Barefoot, we ran up and down the hotel corridors moving the guests shoes, left outside their doors, to different doorways. The Europeans set their shoes outside their rooms at night to be polished by the concierge. We thought we were really very clever!

The next morning, Nils had such a guilty conscience about all of this that he went to a special mass to be forgiven! All but Gunilla felt quite "tired" and were quiet at breakfast. She was very kind, though, and did not lecture our obviously distressed minds.

MARCH 5 Countess Paula Clary and Count Marcus, her husband, and the children arrived. I learned to take care of the children quite eas-

ily. Marcus left Monday. Paula and I rode horseback every day. At a party given by the Chinese Consul Woo, I met Captain Dean Bressler, a very handsome young widower. (Dean was to become one of my boyfriends. In the United States, he had accidentally shot and killed his pregnant wife during a burglary of their house. He had a young son, Michael, living with him in Stuttgart.)

MARCH 13 Friedrich Carl and Gundi arrived today, and later Count Hansi Larisch, Count Ferdinand Arco-Zinneberg and his wife,

Captain Dean Bressler.

Countess Ursula (Ushi is Paula's sister) and Count Hubert Deym. We went for the first time to the International Club, a mixed group of German and American members. Dean took us. Many characters. A count with seven titles and a lorgnette held our attention. Everyone poured into bed about 4:00 a.m. All but Friedrich Carl and Paula left this morning. Went horseback riding and to the club again.

MARCH 16 Met Gunilla in Karlsruhe. Nils was there on his way back to Sweden. Both looked fine. Small party at the club with Dean.

MARCH 18 Gunilla waiting for the Munich bunch, Ushi, Ferdinand, Hansi Larisch, etc. Paula and Marcus arrived, and later Larisch, Ferdinand, and Deym. Decided to make it Dad's birthday celebration. Quite a party. Dean came. About 1:00 a.m., three more people came. Ilse Flöter and two unknowns. Such a motley crew. They were all quite tipsy. Were finally rid of all but Gunilla and Paula.

MARCH 19 Sigi Welczeck and Pümi came. Gunilla left. Dad, Paula, Dean, and I were invited to a party for the Military Governor, Charles LaFollette. So quiet and formal. We came home early to have a better one. Sigi was in bed. After we had a few drinks and some good laughs, we woke her and partied some more. Late night.

MARCH 20 Pümi and Sigi still here and Brita coming. Went horseback riding with Drinkerts and the Governor LaFollettes. My horse ran away twice on the paths. We were riding on the pavement and heading back to the stables when I saw a GI throw a garbage can from the second story barracks window. I hit the ground before the can did, knowing my horse would surely run away again. I could barely manage him from the ground, and had to walk him back to his stall. (These were good German horses, not the army hard-mouthed mounts.) Brita arrived and we all went to a party given by the Iranian consul general celebrating their New Year. Very good fun. Brita was having a marvelous time and was surrounded by a five-foot Iranian.

MARCH 21 Dean drove us all to Babenhausen. Most beautiful day. Dad went out and shot nine pike. (This is a large 24" to 36" bony fish found in the rivers. Unfortunately, the shooting usually ruins the less bony meat by the head.) Sigi and I took a long walk in the fields. Pümi, Sigi, and Gundi are some of the finest Germans I have met so

far. They think along the same lines we do and are good people. For the first time, in a long time, I found myself talking to an open-minded person. (Sigi) We stayed for dinner and then home.

MARCH 27-28 Dean and I drove to Babenhausen early, and Dad was to follow. We went to the castle church that evening and then started to party quietly. Dean had brought some of his German war records to surprise Friedrich Carl. Germany's military music was the most stirring I had ever heard. It is very strong. We waited until things were going well and then played our favorite "*Gegen England*" (Against England). Friedrich Carl became, suddenly, the most human I had ever seen him in company. He seemed near tears and asked us if we would "please" turn it off. It was a song his soldiers used to sing.

After getting over that bump, we talked and waited for Dad to arrive. He never did and I was left to try to explain to Brita why he had failed us. Brita had been looking forward to seeing him. In the morning, he arrived in time for Easter church. We all spent the afternoon along one of the streams having a picnic lunch and wine. We were driving around the fields in our Mercedes sports coupe that Dad had driven. Lots of silly fun but unfortunately we broke the axle on the little car by overloading it with riders. Rode home in Dean's car with Dad and Brita.

MARCH 29 Took Brita to the train to Sweden. We had enjoyed our visit with her.

MARCH 31 Dean's boy, Michael, came down with a bad case of bronchitis. Took them both to the hospital and what a time calming Dean. Men just should never be fathers.

APRIL 2 Farewell party for General Buress, a very fine man. Glad to see his daughter leave, as Dean was too interested in her.

APRIL 3 Paula and children arrived. Went horseback riding. We had several martinis before we rode. I was too relaxed on my horse, he shied, and I rolled easily to the ground. I was quite embarrassed and Paula was bent double laughing. I remounted hoping desperately that the same would happen to her. Sure enough, at the canter she was leaning too far ahead and her horse stopped and she went right over his head onto the ground. Lots of excuses, but we felt very sheepish.

APRIL 4 Mr. and Mrs. Price, and Mr. Nichols, Assistant Manager of Kaiser-Fraser, and his assistant arrived. Took them to George Erion's for cocktails. Very interesting people. She is the cousin of some well-known politician. That night we went boar hunting at Captain Bill Wright's until 3:30 a.m. Bill shot three and I was, as usual, too excited and missed. (We hunted from a jeep with mounted search lights.)

The boar were ruining the farmer's crops. Farmers had no guns and so could do nothing about them. They also would attack the farmers and had killed or wounded several.

These boar can weigh up to six hundred pounds and they have large tusks. They smell terrible and could frighten the most seasoned hunter. The lights did not reflect from their eyes so you recognized them by the odor or the shape. When we would spot one (or a herd), we would drive hell-bent-for-election through the fields. Careening and bouncing, we fired at the hulks and it was surely only by luck that we would hit them. We must have wounded many by this kind of shooting. The meat is dark and heavy and we often trade it for fresh rabbit or sausage.

APRIL 5 Off to Garmisch with Paula, children, Gunilla, and little Toni. Went to two hockey games between the Olympic Swiss team and a German team. Lou Montfort, my boyfriend here, arranged the weekend. We attended a private musical gathering where the Hungarian composer, Georges Boulainger played his composition of "My Prayers." Beautiful. Played six sets of tennis until I became so angry with Lou I ran at the set point ball he hit and drove it through the net. Admittedly, the net was war weary.

APRIL 9 Count Marcus Clary arrived for the weekend. (Marcus had been a prisoner of war when Dad and Paula met.) Went hunting and shot my first boar. Hit him in the heart. A clean shot. They are really hideous beasts-dangerous and very smelly. About two years old.

APRIL 10 Dad is off hunting. Michael's birthday party.

APRIL 12 Spent the afternoon at the welfare office directing the issuing of clothes to the needy. Took off about 5:30 p.m. with Will and Mary Harrison and Dad to Strasbourg, France. (Will was a reporter for an American newspaper and he and Dad were friends.) Mary and I put up with them.

APRIL 13 We shopped all day for material for clothes, a cigarette holder for myself, and phonograph records. Such a relief to have these things available. Back in Stuttgart by 7:00 p.m.

(We had often taken short trips with Will and Mary. We had once driven to Salzburg, Austria, to see the "Mad King Ludwig's castle. It was not a long trip, but Dad was tired so I did most of the driving. We stopped just across the border of Austria to have a drink and a comfort stop. When we ladies came back to join the men at the bar, there was the Colonel fast asleep on the bar sofa. Naturally, anyone seeing him would think he was passed out (and in uniform). Dad had the ability to nap at the drop of a hat. I really envied him, but not at this time. We never said a word and enjoyed our drinks as people whispered about the American officer.)

APRIL 14 Went to the German-American club in Waiblingen. Everyone drunk and disorderly. Hardly a well-formed group. Seems the main attraction for the Germans is the food provided by the Americans, the wine, and partying. (Why else do we go to parties?) Often quite typical, as getting some of these items is still quite difficult for them.

APRIL 15-29 Parties for Will and Mary Harrison as they are going home to the United States. Will miss them. Paula and tribe were here. Marcus was not invited, but came anyway. I think we make it very bad for him, as he does not fit in. Bought a new police dog as my beloved Hasso died. This is Alex and he is very sharp. Police trained. Two years old and not friendly, but very handsome. So far he is ruling the roost, as I am afraid of him. So are the servants.

JUNE 10 Dog is now friendly. He wet on the wall a day after he arrived. Dad reflexively picked him up by the scruff of the neck and the tail and threw him out the dining room window. I expected him to attack, but he accepted the dominance and never did that again. We have had four solid weeks of rain. Dad spent two weeks in America. Was appointed vice president for the Reserve Officers' Association in Europe, and is to form the group. Very good. (Dad then founded the Reserve Officers' Association unit in Europe and was a member for life.)

CHAPTER XVII

ITALY

In the fall of 1948, Ann Armour and her seventeen-year-old daughter, Betsy, arrived for a visit from the United States. Ann had been a friend of Dad's for many years in Los Angeles, California. I remember as a young child going to her parent's (Somermeir) home at 9599 Sunset Boulevard, in Beverly Hills, for dinner. It was a palatial building, prominent on the *strip*, and like a castle inside. It was not as typically *Hollywood* as some of the ornate homes of the wealthy movie people. It was sedately done in lovely woods and stately staircases. The gardeners tailored and carefully tended its lovely grounds. I remember how I gagged at dinner on the cold beef consume, never having such before. This attracted an elbow from Dad to re-

Ann Armour and daughter, Betsy

mind me to mind my manners.

Betsy was a free spirit and someone told me I was to be her chaperone. I failed miserably with this teenager who was man crazy and had a mind of her own. She also had a sharp tongue, when angered. I was an adult to her and she was not taking anything from any adults. We were all right as long as I gave her no direction. Ann was a charming lady who had been married several times yet never seemed to find the man of her life. We took them both on hunting trips and to visit Babenhausen. While on a hunt at Captain Barbers, I lost track of Betsy and she disappeared for the night. Somehow, that never got back to Ann or Dad so I think I gained a few points with Betsy that time.

Ann wanted to tour Italy and Dad graciously let us take the Packard. He could not take time off so Ann hired a chauffeur from Paris. Our driver was an older man named Theobald. The name "Theobald" was too much for Betsy and me and we caused him much torment. However, he was a good driver and came with a uniform. Packed and passported, we took off early one morning. We headed to Memmingen and to Constance on the Bodensea for the afternoon. I think Ann planned this short first day to see if Theobald was a good driver. He passed, and we all enjoyed the stopover. Ann rested while Betsy and I rented a motorboat and "flew" around the lake. We had to stop wherever there were men so Betsy could see if she was interested. By the time we turned the boat in, I had more than enough of Betsy and went to my room to change for the pool. I could not have taken more than twenty minutes before I arrived at the pool. It was not too surprising to find Betsy already there with two Mexican fellows.

At least they invited me to join them and we swam and had a really great time with Tico and Lorenzio. They were gentlemen and we dined and danced that evening. We even delayed the start of our trip the next morning to have breakfast with them. I still have their addresses in Mexico City. After gay farewells, we were off to Venice. This is a city of canals. Ancient, water logged pilings support the town. At that time, there was great concern by the city fathers that Venice was sinking. It is still there so either they "shored her up" or just lived with the situation. There is no doubt that Venice, even so shortly after the war, was (and still is) a very romantic city. It has its own mys-

Theobald our driver.

tique, a charm that seems quite real. Even the boatmen and their often off-key singing were charming.

We had left the car and Theobald at the dock, as we would go by
water to Venice. It is separate from the mainland. We took off in a
launch for the city. By now we were really in holiday moods. I was especially enjoying being away from the scenes of war. Arriving in
Venice, we went straight to our lovely hotel, by gondola, feeling like

movie stars. Well, at least I did. Most of the movie people did not impress Ann and Betsy. We were delighted to see electric stop signs over the canals and our boatmen brought us to full stops for the traffic. Motorboats also passed us, leaving us to rock in their wake. It was a very exciting ride in that ancient gondola to the square where the buildings, shown in my history books, actually stood. The upside down building, was indeed upside down. The architect had designed it and then looked at the blueprints upside down. He was struck with the appearance and decided to build it that way. This was the tale the hotel manager told us. It was a great story, if true.

By now it was getting dark so we saved the rest of the square for morning. Our hotel was old and lovely, and the food was excellent. We called Dad to let him know we were all right and getting along. After talking to Dad, Ann and I found that we had lost Betsy. We went to the bar for a nightcap, and again found Betsy surrounded by men. An older, nicely dressed man was attracted to Ann and I was again with Betsy and her new friends from Palermo. The one who liked me was short and funny and kept yelling loudly, "Viva Palermo," "Viva Palermo." He was *slightly* inebriated. By then I did not care and we had a great time.

Slightly "tired" the next day, we toured the lovely city of Venice. They are known, of course, for their beautiful Venetian crystal. We stopped at a glass place where we watched them twirl and swirl the glass rods. Somehow they made lovely pieces of crystal in this process. Short on money, I picked up a few blobs of crystal from the floor as my souvenirs. These glass makers filled their showcases with exquisite crystal that was to die for.

Of course, we saw the famous bridge of Sighs and many other notable landmarks of history. In the afternoon, we were invited to the palace of Prince Alfons Clary und Aldringen, Paula's father-in -law.. Dad and I had met him at the Löwenstein's castle when I first met Paula. We took a gondola and I wondered how dank and mildewed the palace would be as we were rowed through the not-so-fresh water. We were taken right to the steps of the very old building, and met by our host, Prince Clary. What a surprise to find everything quite dry, lovely, and warm! The prince was very much the gentleman and we were served an excellent tea and cakes. The Princess Ludwine was not there as she was visiting members of her family. Even Betsy was

Betsy, Prince Alfons Clary-Aldringen, and author outside his home in Venice

on good behavior and seemed to enjoy herself.

The next morning, after another evening with our "Viva Palermo" friends, we were off to Florence. I think Theobald was glad to see us, and we were like a family as we piled into the Packard for more adventure. The countryside was beautiful and the climate was warm. Only as we approached larger cities did we see signs of war. Perhaps because of the economy, or the tropical climate, Italy was far behind Germany in rebuilding and cleaning up. We often felt we were in a poor country. It was not always so clean.

Florence was a lovely city with a most beautiful cemetery that had suffered badly from the bombs. We toured it because of its well known, striking, marble carvings and sculptures. The Italian officials had posted signs for "no photos," but they were in Italian, and I do not read Italian. They did not want pictures of the bombing damage to the statuary. One memorable piece was a remarkable statue: a marble bust of a man on a throne-like pedestal, with a step leading up to him. Lying on the step was the marble figure of a woman. I

Cemetery figure in Florence

presume his wife. She was looking up at him adoringly. In the crook of her arm was his head, blown off his marble shoulders by a bomb! I have often thought whoever placed it there was a romantic. Still, are not all Italians? We roamed through this cemetery as though it was an art museum. The marble statues were absolutely gorgeous despite the random bomb damage. Superior craftspeople did every

form, from busts to full-figure, to animals and chariots. It was really an experience in art.

On we went to Rome. In Europe we did not see signboards full of advertising as we have in the United States. Seeing the countryside was lovely instead of someone else's idea of what we should buy. However, they did have handsome iron flowers about four feet tall, with small signs advertising some product along the roads. It was comic to see signs by cafes with unreadable names of Italian foods and pastries and then "Coca-Cola."

As I look back, it seems Rome was quite devastated even in 1948. Signs of bombings were still quite obvious in certain sections, not all. I recall there was a valiant effort on our Allies' part to protect the ancient city, if at all possible. Our greatest thrill was driving down the avenue toward the Coliseum. It looked as though it was right out of my history book. We passed a wall with a series of maps by Mussolini showing what he had expected to do to Europe. I was surprised that the Italians still kept them there.

The next day, after an early evening for Ann and me, we drove to the Vatican with its treasures. Such an impressive place! A city within a city. We had to buy postcards, of course, and mail them to friends with the Vatican postmark. (I still have mine) We were surrounded by people in religious frocks and habits of all descriptions. They were rushing to seemingly important destinations. No glimpse of the Pope, but we did see the treasures of the Popes. Unimaginable riches. Jewels, gold objects, silver pieces, etc. It really seemed quite distasteful at the time, knowing the poverty on the streets. But this was "history." We visited a few shops too, but then the Italian cooking caught up with me. I went to bed while Betsy and Ann toured the caves.

I was feeling much better the next day as we headed on toward Pompeii. It was really tropical so we traveled with the top down, much to the enjoyment of the villagers. Theobald was basking in the attention. We were having some trouble with the usual crowned roads and the tropical rains. The streets would get like glass. Theobald rarely slowed the car, until we had one very scary slide.

Pompeii was a very interesting sight. Workers were still digging, and I presume still are today. An overly-friendly man, who tried to entice us into looking at the sexual side of the ruined city, guided us.

He never gave up and would point at little locked boxes suggesting we pay him to see the inside. Nevertheless, dragging Betsy along, we did the tour. It was obvious that there was a great splendor, years before, to this city. However, the remnants spoke more to the cataclysmic eruption of force from the volcano. Forms made by pouring concrete into holes discovered in the ruins created gruesome figures of dogs and people as they had died. They were frozen in time, no longer useful to themselves or others. We were interested, but glad to escape back to the car and the journey toward Capri.

We left Theobald and the car at the dock again, and boarded a boat for Sorrento and Capri. Since we had decided to bypass Sorrento, we just saw it from the water and dock. Capri was so enchanting as we approached, and it was teeming with tourists. We went to our hotel and then out to sightsee. Hiring a taxi, we headed for the top of the island for the usual grand view. We wondered, after Theobald's trusty driving, if we would survive this taxi's sure death speed. We went at break neck speed around drop offs of hundreds of feet and blind corners. We were all three total wrecks by the time we arrived at the top. After a short walk around the area, we unwillingly went back to the taxi and hid our heads in our arms until we stopped at the bottom of the hill. I would have walked down, but it would have been just as dangerous. Enough of that. That night Ann became ill and we had to call the doctor, who gave her a sedative. No wonder.

I enjoyed the sights of Capri, but we were happy to get back to "our" Theobald and the seeming stability of Naples. Ensconced in an adequate hotel, we put on our new sandals from Capri and went down the back streets of Naples shopping. After about twenty minutes, I felt itching on my legs and looked down to see what seemed like hundreds of fleas feasting on my bare skin. I let out a scream and Ann and Betsy came running to find out what was wrong. They were also covered so we made a quick exit to the hotel. Thank heavens we were carrying emergency supplies of toilet paper, soap, and DDT (an insecticide) in our luggage, We sprayed ourselves, the room, and our beds. But we still felt "eaten up."

We went down to dinner in the hotel restaurant that opened to the street. The waiter approached with the usual white towel over his arm. I always took it to be a mark of office, although I had occasion-

A grotto at Capri

ally seen it used to brush crumbs off the tables. We ordered the least seasoned things we could and concentrated on the great bread. While we were waiting for our food, a bat flew in the door and our waiter went after it with the towel. He knocked chairs over and was a dramatic figure dashing about. We tried to keep our appetites with what we had already experienced. Finally, he swatted the bat to the

floor and, instead of gathering it in the towel, he stepped on it. I can still hear it. We gagged and jumped up from the table. We went right to our rooms and to bed. Bad dreams.

It was a relief to be under way the next morning to the seashore. An electrical storm, typical for the Mediterranean, soon developed. It was so breathtaking along the beaches. Electric blue skies seemed to crackle they were so intense. Lightening played all around us. We stopped for lunch at a restaurant where we could sit and watch the storm. Our meals were in a fresh saltwater pond as we entered. We could choose from lobster, eel, and other strange looking, live delicacies. By now, feeling acclimated to the Italian food, we bravely asked for the usual "extra garlic." We really enjoyed our sumptuous meal alongside the stormy sea. We even invited Theobald to have a glass of wine with us. By now we really were feeling like a family. All along the way on this trip, we had no trouble with the Italians. They had been polite, and seemed warm and friendly.

Reluctantly, we left the restaurant and headed for Pisa, to see if the leaning tower really did! It did, and was amazingly stable at such an angle. We were not able to enter the building. Such a pity! Cowards that we were, we had no intention of climbing anything leaning like that. Also, we saw the tall column with statues of Romulus and Remus being suckled by the she-wolf.

On toward Milan and *The Last Supper* painted by Leonardo da Vinci. We were still in warm weather, but having the top up seemed more comfortable as we headed north. Arriving in Milan, we went right to the building housing the painting *of The Last Supper*. It was amazing that when the Allied bombs hit the building, only the side walls were lost. Thankfully, the two end walls with the famous paintings remained. Workman and artists were repairing these paintings from the shrapnel damage and the weather when we were there. It was an humbling experience to view the original *The Last Supper* portrayed in so many religious pictures. It had great beauty despite its damage. On the opposite wall a painting of a famous battle, was also being repaired. It would have been a great pity to have lost these treasures.

Surprisingly, we were all getting along quite well as the trip neared its end. Betsy was champing a bit to get out on her own, but was not a problem. We even talked about missing old Theobald

when he went back to Paris. I wonder if he shared our feelings. We arrived in Zurich for the night and the next morning, we were off to the German border and then Stuttgart. When we reached the border, the Swiss waved us through. However, when the German guards stopped us at the German border, they held me as I had let my passport run out! I was obviously not very good about identification papers, other than my driver's license.

Once in Stuttgart the Constabulary officers had stopped me when some ladies and I were entering the PX. It was just routine until they found that I did not have my dependent's identification card. They said they would have to take me to Headquarters! I thought it was just a joke. How could they do this to me? I certainly looked American. Nevertheless, they were dead serious. I was put between two of the Constabulary men and had to get into their jeep. It was very embarrassing, to say the least, as they drove me off leaving my friends helplessly behind.

When we arrived at the Constabulary Headquarters, the very serious guards took me into an office, set me in a chair, and quizzed me about my identity. I was feeling quite powerless by then and close to tears in my frustration. Despite my pleas, there was no way they would accept what I was telling them. In desperation, I asked them to call my father, hoping he was in his office. I was convinced they would put me in a cell, for heaven only knew how long. When Dad answered the phone, the Constabulary Officer told him they had picked a young woman up who did not have identification. He asked Dad if he had a daughter named Jean Walters? He said, "no." I almost fainted and began to cry, by now totally worn down.

The soldier explained my plight to Dad and the Colonel relented and admitted he did have an impractical, independent daughter named Jean. What a relief! Thank God for my sense of humor or I would have killed Dad when I arrived home. The Constabulary drove a sheepish lady back to the PX where I, red faced, found my friends waiting for me. Never, never did I forget to carry my ID after that. To this day I think Dad set the whole thing up to teach me to carry that card.

However, here I was without a current passport and at the mercy of the German border patrol who loved every moment of their power over an American. No amount of arguing, or offers of a gra-

tuity, would sway them. I was going to have to go to Basel, to the American Consulate, and have my passport brought up-to-date. I was so embarrassed as this was causing Ann added travel time and was such a stupid thing to have happened in the first place. I remembered, at the last moment, that I knew the English officer in charge of the German town just across the border. A hurried call, but he was not in town nor available. It looked like we were going to Basel.

Ann decided to call Dad and let him know we would be very late. I really did not want her to do this for obvious reasons, remembering the ID episode. Just then the telephone rang and it was the English officer. His secretary had reached him and he told the guards to let me through. "*Yawohl, mein Oberst,*" I heard the guard say, and we were on our way. Again, a red faced, young woman learned the hard way, but what a relief.

We arrived at the house tired, but having had a really wonderful trip. It was hard leaving the good weather, the lovely countryside, and the hotels to return to a winter in still depressing Germany. At least we had Ann and Betsy for a few more days. Theobald was driven to the railroad station by Herr Braun after warm goodbyes and thanks. I noticed Ann gave him a large bonus and he was quite pleased. So it was soon back to life in Germany again.

Ann and Betsy rested a few days. When Ann was packing to leave for the United States, Betsy decided she had other needs. An argument developed and, as usual, Ann gave in. Betsy, with Dad's help, (anything to get her off our hands) (sorry Betsy) managed to work out a plan where she would be a paying guest at Babenhausen. Gundi was given the dubious duty of becoming Betsy's chaperone. I knew how well that worked! I planned other activities to avoid the situation.

It was not long after Betsy arrived at the castle that Gunilla was biting her tongue to remain a lady. Betsy was after all the men, did not accept the pace of life at Babenhausen, and generally made a pest of herself. Gundi was helpless. Friedrich Carl was also furious with Betsy. To give Gunilla time away from her, Friedrich Carl and Gundi took Betsy with them on a business trip to Munich. When they arrived at the hotel in Munich, Betsy was left behind while Gundi and Friedrich Carl went to their business meeting. I am sure they stayed away as long as possible. It did not take long before Betsy

had the attention of all the men at the hotel bar. When Friedrich Carl eventually found her, he told her that they would be on the road by ten the next morning. Both he and Gundi left her to her own devices that night.

The next morning they had quite a struggle arousing Betsy and trying to get her under way. It was no easy task as, of course, she wanted to stay on. Friedrich Carl was tempted to leave her but then insisted she accompany them. Eventually, Betsy made it to the car. As they were leaving, Betsy suddenly announced that she had left her watch and bracelet, both gold of course, on the bathroom sink. Two steps ahead of her, Friedrich Carl knew this was a ploy to get them to let her stay. He told her, "too bad," and he drove off to the great shock and anger of Betsy. I do not know if she ever found her jewelry.

Soon, Babenhausen was no longer interested in putting up with dear Betsy. She somehow made it to Kitzbühel, where she fell in love with a German ski instructor. They were married for a short time and had a lovely daughter. I saw Betsy again some eighteen years later at my father's resort in Mexico. She was mature, pleasant, and friendly. Not at all the rebellious teenager I had known. Somehow, I missed the young Betsy.

CHAPTER XVIII

THE FUGGEREI

In the Fall of 1948 the reconstruction of the Fugger owned houses and apartments in Augsburg was complete. Dad and I were invited to the reopening ceremony. We drove with Friedrich Carl and Gunilla. Both were dressed in their best for the festivity. This was the *Fuggerei*, a large section of Augsburg built by Jakob Fugger in 1516. There were many apartments housing the poor, unemployed, and the retired people of Augsburg. This was Jakob's idea of sharing his wealth with the "commoner." He also felt a duty to repay, in some way, those who had been loyal to his firm and to the city.

The bombing had burned and/or destroyed the *Fuggerei*, in the heart of Augsburg, during World War ll. The three branches of the House of Fugger had felt compelled to reconstruct this part of their family history. Later, they would sell the Fugger brewery at Babenhausen to help refinance the remodeling and addition of more apartments to the foundation. The *Fuggerei* buildings were well made accommodations, not an institutional presence. The families were very proud of their accomplishment in this restoration.

Friedrich Carl and Gunilla introduced Dad and me to Prince Joseph Ernst Fugger von Glött before the ceremony. The Nazis had arrested this prince for his role in one of the failed attempts to kill Hitler. He had spent three years in prison and was very lucky not to have been executed. After his release, he became a primary figure in the reconstruction of the new German democracy. These were important times and Dad and I were fortunate to be a part of the history, both old and new. At this ceremony, various members of the

Fugger family made speeches. I took pictures that were later printed in the local Stuttgart newspaper.

Following the ceremony, we drove to Munich for the celebration of *Fasching*. This affair was similar to our Mardi Gras and is a wild, raucous time for all. I do not believe Gunilla was with us, having retired to their smaller castle, Wellenburg, nearby. Just as well. We went directly to one of the more famous beer gardens. We were ready for some serious relaxation after being our serious selves at the Fuggerei. It did not take long, with the rich German ale, to begin to become one of the merry group. Nationality and position no longer counted at this time. People dressed in many different costumes and masks and acted out as they wished. We were having a great time, although we were not in costumes. Dancing folk dances, singing old German songs, we were one!

Suddenly, a person came up and grabbed me. "It" was dressed in a huge raincoat, pants, and a mask. I have no idea if "it" had anything else on. I was bent over backwards and given a huge kiss. Flustered and speechless, and hearing Friedrich Carl laughing unmercifully, I turned beet red. However, I was soon dancing a wild polka and trying not to get dizzier than the marvelous ale had already made me. To this day, I do not know whether a man or a woman kissed me! We drove back to Babenhausen that night and, I swear, the whole time Friedrich Carl never let me forget the "thing."

SPAIN

It seemed to me that Dad and I would get along very comfortably when traveling. I have tried to puzzle this out. Usually people in cars heighten their differences. The driver is the "authority," and the passengers interact accordingly. We always seemed good comrades as we sailed along the various routes of our travels. It was too bad we could not have spent more time traveling, although we certainly did our share. I know part of it was our mutual ability to enjoy strangers along the way, and to see the beauty in the countryside. It was always a favorite occasion for both of us to pick out a small shop and purchase local bread, cheese, and wine. Then we would stop at some scenic spot to enjoy our fare. We could both talk about our lives and friends and really enjoy each other. I think when we would return home, he became the father again and that was the end of the cama-

raderie. Of course, I also became the stubborn daughter.

Dad and I decided one day to drive to Barcelona, Spain, where cousin Robert Ades was working in the American Consulate. We left Stuttgart in the Packard about 8:30 a.m. on icy roads. I think we both had premonitions of bad roads ahead. However, by 10:00 a.m. the roads were clear and we sailed smoothly along. Dad was always a good passenger. I did most of the driving and he usually slept in the back seat. If I saw something interesting, it was all right to awaken him. Heading south through Switzerland, we stopped at Zurich first. It was wonderful to be, again, out of the war torn and poor areas of Germany. It made Switzerland seem exceptional. She always seemed so clean and orderly anyway. We filled the gas tank here, a rare privilege in Germany, for sixty cents a gallon. The gas was full of denatured alcohol to increase it's volume and the car was soon full of alcohol fumes.

We had cleared four border points and at each had to especially declare the money we had with us. We also had to show our passports (mine was up-to-date for a change), the papers for the car, and what we might be carrying. No problems, but it was time-consuming and a bother. I asked for the best road to take us to Berne from Zurich. We were directed to a road that took us right back to another border station! The road went back over a strip of Germany so we had to pass four more control points! We were both quite upset with the Swiss. However, the new route turned out to be an especially beautiful one. We quite enjoyed Luzon, a small city with a peculiar style of architecture. The buildings had archways over the sidewalks and streets. Stores and businesses were under these arches. It looked like a town built beneath an endless bridge. The town is on the shores of Lake Geneva and is known for its famous university.

Skirting the lake, we drove into Geneva. The city seemed much like an American one. It was busy, and there was heavy traffic. We gained the impression that these were industrious people. As the gas gauge had registered empty for the past half hour, I decided to be on the safe side and stop at a station. I should have been more cautious, especially as I was still angry about the added border crossings. I drove into a Shell station built like a small castle, and stopped at the first pump. The attendant very impolitely waved me to another one. Then he sneeringly said, "okay." Whatever it was that he put in

the tank, we will never know. It might have been ginger as the car began to surge and fly along the road. Just as suddenly, it would stall as
though shocked by its own behavior. A smell like antifreeze or lighter
fluid filled the car and was choking us. As cold and crisp as the
weather was, we were forced to drive with the top down. It must have
been quite a sight for the natives. Despite the car's gyrations, we
made it into Lyon by 10:00 p.m. that evening.

Our French hotel was so typical for that time. It was shabby and
old but with a certain genteel quality that made it all right. Massive
and ornate beds, threadbare rugs, very large gilt mirrors, and heavy
carved furniture seemed mostly standard then. The smell and activities of the former guests seemed to linger, and I rarely found things
overly clean. The bathrooms were a jungle of peculiar instruments of
assorted sizes and shapes that only a Frenchman could understand
and need. Our hotel was the Grand Nouvel, at a cost of four dollars
a room, or one thousand francs. The exchange rate was very good
for us.

That night, needing gasoline "tickets," we inquired of the clerk if
the Automobile Association would be open the next day, Sunday. He
informed us, "Oh yes about 9:00 a.m." So the next morning, after a
good breakfast costing about two dollars for the two of us, we
headed for the auto office. At 10:30 a.m. we were back at the desk demanding to know when the office was to open. We were then informed, by the morning clerk, that the place was never open Sunday.
Consequently, we paid dearly for our gas across France–at one dollar
per gallon. We were traveling with the usual five gallon cans of gasoline in the trunk. However, we always kept them for any emergencies
ahead.

Halfway to the Spanish border there is a direct change in the
countryside. Almost dramatically it changes from a lush green to a
dry, arid environment. The architecture also changes from what I
call European to the Spanish influence. Stone and brick architecture
with tiled roofs. The Spanish seemed to use a great deal of whitewash
(thin white paint) on their buildings. There were always plentiful
pots of colorful flowers on balconies, at doorways etc. We saw many
more people in uniform, which made us a bit uncomfortable. However, the climate was becoming warm and pleasant. This was their fall
season.

About 5:00 p.m. we drew into a small cafe for dinner. It was the usual not-too-clean but passable place when a person is hungry. We tolerated these situations considering them as part of the local "atmosphere." We were to find that the rooms we insist be clean, are not in the hotter climes. Also, the lavatories along the way were very primitive and not at all sanitary. They usually consisted of two cement pads over a hole. We found these so horrible that we risked a trip in to the woods to avoid their use.

Dirty faced children delivered the food and cats and dogs vied for whatever they dropped. Dad and I tried not to notice some of these things. I purposely sat with my back to the bleak appearing kitchen. I had hung my coat on the back of my chair and it had half slipped to the floor. I heard a strange noise from behind me and turned to see what was happening. There, on my coat, was a young cat giving birth. We had at least finished most of our meal before this took away what was left of our appetites. The owners rushed over and took the cat and newborn kittens away. They were gesturing and making dabs and swabs at my coat. We departed with many apologies from the owners who, in broken English, made it known that they would name one of the litter "America!" I rolled my coat up and put it in the car's trunk. It spent the rest of the trip in there with the containers of gasoline.

On the road again, we passed many hunters on bicycles as this was their bird hunting season. Their hunting dogs rode in boxes tied to the back fender of the bikes. We saw many hares– the very large European rabbit. More than once we would mistake these large animals for the small deer we hunted in Germany. Later, because of an overabundance of these rabbits, someone introduced a disease that wiped them out entirely. Many angry hunters let the government know what they thought of this travesty.

As we neared the border, the roads were becoming very narrow and twisting, but they remained quite smooth. We crossed into Spain about 6:30 p.m. with about 120 kilometers to go. At the border we met one of the "black cardboard hat" uniformed officers. These peculiar hats bore a great resemblance to Napoleon's famous one. These were the land police. Whether it was the funny backward hat or the darker complexion, the men really looked mean. Like *banditos*! However, they were very kind and I wondered if it was my *La*

Femme Fatale aura that caused this? Wishful thinking but they could be quite gallant. They even gave us some good tips on how to avoid paying the government tourist tax of fifty *pesetas* per day. One dollar bought eighteen *pesetas.* If we spent a certain amount while in Spain, the government would waive this tax. They told us to save all receipts, whether ours or not, to present at the border on our return.

Everything was found in order, and we passed over the border into our first Spanish town. Although it was growing dark, the immediate change in architecture was outstanding. We encountered many narrow streets as we drove along. These allowed only one car at a time. A pedestrian had to press against a building to avoid being squashed. Their buildings were built right next to each other, and all had flower covered balconies. It seemed the smell here was somehow different. Fresher perhaps? This all had a definite romantic flavor somehow.

Three or four miles down the road the black hats again stopped us. Again, they were polite and friendly and we passed with no problems. However, they showed great interest in our passports for some reason. I know they could not read one word of English, but they checked every page. Finally, they allowed us to drive on and we then came to two more check points. By then, we felt quite sure that this was a heavily police-controlled country. Bob and Christine later verified this.

Narrow roads and an evening fog made us lose time so we did not arrive in Barcelona until midnight. I had asked Dad how we would find Bob's apartment but he was not concerned then. Now that we were in this large, foreign city it was evident that we had a problem. Never mind, my father had studied his Spanish dictionary and he would ask directions. I have mentioned in another place that he was not clever with languages. Spying a man coming across the street, Dad called to him and, in his best Spanish, began with "Senorita." I knew what that meant. The man seemed to forgive the reference and began waving his arms and giving us a torrent of Spanish. We smiled, thanked him, and went on in complete confusion. It was at this point that I learned Dad had memorized the "where is" but would not understand the answer.

We hailed a taxi (the streets were almost empty) and Dad used his very poor Spanish. With a quizzical look, the driver reflected his bewilderment. Dad finally showed him the address and the driver

then indicated that we were to follow him. Exhausted, all we could think of was bed. I drove along behind the taxi. We could easily have been following a killer to our ends, but we went willingly. A few turns and there we were at Bob's apartment. We expected to pay through the teeth for this help. However, the driver stuck his head through the window and said, "goonite," and drove away. A generous man.

We found our way to the door of the apartment house only to be confronted by an armed guard. It seemed, because of political problems, they locked everything up at 10:00 p.m. Bob had told the guard that we might show up so we were directed to their apartment. How good it was to see the family again. Even the children woke up to greet us.

The next day their Bolivian maid greeted us. She had been with Christine's (Bob's wife) family in Bolivia for years. This lady had been a peasant and had never seen the lake twenty miles from her home. Christine had brought her with her when she came to the United States to live. On the ship in the middle of the ocean, the maid had asked Bob, "Senor, how can all of this water stay in one place without running off?" She was so excited to see us again. She animatedly told us something in Spanish that one of the children interpreted for us. The maid had said that she felt we were her family.

The next morning, after catching up with our many happenings since our last visit in Paris, we went with Bob to the American Consulate. There we met Mr. Ford, the Consul General and his staff. We were well received and they extended invitations for dinner and plays to us. We learned that there were few Americans in Barcelona then so we were instant celebrities. The Barcelona newspaper later interviewed us and we received a very good write up as "dignitaries." They took a flattering picture of me, none of the handsome Colonel! We rapidly learned that the Spanish were late to rise, started work around ten, and closed for two or three hours at noon. Then, back to the office until six or seven. Next was the cocktail hour and dinner was about nine. We would go on to the theater or parties after that. It did not take us long to adapt.

Barcelona was a busy and modern city with all of the latest fashions. I broke Dad's arm and was allowed to catch up on my wardrobe, to a degree. Being able to choose from a variety rather than

Cousin Bob Ades and author in Barcelona

just one style was so delightful The buildings here varied with often a heavy baroque architecture which I found rather ugly. The streets were broad avenues and new cars were everywhere. The people were quite well dressed and we were with a very charming social group. The streets were colorful in festive decorations of flowers and tinseled rope.

Horses and wagons, also handsomely decorated, were everywhere. The wheels on the wagons were about six feet high. Tinseled or colored ropes were often interwoven in the spokes of these wheels. Surprisingly, there was much advertising all along the streets. This was rare in the northern countries. We saw many small billboards, and the building's walls were covered with ads. Not too neat. We found many outdoor markets with all kinds of local products. I was surprised by the many bird cages with native wild birds for sale. Although there were many summer villas, apartments seemed the most prevalent style of living.

We attended many cocktail parties, toured the museums, and saw a district where they displayed all of the architecture of the country. I do not recall the name of this area, but it had many liveable homes representing each architectural style. It was quite fascinating. One evening we attended a light musical. The consul general was our host and we sat in his elaborate box, with an attendant serving drinks.

We were told of the bombs that had damaged this building and others in the city. This had been during the recent revolution and many people had died. It was our hope, as we watched the program, that there would be no bombs that night! The cast in this musical was very casual, talking to each other while the opera was on and even going offstage. They had a peculiar style of singing. It came from the stomach in a great push, and was guttural in quality. All in all, very interesting.

This was a wonderful visit with our cousins. Our only problem was the spicy foods so late at night. Dad and I both decided we could not live in this manner. We reluctantly left our cousins, after five days, and had an uneventful drive home. There were no problems at the usual border stops and no tax when we showed our receipts, some of them Bob and Christine's. We drove on into the colder weather and the signs again of the war-torn land we had forgotten for a brief time.

CHAPTER XIX

HONORS AND MEDALS

Dad continually looked for some way to get recognition for his efforts in World War 1 and World War ll. The Military Government officials had informed him that there were going to be United States warplanes destroyed as excess or outdated weaponry. He saw an opportunity to get some acclaim. He contacted some French officials he knew and asked if they might be interested in these planes. In the back of his mind was a hope that the French might show their appreciation by a medal of some sort. He could picture himself at the ceremony receiving it. Dad had waited a long time for this.

At first, he would not tell me how he planned to get these craft to the French. He began the work of planning the presentation ceremony with the French officials. This seemed a little premature to me, but he did not want my advice. The planes were to be presented at a small town in the French zone. Our "sometime" German driver (I believe his name was Leroy) was a young man who had a brief flying career before the war ended. I was thoroughly of the opinion that he must have flown better than he drove, or he would not still be here.

Leroy was to fly the planes, one at a time of course, to the small town prior to the ceremony. I pointed out that the French and American authorities might object to a war plane manned by a German pilot flying over the Zones. That is when I learned that this was to be a secret affair and that Dad hoped to pull it off before anyone stopped him.

On the day before the presentation, Leroy and Dad drove to the

airport where the planes were stored. Dad was really elated and, like a kid, felt he would finally get his recognition. Leroy would be flying and Dad would be driving to pick him up and take him back for the next plane. When they arrived at the storage point, the planes were gone! They had been flown to some hidden place and had been destroyed. Poor Dad, he really had been a hero during the first war and saved a small French village with his regiment. Now, he had nearly created an international incident when the French learned they were not to get the planes. They called him on the carpet, and it took sometime before the French let him forget their anger.

Another time, Dad and I drove to a small German town, Höhr Grenzhausen, in the French zone. He had helped capture this place in World War 1. His soldiers had begun to ransack the little town and Dad had stopped them. He had managed to get a truce for the town and the citizens had treated him as a hero. On this day, he did find a family that remembered him and we were invited for their evening meal. Much gesturing and arm waving helped us all communicate as they had a strong German accent we could not interpret.. They treated us very well and visitors came to greet Dad, including the mayor.

This town was well-known for its production of very beautiful steins. Dad suggested, in his usual poor German, that it would be nice if he could have one. The mayor immediately said they would present him with two steins for his heroism toward the village. Dad was ecstatic and after a few more glasses of wine to cement the offer, we retired to our very shabby, little hotel for the evening.

The next morning we had breakfast with the mayor and some city officials. The latter seemed a bit bored but friendly. Dad wrote down the information about the time and the action for the inscription on the steins. After much ado, we were on the road again to Stuttgart. Dad was very pleased with himself.

Time passed and no call came regarding the steins. Dad kept saying how these things take time, although I think he was worried. After four months, he had his secretary send a letter to the mayor. Again, two months passed. Finally, Dad said we would drive back to the town and see what had happened. Arriving in the town, we went to the mayor's office and were shocked to be greeted by a stranger. It seems there had been an election and the old mayor was no

longer there! No wonder we had not heard from anyone.

Dad again explained his heroism and that there were to have been two steins made for him. The new mayor was quite pleasant and took us to the factory where they made the steins. The director of the factory took us to a room and they served us coffee and cakes while we waited for them to search for the steins. After a short wait, he appeared with two very, very large pitchers. They were a type that were used for milk storage in the cold cellar and were called *krugs*. The potters had decorated them very elaborately. Each had an inscription regarding Dad's rescue of the little town. I felt so sorry for Dad as he was really disappointed. They were not the steins he had wanted. Worse still, he had to pay for them!

We rarely mentioned those pitchers. I used them to make martinis or that punch mixture that had such an effect on all the guests. I still have one left. The other was broken somehow. The inscription reads, translated from German, "The Lt. Col. Eugene P. Walters is kept in memory from when the Field Artillery Regiment 148 was stationed here in 1918. He is greeted by the people of Höhr Grenzhausen and saluted in May 1947. The Mayor Grees."

BORDEAUX, FRANCE

Dad's and my last trip together was to Bordeaux, France, in April of 1949. Despite our mutual disagreements, Dad wanted me to go with him to Bordeaux where he had spent Easter in 1918. Such a romantic. I think perhaps the first World War was his time of independence and proof of his maturity. Whatever, he had many fond memories of the French, although I think he had given up any idea of medals or honors by then.

We piled into the Packard again and set out for France. By now, things in Germany had greatly improved. We saw fewer signs of war and this was a beautiful time of year in the country. There were no problems at the checkpoints and we were, by now, quite versed in these procedures. The uniformed guards always enjoyed looking over the Packard, and perhaps its driver? Even gasoline was easier to find, and not altered, so that the car ran smoothly. I think in a way we missed some of the old struggles we had earlier, but seeing the improvement all around us was delightful. There were fewer war scenes. The ruins of ancient times, with their decaying but historical

bricks and mortar, seemed a measure of the devastation that had been. The narrow cobblestone streets of the villages were so picturesque and the fields of grape vines stretched for miles on the hillsides.

The buildings were so very old, but brightened by the usual geraniums. This was an architecture of external white plaster and dark stained boards of the Norman period. Oxen plodded along hauling heavy carts of various kinds. The famous "honey" wagons were something to avoid following too closely. These were the manure vehicles that carried sewage (mostly from the cattle) to the fields. Often there were thatched roofs and houses that incorporated the barn so that the heat from the fires, and the animals, kept the home warm. The bridges had been rebuilt so there were few detours. The usual scene of men relieving themselves by a tree had not changed. This had always shocked me. Even at our house, when the German children were playing outside, they did not bother coming inside to the bathroom. At one time, Paula had some ceramic tiles made for me with scenes of our times together. One of them was of a man at a tree with me looking quite shocked. Meanwhile, Dad and I were stopping at little shops and buying the excellent land wines, bread, and wonderful cheeses. It was not difficult to find a picturesque spot to stop and enjoy our usual picnic. The weather was warm and comfortable. Looking back, this was one of our best trips together, although we were having our problems.

We arrived in Bordeaux, a very old city, by afternoon on the second day. After a well-deserved rest, we went down for dinner in the small inn. The people were especially friendly after the Colonel's halting French explained his reason for being there. They treated us to good wine, and the dinner was on the innkeeper. Someone found an old man who remembered Dad's stories about saving the town from the Germans. Although I spoke very little French, with Dad's help and some poor English on their part, I kept up with the group. Besides, the wine was strong and the company was cheerful. We poured into bed late, but happy.

The next morning, a bit groggy, we ate a good breakfast of smoked ham, underdone eggs, and excellent bread. However, we did refuse the offer of wine. After all, we were going to church, the same one that Dad had attended many years before. I could tell he was

enjoying this "reunion." We drove to the prominent cathedral that seemed to dominate the city. It was lovely with its spires and old walls. Inside, there was a crowd of worshipers. This was a very large church, with huge columns supporting the rampart ceiling. They ushered us to a place behind one of these columns, where we could only stare at it or crane our necks into our neighbor's space. No one seemed to mind.

I presume this was a Catholic church, as French seemed to turn to Latin as the priest went through his routines. People filed up for the communion, but Dad and I had enough wine the night before and stayed put. It gave us a chance to look more closely at the golden statues and gilt work. The stained glass windows were works of art. Everything did need a good scrubbing of soap and water though. After the communion, the ushers took up the collection. A woman, who reminded me of one of the hags in *The Tale of Two Cities*, came down the aisles with a basket on a long pole. It was well filled by the time it came to us.

Neither the Colonel nor I had thought to make a donation, thinking of ourselves as just tourists. We innocently stared ahead, avoiding her sharp piercing look. It did not work. Dad soon had the basket pushed into his stomach with a shove and something was loudly expressed in French. It was probably, "Give, or face the guillotine." He quickly reached for his wallet, always in his back pocket, and hastily dropped some francs in the basket. I am a quick learner and had my francs in hand when she glared at me. It may have dimmed Dad's fond memories a bit, but we later found it quite funny.

That evening, after some sight seeing and enjoying Dad's tales of his war experiences here, we avoided the bar and retired early. We were to start our return to Stuttgart the next morning. Mission accomplished, we had an uneventful trip home.

CHAPTER XX

DIFFICULT TIMES

The trouble brewing between Dad and me was accelerating by July of 1948. He was leaving the War Department and was reluctant to go into the State Department. He was given a full "Colonel" rating which helped his retirement from active duty. Nevertheless, I think the change in departments meant a cut in pay and he had enjoyed the army and all of its protocol. It also meant a change in his work

High Commissioner John J. McCloy & the Colonel

and his position there. The War Department was returning the houses, requisitioned for the occupying forces, to the Germans. Most Americans were being directed to army billets or supervised housing areas.

The newly appointed High Commissioner, John J McCloy had arrived in Europe. Dad and I had greeted him and his family when he visited Stuttgart, They had been our guests for lunch The State Department was just using civilian employees. The German government was taking over their own controls, and there was less need for Allied supervision. By 1949 the occupied areas were changing hands. Dad's favorite town of Karlsruhe became part of the French Zone. I know all of this seemed depressing to the Colonel.

Many friends and fellow officers were leaving, and it was a difficult time for him. He became more irritable with me about my financial situation. As I look back, I believe he was having problems of his own regarding future decisions and did not need a "dependent" adding to his problems. For some reason we never talked about how we might feel, instead it seemed to be just a series of breakdowns in our communication. The situation did not get better, and continued to worsen.

I was feeling ever more homesick for my family in Everett. I could never save enough money for a vacation trip home, and the Colonel would not help me. He would take several trips to the United States every year, and tell me to earn my own fare. He was right. However, if I took one of the many jobs that I was offered, I would have to work another year before a vacation. I remained determined that I could somehow make sufficient money with my photography. It did not happen, although I worked quite hard at it. I began to try some devious ways of getting money. I arranged with several friends to charge their commissary items to Dad's bill and pay me the cash. They were willing to help me, although they knew the "Colonel" would also be angry with them if he found out. He never did and I was not proud of what I was doing.

With the devaluation of the mark, and the resultant availability of more goods, the black market was even slimmer pickings. From letters written home and invitations received, it was obvious my social life did not suffer. Dad and I started going our separate ways by 1949. He had left a letter for me when he had gone on a trip to the United

States. It cut me quite deeply. It was dated May 23, 1949.

My Dear Jean:

It is no wonder that Flöter (the photographer), or anyone else, depends on you to do what you say you will do. You were supposed to be back by 1500 today to pick up a package for Paula's pictures tomorrow. I doubt if you all even make it back in time for them to take pictures. So that being the case, Hubs will probably not be able to meet a deadline for delivery.

It is very evident by the events during the last few months that you've got too much of the play girl and not enough of trying to do something with your career. So, for the last time, I am telling you that by the time I get back I want you to have made arrangements to get out on your own. Now if you don't do it, I will have to do something unpleasant for both of us.

When you reach the point where you begin considering others more than you do yourself, then we will consider things again. You would be wise to take some notice of Ina's words, don't kid yourself into thinking they were completely to blame. I'm afraid the company you have been traveling in, lately, has been going to your head. Too bad.

Hubs kindly loaned me his Robot (camera), but being that you are not here I cannot find only one spool (sic), (film) so I have to leave it behind and proceed with no camera.

Under no circumstances drive the car to Paris

I suggest you get a job with the occupational forces.

Dad

I know that Paula, Gundi, and I had left for a party in Frankfurt. Dad was very angry with us for not seeing him off at the airport. We evidently had to arrive in Frankfurt about the same time he was to fly. He said very little to Paula, and I received the brunt of his anger. So, when he returned, I was sure he did not want to see me and we did not meet him at the airport. As Paula was with me, that made it even worse. We were in very serious trouble. Dad forgave her, but I do not think he ever really forgave me. For years, he criticized almost everything I did or said, relenting only as my professional career began to develop. Even then, he never allowed me into the family business, and made my brother the "Prince." So, I paid a very high price for my independence (or whatever it might be called).

By now (June of 1949), with her husband Marcus' arrival home in 1948, we were seeing less and less of Paula. I am sure this was very difficult for Dad and was also causing some of his shortness with me. He loved Paula dearly so the loss of this relationship took it's toll. The changes coming as the State Department gave up much of its control of Germany, also bothered him. Paula was pregnant and expecting her baby in July of 1949. They were living about two blocks from Captain Barber's where I had gone to hunt and to visit her. Captain Barber was an entrepreneur. A hustler of whatever opportunity presented itself to make extra money. It was rumored that he had a truckload of German marks when the surprise devaluation came and could not present them for the exchange without risking arrest. Barber always had a resource for anything. A valuable friend, but often risky business.

Paula was to meet me at Barber's. He had invited other guests, so it would be a busy weekend. Paula and I shared a room and a double bed as things were really crowded. Paula had also been painting her flat and the fumes were too much for her to stay there. She was "very" pregnant and uncomfortable, but this lady was always game to keep up with whatever the rest of us were doing. She was not a hunter and stayed at the house with the other guests. They assigned me to take a visiting major under my wing as he had never been hunting. I knew the woods quite well as we had been here often. I planned that we would just drive around the forests and he could shoot by the car. I would not let him shoot from the car, as I had almost lost my hearing on several occasions when someone had done this.

We drove through the lovely, clean woods and were looking for a buck of good quality. We saw a doe and a spike buck. However, it took some time before sighting a good rack. The buck was standing about 75 feet from us and looking off to the left at a doe. The major was in the backseat and I whispered to him to quietly step out of the car on the off side, move slowly to the car trunk, and shoot. He had a perfect shot and at a standing target. I was breathing hard, not moving, and waiting for the shot that was a long time coming. As I slowly turned to see what the major was doing, he fired. He had developed "buck fever," and was shaking so badly he had hesitated to shoot. The buck went down, but was struggling to get up. The major

had hit him in the back. Taking care of a wounded deer was not my area of expertise. The forest meister's or my guides handled these situations.

Wishing to give him a tongue-lashing, but aware of "buck fever" that had left me palsied at times, we went to the poor buck to dispatch him. At this point, the major asked me how we were to do this! The buck was struggling, the major seemed helpless, and I searched for an answer. A rifle shot at this distance seemed risky to me. I remembered seeing, ugh, the foresters often insert a knife at the base of the skull to kill a wounded animal. The major used his hunting knife, but only a surgeon could have found the entry spot. This buck was not lying quietly. We finally went back to the car. He steadied himself with elbows on the car trunk and fired a shot to the head. At least this ended the buck's misery and ours. I was feeling very upset by this time and was not too polite to the man. But we had meat for the evening meal and the major had a nice rack.

Back at the house, cocktails put an end to my gloom, and we were soon telling hunting stories. Barber had three or four large German Shepherds. He always had pure black ones. The dogs were his babies, but were a bit overwhelming when they were all allowed in the house at once. They were enjoying the attention, when Barber picked up a paperbacked book. He showed how the one dog liked to try to grab it as he did not like the rustling of the pages. In the spirit of the moment, or out of sheer stupidity, I picked up the book and showed it to the dog.

I then tossed the book to Paula. It landed in what was left of her lap. The dog landed on her with his paws on her very pregnant front. Obviously, this was a very stupid, thoughtless mistake of mine to have done this. Paula let out a groan. I expected to see her fall to the floor. The other guests gasped, but Paula pulled herself together with the determination that is so strong in her. She said she felt fine. I felt absolutely abysmal, and it was quite evident this could have had disastrous consequences.

Paula seemed all right through dinner so I was very relieved, but still feeling quite guilty. She tried to reassure me, but not too successfully. We made it an early evening as Barber had planned a big hunt for the next morning. I went to bed with a book. Paula took a bath and seemed somewhat preoccupied. Looking back, apparently she

was preparing for delivery of the baby. However, then, it just seemed like untimely behavior when she came into the room asking if I had some polish remover. She somehow had to get nail polish off her nails. I asked her why and she just glared at me. I quickly gave her my remover and I think I even helped her remove the polish. She came to bed eventually and seemed to fall asleep. I was still reading. Suddenly, she sat bolt upright in bed and said the immortal words, "I have lost my water."

When I was in college, I had written a paper on the process of the birth of a baby. The movie on the same subject, "Birth of a Baby", had a profound effect on many of us. It was a subject not openly discussed in those days. After tedious research, long hours of writing and rewriting, I had received an "A" on the paper. From then on I was quite confident that I could deliver a baby, right to the cutting of the umbilical cord. I even bragged about it! Now, here we were and I had never heard of "I have lost my water." I asked what she meant! Paula said she was not feeling pains but that this particular situation preceded delivery.

I shot out of bed and called for help by waking Barber and the guests. Barber asked if we needed anything. I said, "Yes, a beer." He replied that he did not think Paula should have a beer at this time. I told him it was for me! I was really quite shaken and still feeling guilty regarding the dog and the book. It was obvious to me that this was what had caused the labor to begin.

Paula now announced that she was having labor pains and we timed them at five minutes apart. She asked me to call her physician in Stuttgart, although we both knew it was too long a trip. The doctor concurred and suggested the local physician should be called. Paula wanted to go to her apartment as she had everything ready there for the birth. Barber called the doctor and then drove us to Paula's apartment as the pains became more intense.

Poor Paula was now surely in full labor as we struggled to get her to bed. I remember one lady, who was supposed to be helping me get the linens, towels, and other supplies, suddenly doubled over with sympathetic pain. She could not do a thing and had to leave the bedroom. It was just the two of us now, and suddenly I could not remember what came next! However, the doctor finally arrived and I was reluctant, but glad, to give up my responsibility. He also had a

nurse who arrived within moments.

Paula was now in serious labor. I do not know if we told the doctor that this was her third child. He gave her a shot to hurry the delivery which seemed to me to be moving quite rapidly anyway. I was staying because Paula had asked me to, and because of my own curiosity about the birth process. Perhaps I might really learn something other than what I thought I already knew. I also kept the rest of the group, waiting in the living quarters, informed about what was happening. It surprised me later to learn that this whole birth of this baby had taken about six hours. It seemed to me it had all happened much more quickly.

After the shot, Paula's pains escalated and suddenly the doctor announced the baby's head was showing. At that point, the baby just shot out, as though propelled! It was a very lucky thing too as the cord was wrapped around "Christian's" neck and could have caused serious harm if this had been a prolonged labor. As an onlooker, I was simply awestruck by this whole process. It seemed a wonderful thing to see new life, yet wonder how this fragile baby could have survived the ordeal. It seemed miraculous to me that something so new could then be spanked to start breathing, have his throat cleared of mucous, and then be immediately subjected to our cigarette smoke. Paula even had a cigarette.

She was still quite alert and asking about the health of the babe. The conversation was all in German, with the doctor and nurse having heavy accents. Yet I could easily comprehend. Mother and baby were healthy. I was exhausted and, after giving Paula a good hug, retired to let the doctor and nurse complete whatever was now required.

Marcus and the family nurse soon arrived. They took Paula and the baby to the nearest hospital. The hunt was, of course, canceled. After a few hours sleep, I returned to Stuttgart to report the activities to the Colonel. God only knows how frustrated he might have felt, but he said little. I am quite sure I left out the book and dog part. However, that was surely the cause of Paula's early labor. It did work out well though as that cord could have caused lasting problems for Christian. Or am I, perhaps, rationalizing away my guilt? That was the only time I saw Christian, whose nickname is "Tita," until Paula and the children came to Rancho Buena Vista when he was eighteen. I have not seen him since.

CHAPTER XXI

LEAVING GERMANY

Dad's trip to the United States in the spring of 1949 had been to attend the Reserve Officers' Association meeting and to look for possible business ventures for Europe. His fraternity brothers were always loyal and gave him leads for possible sales opportunities. He announced in July that he would be closing the house in September and that I had a choice. I was to find a place of my own, or return home for good at the cost of the government. The government had sent me over and had to return me and my household goods. Finally, a way to see the family again. Nevertheless, this would be the end of my life in Germany

It was a surprisingly easy decision to choose home, despite losing my many friends and this wonderful life. Dad was to remain in Europe. He eventually found a living by selling products there that Germany did not have. He did well in his endeavors. At some point he and Paula had a "final" falling out and he then married Bebe Jorgenson, his college love. He returned to the United States in 1957 when Bebe died. Dad bought his Mexican Resort, Rancho Buena Vista, with the proceeds from her estate.

I was given many farewell parties, despite my attempts to say that I was just going on vacation. Even with the parties it was a difficult time for me. I had made this country my home and loved my many friends. However, I remember my last birthday in Germany all too well. Dad did nothing, not even a "Happy Birthday." He had invited some of his friends over and they excluded me. He had planned it well, how angry he was with me! Despite calls and cards from my

friends, it was quite painful. Still, his behavior helped to hurry me on my way. Two days later I attended a party at the Consul General's house and was pleased to find myself the object of a surprise birthday party. At least my friends had not forgotten me and realized my difficulties. Later, I spent my time traveling around to say goodbye to the families who had been so kind to me. I saved Babenhausen for

Friedrich Carl in a relaxed moment

A last gathering, Count Ferdinand Arco, Paula, Friedrich Carl, beautiful Gundi, two friends and the Colonel

the last. That would be the most difficult.

Dean drove me to Babenhausen for the weekend and the last hunt. Gunilla was very pregnant with Markus and not feeling well. We kept our festivities quiet. Everyone talked about the many memories we shared of our times together. The possibility that I might come back helped to soften the parting a bit. Our final hunt was with beaters and was for rabbits for the table. It was very early into the deer season. We were using shotguns and we were positioned along a straight stretch of road. The beaters were moving noisily toward us. Foxes were being shot and many rabbits.

Suddenly, a large handsome buck bounded toward me and almost into my lap. I reflexively pulled the trigger at about twenty feet and the buck went down. He then stood up and staggered into the woods behind me. I felt disgusted with myself as shooting a deer with a shotgun was unforgivable. The forest meister said it was all right, but had us all wait where we were for twenty minutes before he went to track the deer. This period of waiting is to keep the animal from running away from pursuit and makes the tracking simpler.

When he found it, it was dead and he also found that it was Friedrich Carl's best buck! It was not supposed to be there. If they had known that this buck was anywhere nearby, they would have had us hunt elsewhere. Remember that we hunted to cull, not for big racks. Friedrich Carl was furious with his foresters (luckily not at me)

so we all stayed back as his anger was awesome. Because of this error, I was not to take possession of the rack until Friedrich Carl decided what to do. He later agreed that it should be mine and had the horns taken to Memmingen for mounting. I never saw this buck or the horns as I left before the mounting was completed.

For a year or more, I tried to get the Colonel to send the horns to me, but without success. He kept making excuses. I believe that he had already given the rack to Friedrich Carl or the latter had picked it up himself. Eventually, Dad talked me into "letting" him take the horns to the castle, Wellenburg, where the mount would be forever on the castle wall. I was to feel happy that my name would be on the plaque. Actually, I was.

Meanwhile in Stuttgart, the process of packing and dismissing the servants was also an ordeal. Ina and Eugene had often been caught in our battles and I think they were more than ready to leave. We were fond of them and I hope Dad gave them a pension of some kind. They went to live near some relatives in Northern Germany. I was to hear from them several times. Eventually, the whole army seemed to move into the house to do the packing. I was supposed to supervise, but could not be in all of the rooms at once. However, to my knowledge, only one thing never made it home with me. A large navy telescope of Dad's did not make the trip. When the crate of belongings arrived in Everett, Washington, it filled the entire garage at grandmothers'. My two dogs, a German Shepherd named "Alex," and a Dachshund named "Popo," were put in dog crates and sent to Bremerhaven for the sailing.

True to himself, Dad did not appear when I was leaving the house. He also left me no money. I had eighteen dollars and a box of dog biscuits to get me home. I ate dog biscuits that night in the army barracks before boarding the ship the next day. Once I was on the ship, my meals would be free. I still had a long train ride from New York to Washington state so I had to be very frugal with the eighteen dollars. It was a very sad lady who looked back at the house on Richard Wagner Strasse.

As I was being driven through the streets of Stuttgart to the train depot, I thought how much the Germans had improved their lives and surroundings in such a short time. It was beginning to look as though there had not been a war. Only an occasional building or

wall still showed signs of shelling. There was a great deal of rebuilding and new building. People walked with their heads up and with purpose. Their clothes were still in colors of dark blue, brown, or black, but that seemed all right considering the progress being made.

I remember very little about my trip through the familiar German countryside. When I arrived in Bremerhaven, I was given a private room in the barracks. There were no loud women in the other room giving me a bad time. I do remember feeling desperately alone. The next morning I visited my dogs at the port and tried to reassure them that all was well. They looked very miserable and had a long period of confinement ahead. I left one of my gloves in each of their boxes to remind them of a familiar smell. I do think they were eating better than I was.

I also kept hoping to see a familiar face of someone coming to wish me well. However, there was no one. It was just as well, as I had said my goodbyes, and would now begin accepting the great change coming in my life. The next day, as the ship hooted its departure, my mind flashed back to my arrival at these docks and my stumbling entrance onto German soil. How much had happened and such a rich life for me in only a few short years. It would remain the outstanding time of my life. Could anyone have asked for more? I think not.

Author in 1975 (credit Leslie's Studio, Aberdeen, Washington)

CHAPTER XXII

RETURN TO GERMANY

1977

Many years later, in 1977, the Colonel was the *El Patron* of Rancho Buena Vista, a popular fishing resort in lower Baja, Mexico. My brother and my sister-in-law, Charles and Toddy Walters, had joined Dad about 1960 and had helped to develop the resort. They would invite me down several times a year, but they never allowed me to be a part of the operation. However, we had good times and Dad was less antagonistic as he aged. It was always my job to take care of him whenever he was ill or was recovering from surgery. At those times he would come or be sent to my home in Montesano, Washington. I had moved to Montesano in 1967 to establish a two-county mental health program, and was the Executive Director. Dad liked that.

The Colonel never let me forget, however, that I should have worked on the East coast where the "important families were." He was never satisfied with my decisions or, for that matter, my brother's. He also had a way of getting Charles and I pitted against each other. When either of us would go to him for help against the other, he would utter the dreaded words, "consider the source." This made it a round robin and never answered our problems. Yet, as he aged, he mellowed and became more dependent in a way.

Dad had a lovely silk standard (or tapestry) that he found in Memmingen during his service there. It hung in his house at the resort and was suffering from the humidity and the fact that it was several hundred years old. It had been handmade by an ancient order

The Colonel with my mother, Eunice Davis 1975

of nuns. It was for the hundredth anniversary of a military regiment of the time. I repeatedly urged him to get the standard and his priceless oriental carpets to the United States and out of Mexico's humidity. Perhaps a guilty conscience finally made him decide that the tapestry should be returned to Memmingen. He had never told me how he had become its' owner.

For some reason he decided that I should present it to the officials of Memmingen–perhaps the mellowing? He had my brother make the travel arrangements and send me sufficient money for the trip. Chuck did this grudgingly, always feeling that I was getting the best choices. I was to stay with Paula in Baden Baden. A Baron Dieter Malsen was to arrange the "returning of the standard" ceremony with the recent mayor of Memmingen, Herr Doktor John Bauer. Dieter Malsen had occasionally visited Babenhausen when I was there and, without my knowledge, had a "crush" on me. He was several years my junior and that was perhaps why I paid no attention to him. I had, as he continuously reminded me, never known he was there. He had recently visited with Dad at the resort. Dad had asked him to arrange the presentation and see that the standard was repaired. Dieter lived near Memmingen in his small castle called Osterberg.

The standard was sent ahead of me to Dieter, who arranged for its cleaning and repairs. I flew from Seattle to Frankfurt where Paula met me at the airport and drove me to her flat in Baden Baden. We

had been seeing each other at the resort and at my home in recent years. However, it had now been two years since we last met. There had been some problems between her and Dad, mostly because of the changes in him through the years. Paula and I started out well in this lovely town. I so enjoyed walking about its' park and along the river. This was my first trip back since 1949 and the sights and sounds of Germany were like music to my ears.

One evening I went to a rather formal party with Paula. This was at the home of one of her friends. I was not willing to try my German vocabulary in this small group of counts and countesses. I soon felt left out as they were all speaking German. There seemed to be some hostility, or so I thought. Usually, manners require that a host speak the language of their guest. Perhaps this was a chance for the Germans to get back at an American woman who had been among the conquerors? At least my feelings about the situation soon proved to be a correct assessment .

Eventually, one of the men asked me why I did not speak German? I said that I did not speak it well and so did not wish to make mistakes. He disdainfully said, "Well, I would not travel to a country where I could not speak the language." There was a hush in the room, as though this was the plan. Perhaps I was just being too sensitive. Paula did not step in to help me. I really did not need her help as I can stand well by myself. I was angry though, but I diplomatically said, "Do you mean that you would not go to Greece because you do not speak Greek?" This rebuttal of mine was just the ticket! I was an instant success and from then on they all spoke English. This reaffirmed my belief that the German has respect for the person who does not back away from confrontation. We had some very lively discussions about our cultures and politics for the rest of the evening.

My dress for the evening was one of the then popular Kimberly knits and was full-length. I had purchased it for the trip and this was the first time that I had worn it. I stood most of the evening. The heavy knit began to get longer and longer and longer, and settled around my feet. No one seemed to have noticed so, gathering it up like a bridal train, I sat down and stayed down the rest of the evening. When I finally stood up to leave, I again gathered it up in my left-hand and managed to get out of there before I had lost my hard earned composure. I did not want to give anyone the opportu-

nity, or reason, to ridicule me again.

While I was with Paula, Princess Gunilla Fugger came to visit me. She had a small apartment in Baden Baden where she came for the baths. Baden Baden is famous for its lovely baths with their curative powers. People have come to these heavily tiled and statue filled buildings for ages to bathe. I enjoyed seeing Gunilla again. She had two of her sons with her, Count Hubertus, who was two when I last saw him, and another son, Count Markus. She had been pregnant with Markus when I left Europe. Hubertus was very handsome and charming, as was Markus. Gunilla looked very well and was just as regal as always. We had a wonderful visit, although short. There was time to remember some of our good times at Babenhausen. Gunilla invited Paula and me to Babenhausen for a visit. We planned to stop there on our way to Dieter's for the ceremony.

Several days later, on our way to Osterberg, we stopped at Babenhausen for tea. What a lovely sight for me. There was the castle in the distance and the fields where we used to hunt. I felt very nostalgic as we entered the courtyard. Gunilla, dressed in a German dirndl, and Hubertus, in his Bavarian suit, met us. They took us to a newly restored part of the castle, not the middle part that I had known. When the family had recently restored these rooms, the workmen had found a hidden ceiling of beautifully carved wood. The elegance of this part of the castle seemed to embody the history

Paula, Count Hubertus Fugger-Babenhausen, and Gunilla at the castle

of the Fugger family..

Prince Friedrich Carl was not living at Babenhausen anymore. He was at his smaller castle, the lovely Wellenburg, by Augsburg. He was seriously ill with emphysema and needed to be closer to the hospital and doctors. We planned to visit him also. After tea, served with the usual elegant silver, Gunilla took us to look again at the old part of the castle. This was where she had her apartment and where we used to stay. Such memories came flooding back! We recalled many of the better times and then it was time to go on to Osterberg.

Paula and I both seemed uptight and argumentative as we drove to Malsen's castle. We were not like the old friends of years before. I had a terrible cold and blamed that for my shortness. I did not know what her reason was. We were met by Dieter and his new wife, an Italian countess. Dieter's castle was small but lovely. He had been remodeling it and had done a very good restoration. When he took us for a tour, I coveted the beautiful, ancient furniture. He led us through the charming rooms and up to the third floor, which was unoccupied. He planned to also remodel it. I was struck by the millions of flies in some of the rooms. In places they seemed at least six inches thick. It seemed to me it would make a good setting for a murder.

Paula and I were staying in the guest house and, as I had a cold, I enjoyed having some privacy. I also wanted to write my presentation speech, which I had decided would be in German. I was to give this speech when presenting the standard to the City of Memmingen and the city officials. Dieter had arranged the ceremony and the invitations. Gunilla and Hubertus would also be there. As a surprise, little Rödle Kreuzer, our party friend from Babenhausen, was invited. He was so pleased that I remembered him. *Rudi* was always ready for a good time and companionship. By trade, he was a photographer and printer.

Dieter was a gossip and a pincher. He was very impolite with me. Once when he and Paula were talking and I joined in, he told me not to interrupt them. Again Paula said nothing. I was left to believe that this was retribution for my not being interested in Dieter twenty-some years before. What else could I believe? It was very uncomfortable and I could hardly wait to get away from there. I did have to rely on Dieter to help me translate my speech into German so that it

would be correct. I did not ask Paula as we were hardly talking. I could not trust Dieter and was afraid that he would change the meaning of my sentences as an attempt to embarrass me. He did not, and for that I thank him.

There was a good crowd for the presentation. Dieter had the standard cleaned, repaired, and placed on a stand. The mayor, Herr Bauer, opened the ceremony with a history of the standard and of Dad's work in Memmingen. Several officials who had known the Colonel said some pleasant things about him. It was a pity that Dad could not be there because this was the recognition he had wanted for so long. I gave my speech in good German, (or so I was told) despite the cold and the runny nose. Afterward, the mayor gave me a lovely plate with a picture of the city of Memmingen on it. I also received a book about the history of the town. Following the ceremony, we went to lunch in one of the beautiful, colorful, Bavarian buildings. There were more speeches and the good German food was welcome.

I had a brief chance to talk with Gunilla again before leaving and encouraged her to come for a visit to Baja, Mexico and to my home in Montesano, Washington. It was then time to leave and I felt a tug at my nostalgia as I said goodbye to this good friend. Then back to Osterberg (ugh!). I was so glad when we left the next day and went to see Friedrich Carl. I would enjoy seeing a friendly face after the

Author receiving a plaque from Mayor Herr Bauer, Baron Malsen at right

last evening with Dieter.

When we drove into the courtyard at Wellenburg, the whole family was sitting in front of the castle door waiting for us. Protocol took us first to the Princess Elizabeth Fugger-Babenhausen, Friedrich Carl's mother. I had not met her before. She was a beautiful, elderly woman with lovely, large brown eyes that seemed to reflect an inner serenity. She also had a quiet, regal quality about her. This was perhaps why Friedrich Carl married Gunilla instead of Greta Garbo, as he liked to intimate. Not only were there similarities in Gunilla and the elder princess, but they were also very fond of each other.

Next was Manu, Friedrich Carl's sister, who had given up her title to marry a man from a very well known noble family, Wilhelm von Hagen. Manu and I had often met at Babenhausen. I then went to Friedrich Carl who looked terrible, ashen pale and struggling for breath. What a shock for me! I so hope I hid my reaction from him. He had his two men servants help him to his feet so that he could greet me. This time I was ready for the kiss of the hand, and he also gave me a most welcome hug that meant a lot to both of us.

We were able to chat for about a half hour before he was obviously beginning to tire. He told me while we were talking that he was a "wimp" and needed *mit arbeiters* (helpers) to help him have romance. Always trying to shock me, but he could not do it. We had always had a private joke about the steelhead trout. He did not know about the fish when I had first mentioned it to him. I had explained to him that the fish would follow the female salmon during spawning and bump her belly to knock the eggs out of her. He, who had never been anything but a gentleman with me, would threaten to give me the steelhead treatment. He loved to refer to some pompous person as needing the treatment. He would threaten his mother-in-law, the Countess Brita Bielke, but always under his breath so that she could not hear him. He had a great deal of respect for Brita, He reminded me of our joke at this time.

They had planned on our staying for dinner but, because of Friedrich Carl's condition and the long trip back to Baden Baden, we declined. That would have been my first chance to see the rack of the deer that I had shot so many years before. We talked about that too. I said goodbye to my dear old friend, with promises to tell "Daddy" (the Colonel) to be a "good old boy" and his wishes of the

best for him. We knew this was the last time we would see each other. I received another hug and we both had tears. I thanked this lovely man for all the wonderful memories he had given me. He died two years later. I had received letters from him as he grew more morose and irritable as time went on. He was grieving and lonely after his mother's death. She died a year after we were there. His life had ended very sadly. *Auf wiedersehen*, Prince Friedrich Carl Fugger.

The following is a letter from Friedrich Carl dated April 25, 1977, exactly as he typed it.

Dear Jeanna,

Many thanks for your nice letter dat. April 14th.

No news from the family except that my wife spends quite some time in Bonn when she took over the household of her brother. Next year she will travel to Africa where he will be the representative to Sweden in some tiny country.

My number one I don't correspond with, number 2 is a learner, so has to be able sooner or later to run the Fugger business. Markus (number 3) has started quite a few things and now studies as a naturecure practitioner. Johannes will be at school at least one more year, then military service, after that banking. Tatiana doing quite well in her school. She, of course, is everybody's pet.

Glad to hear that your old man seems to be more or less well. Also good to know that you are on your feet again.

My sister with her children and grand children is more or less feeling well except that one of the grand children usually has some bloody *Krankheit*, (sickness), some kind of *Kinderkrankheit* (child sickness), so quite often I cannot connect (contact) George and his wife, being afraid, to pick up some *Krankheit*, which you usually if you get it don't survive in my age.

I refuse to tell you something about my health. It usually is below 0 and I have a passport which says I am 100% sick.

Hubi is a big success *mit alle Mädchen und Frauen*, (with all the girls and ladies) what stops him from concentrating on his work. He has far as I know not found *eine Braut*. (A bride)

After the death of my mother, Wellenburg is very lonely so I wouldn't mind if the old fellow Hubi got married sooner or later and would come *hier* in Wellenburg with his Frau.

It interested me to read that you didn't speak with your brother for 4 years. Here things are even worse as my number 1 married with a French girl, is living on one of my former states about 40 kilometers north from Wellenburg. Nothing more to say to that problem.

Nix mehr (no more) able to travel, I stay either here or in Babenhausen, not seeing much of the world.

Das ist alles. Show up sooner or later.

Viele herzliche grüsse (many heartfelt greetings) Love, FC

My stay at Paula's was shortened at my choice, as we really were not getting along well. She was so bitter about the Colonel. I believe she was having financial problems as well. Her family had run into some kind of banking problem and I doubt that Dad was helping her much, if any. I left and flew to London for three days and then home.

After a bit of rest, I organized my "loot" from Memmingen and the pictures I had taken. The society editor of our small newspaper was very interested in my trip. She did an excellent full page write-up. I sent it along with the plate and book to Dad. For once, in a very long time, he was pleased with me and felt that I had done a "bang-up" job. I later received an invitation to Hubertus and the Baroness Alexandra's wedding. I could not talk myself into making another trip so soon and had to decline. Now, looking back, I wish that I had gone.

CHAPTER XXIII

EUROPE 1995

It must have been about April of 1995 that the magnitude of my coming 70th birthday hit me. Instead of being proud of achieving seventy, I found it a bit overwhelming. I looked at my present life and circumstances and decided some changes were needed. I have a phobia about flying. I had not been off the ground since 1981 when I had flown to Mexico to help my brother who was dying of cancer. In fact, I had not been anywhere for more than five days, and always within driving distance from my home. Europe, especially Germany, has always held a great fascination for me. It appeals to my romantic side, which is usually quite well hidden by my stern and businesslike characteristics.

I have many fond memories of the days from 1946 to 1949 spent in Germany and so I decided a return trip was necessary. I also wanted to see if I could enlist the help of Princess Gunilla Fugger of Babenhausen and Countess Paula Clary of Baden Baden in writing this book. I had only had Christmas card correspondence with both of them since the 1977 trip. I needed to reestablish contact with them and my "near daughter," Kathleen Vanderlinden, in Bruxelles, Belgium. Kathleen had been an exchange student here in 1981 and she had fallen in love with one of my horses. She and I had become good friends, despite our age difference. She had subsequently been here twice to visit, but I had never met her husband and two children.

I know my close friends made bets that I would cancel the trip. However, with purpose, and a need to free myself to travel again, I

was determined to go. I contacted a really excellent travel agent who led me through the maze of airlines, motels/hotels, insurance, train reservations, etc. Arranging schedules with my three friends was a difficult process. I could not reach Paula by telephone or letter so I booked a reservation at a hotel for two nights in Baden Baden. This would allow time to visit Paula, if she was home, and give me a chance to see Baden Baden again. I then scheduled five days at Babenhausen. Perhaps this would be too long a visit with Gunilla, but at least the schedule was finally in place. My departure date was set for September 21 and I was to return on October 5. I asked for a non refundable airline ticket to lock myself in. I knew that I might lose my nerve and try to find a reason not to go. However, with that amount of money at stake, my Scotch blood would keep me on track. These phobias can be difficult and unpredictable.

There was a flurry of planning, anticipating everything that could go wrong, and shopping. I am not a shopper by nature, and, living on a horse farm, I needed a new wardrobe. What a shock to get out into the non equine shopping world and find the many changes. Changes not only in styles but prices. Within a short time, I was spending freely, i.e. a five hundred-dollar sweater set. This latter purchase then required innumerable trips to find matching skirts and slacks. I eventually had to put the brakes on to leave some money for the trip itself. I was certainly well color coordinated, and as the book says, "old ladies wear purple." I even made a last minute stop on the way to the airport to purchase purple stockings! I had purposely lost twenty-three pounds by the time I was on my way, and three more while in Europe.

Speaking of pounds, I did not heed the advice of my well-traveled friends and packed for variety and not for lightweight. I was soon to find out that no porters exist in most European train stations. The stations all seem to have at least three flights of stairs down and three flights of stairs up. The travel book also said not to let anyone help you, as you might never see your luggage again. My apologies to all the pleasant, honest men that did offer as I struggled with what seemed like an eighty-pound suitcase.

I am sure no one was more surprised than I that I remained calm and certain of my departure. Two nights before I left, my mare surged forward and caught my right leg with her front hoof. She

lifted me off the ground–spinning like a top–to crash down on my left elbow and shoulder. As I lay on my back, taking stock of my condition, my first thoughts were, "I am going, I am going." (I am leaving out the swear words.) I was even more upset when the mare came over and snorted at me as though I was some strange creature from outer space. I managed to get up and had just a sore leg and shoulder. I thought if this had been several years ago, I would have had a convenient excuse not to go! As it was, I never felt pain from the fall during the trip.

The big day arrived. There were many calls from good friends wishing me well. I had written endless notes to Chuck, the man caring for the house and animals. All of my errands were completed and, after lunch with my friend, Vera Stewart, I drove to Olympia to meet the limo to the airport. I managed to leave my car at the motel where I was catching the limo to the airport. It seemed a good plan as it was free!. It felt as though the limo took hours in coming. However, we eventually were tearing up the highway. I had no anxiety, only a sense of excitement to be finally under way. At the airport, although I was two hours early, I was surprised to find people were already checking in. There were three different counters, each sporting a name that only confused me. I chose the nearest one, "World Traveler." It really did not represent my more recent life, but I liked the implication.

It dawned on me, for the first time, that I had not asked the agent about the class in which I was traveling. Three times people came up to me and told me I was in the wrong line and should be in "first class." Even if they had been right, I would not have moved as that heavy suitcase was already a problem. At least I felt properly turned out since they had that interpretation of me. When I reached the desk attendant, I told her of the large bruise on my leg from the horse incident. I explained the need to elevate that member. This advanced me to the "Frequent Traveler" area and a convenient footrest. I was also next to the restroom. What a relief it was to check that heavy suitcase through. Little did I know what lay ahead with that load.

Still not anxious, but not wanting to risk my phobic reaction, I did take my first tranquilizer. I had a marvelous book with me, so I sat near the boarding gate to read. The book was *Berlin Diaries* by

Missy Vassiltchikov. It dealt with life and the bombing in Berlin dur-
ing the second World War and named many families that I knew.
Mentioned were the Fuggers (Foogers), Clarys, Saurmas,
Hohenlohes, Bredows, etc.

Soon, it became a little difficult to concentrate due to the pill. I
walked to the magazine shop where an English couple stood ahead
of me in line. They had two candy bars, but not enough change. I
paid the twenty cents owing and was then pointed out as "that nice
American lady who paid for our bars." I heard this five or six times
and was even pointed out as we entered the plane. A very cheap way
to become a United States diplomat.

The trip was uneventful, and I had not one trace of my phobia.
Lots of food and drink, which my fellow passengers thoroughly enjoyed. The plane seemed primarily full of Britishers, all having many
drinks and telling some often not too flattering tales of the United
States. I was rather unhappy to see that the flight attendants were
wearing uniforms very similar to my new dress, a Pendleton. The
night seemed very long, but it was a beautiful dawn over London. At
that time of the morning, the city seemed bathed in soft yellow and
orange and the buildings' windows were lighted like stars. The landing was smooth, not a glitch in the whole trip. After getting off the
plane, I found it was necessary to take a bus to Terminal 4. This was
where I was to catch my Bruxelles flight.

I soon found myself hanging precariously from an overhead strap
as there were no seats available on the bus. I was straddling my small
flight bag and a box full of gifts. We drove at breakneck speeds
around corners and on the wrong side of the street. It was hair-raising, and not one seated man offered me his seat. Well, I guess we
women wanted to be equals and that is one way the men can show it.
At least my heavy suitcase was checked through, although it might
have given me a little more stability on this ride.

I had a two-hour wait for my plane to Bruxelles so I chatted with
several other waiting passengers. I found such an interesting mix of
different races and cultures. A group of young people sitting near
me was speaking a language like German. I understand German
fairly well, but prefer not to speak it due to my many errors. I could
not understand their language and I asked the nearest fellow. He
told me it was Flemish. Dressed and speaking like an American

(hopefully my mental lapse was due to the jet lag) I asked him if he knew what nationality I was. Clever! "Hello Hillary," he said. We both laughed, although I felt a bit undone by the reference! I was to learn that Belgium is having a difficult time as the Flemish want their own section of Belgium. To add to the conflict, the French want their share. The country may be split in three ways if these people have their way.

It was a short flight to Bruxelles and then a lot of confusion finding the proper carousel. No readable signs. I was surprised to find no customs here or in London. It suddenly dawned on me, as I looked at the sea of suitcases, that I really was not sure what my new large case looked like. I had just packed it and had not studied it. It was large and black, but so were half the others. I was excited about seeing Kathleen, but forced myself to wait until things thinned out a bit. After seeing one bag go around quite a few times, I decided it was mine. Lucky me!

As I walked toward the exit, I could see Kathleen waving. Her two pretty girls were beside her looking a bit shy. It was so good to see my dear Kathleen. However, her first remark was, "you look like a hunter!" Now, this pertained to my large, chic and expensive, white plastic raincoat. I had checked with my friends and ended up with a consensus of 50/50 regarding wearing it to Europe. The best remark was from my friend Jo Pickering, who said, "do you feel a little overwhelmed by it?"

After that statement, I had driven more than a hundred miles to a French lady who has a tremendous shop full of French, Italian, etc., material for her rich clientele. She had added a long, expensive silk scarf that made it "*tre chic!*" So, I wore the coat. It also traveled well as it could be rolled up and stuffed in the overhead without being wrinkled. It was, however, like a steam bath when I became excited, rushed, or was simply carrying my heavy luggage. The thing did not "breathe." I asked Kathleen later what she meant by her reference to "looking like a hunter." She explained, with a twinkle in her eyes, that their hunters wore coats like mine when skiing. I wonder.

Our drive from the airport through Bruxelles was hair-raising. There seemed to be no speed limit in the city. Everyone drives with one foot on the brake, the other on the accelerator. This gave the ride a surge-stop sequence. The girls played in the backseat as if

quite used to their mother's driving so I tried also to relax. Maya, aged five, is dark and has dark eyes like her Moroccan father, Fouad. She is a clown and is always entertaining. Laila is nine, a great reader and talker, and rather more quiet than Maya. They get along very well and Kathleen and Fouad are excellent parents.

I found Bruxelles a beautiful city. It has many modern buildings, but they have scrolled or decorated them to break the hard lines of the modern look. I saw many parks as we drove and this seemed to soften the city look. In the old squares there is constant renovation of the ancient buildings with their usual gold or gilt covering. People dart in and out of the traffic with death defying abandon. A very busy city. Even the King's Palace seemed to have a modern square look despite its age.

Kathleen and her husband, Fouad, own a duplex house. It has four stories and is like the narrow town houses in the eastern United States. The two houses have a common wall, but each has a different architecture. This type of housing is due to the high cost of building lots. Their home is very comfortable, yet, typically, the toilet is in a closet downstairs and the bathroom is upstairs. My bedroom was on the second floor so a trip down the stairs, in the middle of the night, seemed a long one. Their dog, Vodka, sleeps at the door of the closet and only the wagging tail let me know he was not on guard.

I felt so sorry that I could not speak to the children, as I had learned very few words in French. We just nodded or pantomimed. I could manage a *Bon Jour*. Fouad worked late each day. I learned that there was some anxiety as to whether he would like my "capitalistic mentality," or I, his Moroccan ways. We took to each other immediately and, as he is a psychologist, we had common ground. Kathleen might have actually felt left out at times. Fouad was working with Moroccan street teenagers. He had a marvelously positive attitude about what he does, despite the fact that he faced difficult odds. In fact, he was working on a paper to be given in India the following month. I was able to help him a bit with the paper. However, most of all, I admired his ability to work with what must often seem an impossible task. Many of the Moroccan youth seem to quickly lose their culture when the families move to foreign countries. They become delinquent and adopt the gang cultures of their host country.

It did not take long for jet lag to catch up with me. I decided, at that point, that I will stay somewhere for three days on my own on my next trip. The lag certainly saps your energy when you need and want to keep up with the others. Kathleen is a marvelous cook. However, I would often cave-in and head for bed, not able to enjoy the meal. Actually, Kathleen thought I was doing quite well to be over the lag in three days. She has a much younger American friend who takes five days to recover. That made me feel better.

We drove around sight-seeing and shopping for my "precious" horse bits and bridle rosettes. I am an avid collector of these antique horse articles. We chatted, "antiqued," lunched, and enjoyed each other. Some of our shopping was in Les Grand Place, a beautiful old square with very ancient buildings with spires and gilt statues. The streets are cobblestone, romantic, and difficult to walk on. We had lunch there in a four hundred-year-old building.

Kathleen and I had a great deal to talk about. Kathleen has a very unrewarding job finding resources for prisoners when they leave prison. She has always been a free spirit, a romantic aesthetic who never wanted to become conventional. Now, that part of her is buried, but chafes to be expressed and not locked into everyday life. It

Kathleen and Fouad

will be interesting to see which child, I would guess Maya, will be like her.

One evening Kathleen's parents came for dinner and brought me some lovely flowers. Mrs. Vanderlinden, does not speak English but Fred, the father, spoke some. At least we could exchange a bit about how I had come to know Kathleen, etc. For dinner we cooked our own thinly sliced meats on an electric platter. There were delicious rolls and a great salad and casserole. Mrs. Vanderlinden had made a prune pie, intricately decorated, with more of a cake-like crust than our pastry. It was all very good.

I stayed five days. As my last day neared, we drove to Brugge, a little over an hour away. This lovely old city had been a seaport many years before and is now landlocked, but with canals. The buildings are very old and the town is wealthy due to the heavy tourist trade. I had not seen many well-dressed people until this city. Some were in Dutch costumes and clogs. We had tea and a pastry and then walked around looking at the beautiful architecture.

Many flowers decorated the houses, and a canal wanders through the city. We finally decided to take a horse drawn cart through the streets. Kathleen loves horses and is an excellent rider. As we were choosing our rental carriage, the horse tried to bite her. She then decided instead we should take a canal boat tour. She also turned out to be a reluctant boater and was a little green. However, it was such a pretty trip with the very old buildings covered with geraniums and ivy. We thoroughly enjoyed the whole venture.

That night Kathleen and Fouad took me to dinner at a small French restaurant where I had the best salmon I believe I have ever eaten. Although I am from salmon country, this was exceptional. It was from Scotland, grilled crisp, and had a superb hollandaise sauce. I tried to pay for things, but they took it as an insult, so I did not press the point. I never did find out how to manage the low dollar/franc exchange, but it was expensive. I thought I was leaving Kathleen many francs for her birthday by cleaning out my purse when I left. Still, I wonder.

It was difficult saying goodbye. Kathleen wanted to drive me to Baden Baden to my stepmother's, the Countess Paula Clary. However, I already had my reservations on the train and was looking forward to the trip. I also felt she just wanted a few more hours with me

and would have been facing a long drive back. Reluctantly, she agreed about the train. As usual, I pushed to be early at the depot, concerned about the heavy traffic and my "set-in-concrete schedule." The girls came with us and they were quite bored by the time the train arrived. Bless Kathleen as she was somehow managing to carry my heavy suitcase. I had mixed up the presents I had for everyone. I had given Kathleen and Fouad, Gunilla's gifts so at least my load was lighter in my hand luggage. As usual there were no porters and there were the usual stairs. From here on, I would be on my own. Ugh! Kathleen came aboard with me and slung the suitcase over-head. I wondered how I would ever get it down.

When it was time to say goodbye, she hugged me for so long and cried. I finally realized she thought this was the last time she would see me. I remember when I was young and we went to visit old relatives and I thought these same thoughts. Nevertheless, I was not ready for this and reassured her I was going to be around for a while. In fact, we had talked about a trip to Scotland, hopefully that next year. If I had ever had a daughter, I would like to have had one like Kathleen. She is not easy to deal with at times, but then, neither am I!

I love the European trains and would like to plan a trip to ride them at night. Then, in the morning, get off and explore an area during the day. After a day of sightseeing, I would board the train for the night. The trains are so comfortable, clean, smooth, and have excellent food. It is necessary to be quick about getting on them or getting off. They waste little time in the stations. The Europeans really use their rail lines. Every train I was on was crowded. I was traveling first class and had excellent reservations. We seemed to roll quite effortlessly through the country sides, which are beautiful before and after the towns. As usual, they do not give train tracks the prettiest passage through populated areas. We went from Bruxelles to Luxembourg. It really would have been a good idea to study a map before the trip, as I often thought I was on the wrong train. I have never excelled at geography. When we left the Luxembourg station, we were traveling backwards, which caused consternation for some. Two young American brothers were traveling with so much luggage there was little space left for anyone else. They seemed to need reassurance that we were traveling in the right direction. They were exhausted and a bit disoriented from lack of sleep. The young-

est told me that they were on their way to Munich. I told them about a few places in Bavaria that I had enjoyed.

From Luxembourg, we began to get into the pretty fields dotted with stands of trees. All the grass appeared mowed and trimmed. I saw one red deer, so small. These were our hunting targets in the forties and the only fresh meat we had then. On into Strasbourg, a half hour late. At Strasbourg, I had to change trains to Baden Baden.

The American boys helped me get the heavy case down and I dragged, pushed, and wheeled it up the steps and down the steps to the next train. The one for Baden Baden was just arriving. That damn coat, as previously stated, does not breathe. I was soaking wet by the time I found my seat. This was a brief trip across the river Rhine and then we were in Baden Baden. I was excited and looking forward to seeing Paula for the first time in twenty years. She is five years older than I, but has always been active and in trim condition. We were on time at 6:30 p.m., but no Paula.

Again I struggled up the steps, hot and tired. No Paula. I had a reservation for the *Bad* Hotel. (Do not worry, *Bad* means bath and the town is famous for its baths.) I had not reached Paula when I set my itinerary. When her letter of welcome had finally arrived, I had canceled the hotel. She wanted me to stay with her. Now, I was becoming concerned as I checked the parking lot and the station. About twenty minutes later, a lady passed me who looked vaguely familiar and I called, "Paula." The lady turned to me and it was Paula. It was so good to see her again. She was struggling with some Parkinson-like symptoms, which at times affect her balance. I did not know this.

Paula is the Countess with whom my father had fallen desperately in love many years ago. They had married, unexpectedly to my brother and me- and Paula. Dad had arranged to pick her up at the airport in Mexico City and then rushed her off to a wedding ceremony. He had brought along his attorney and the attorney's wife and poor Paula had felt unable to stop the ceremony. The wedding was sometime in the sixties. She and I have been friends since 1947. She had visited my home and my father's resort in Mexico. I do not believe Paula has ever really recognized their marriage as it was so unplanned. In ways, I think she viewed it as unwanted and too late.

We drove to her apartment above Baden Baden. Of course, a

flight of steps up to the second floor level awaited me with that heavy load. She has a delightful apartment. It is nicely decorated with pictures from her mother's estate. There is a lovely portrait of Paula in the entrance hall. The rooms are very comfortable. We started remembering the past and trying to bring each other up-to-date. She had planned the next day in Strasbourg, but thankfully (I was tired) changed it to lunch with some friends and some sightseeing in Baden Baden. That was the best night's sleep I had on the trip.

The next day a friend of Paula's, Marai von Bredow, joined us. She drove Paula's car and we went to pick up the Princess Helga-Lee zu Schaumburg-Lippe at her hotel. The princess is eighty-four. She does not look or act it, and is constantly off to parties or traveling. She carries pictures of her estate, Schloss (castle) Pfaffstatt in Austria. She autographed one for me rather like a Hollywood star. She was full of stories about all the people she had been seeing and the parties she had attended. She kept us quite entertained. Marai von Bredow tells you almost immediately that she has had to work for a living. She also explains that she has clothes that she buys secondhand. She is a most likeable, kind lady, and she is a great talker. She takes good care of Paula. Others have remarked about her "marvelous breeding," and she is well accepted by these ladies.

We drove for lunch to a restaurant, the Forellenhof, in the woods outside Baden Baden, where they are known for their trout. This is a lovely old building with great charisma and very good food. Paula insisted on taking me to lunch and ordered the trout. I sat there listening to their stories about the famous families of Germany. I felt transported from my life on the farm and my small community to another world that I had missed. The European nobility seems to have tremendous circles of acquaintances and friends, and seem to know so much about each other. Birth and/or marriage also invariably relates them.

When my fish arrived, after a wonderful salad, I almost lost my appetite. The trout was large and had been steamed whole. The skin hung loosely in a silvery blue. Its white eyes were bulging out and its tongue protruded. No one else seemed challenged by it. I half closed my eyes and peeled it so that I could take a bite without losing my dignity. It was excellent!

Paula 1995

When Princess Helga-lee heard that I was going on to visit the Princess Fugger, she told a story about years ago. Gunilla had not been married long to Prince Friedrich Carl at the time. They were all at a party where Helga had "flirted" with him "just a bit." This had angered Gunilla and they had not spoken since. Gunilla later gave me another interpretation of the situation. She explained that Friedrich Carl was going on a hunt in Austria and teasingly told

Helga-lee to come along and "cook his soup." When Gunilla and Friedrich Carl arrived at the hunt, there was Helga-lee and her husband. When Helga-lee found out that Friedrich Carl had just been joking with her, she was quite angry and became *hysterical.* Gunilla was left to mollify her while the men went hunting. Well?

Everyone spoke highly of Gunilla and all seemed to respect her. The luncheon was most enjoyable and we were to meet later for tea at a fashionable tearoom in town. At my request, Paula and I went to the park and walked along the river to the place where they play chess with child-size pawns. I had enjoyed watching these players on my last trip. Paula seemed better and steadier on this day and we were getting along very well. This was so pleasant for me.

I had so enjoyed this lovely town before, and wish that I could live there. The buildings where the famous baths are found are ancient and roman-like with their colorful tiles and decorations. It is an exciting town where one can meet the elite of Europe. Paula and I also stopped at the gambling casino, a richly appointed building, but it was closed. We were able to go into some rooms where we had played twenty years before. We then went to join Helga-lee and Marai who had been shopping.

The tearoom is a social place where ladies have their doggies at the table and engage in the usual gossip. The Europeans are not paranoid about smoking as we are, and the ladies were puffing and chatting away with gold and silver cigarette holders waving. Fancy cakes and excellent ice creams of all varieties were served. Everyone seemed to be involved in animated conversation. After tea and photos, we took Princess Helga-lee back to her hotel and said good-bye.

I told the princess, out of politeness, that if she were ever in my area, to please feel free to call. I knew the last place on earth she would travel would be where I live and so I felt I was quite safe in extending this invitation. Not that I would not have, perhaps, enjoyed this lady. However, the protocol required is not something I would take on for a stranger. She quickly explained that she was really quite busy traveling, a sign that our day was over. I guess I just do not learn. When I lived in Germany in the forties, I would politely, or casually say, "drop by sometime." This, Americans usually consider just a polite way of saying good-bye. However, there the German accepted it as a bonafide invitation. Also, there was usually no call before they

arrived and any number would drop by. This did not occur with our close German friends, more the casual acquaintance. I quickly learned to stop saying that.

Paula had Marai drive us out of town to an antique shop where she thought I might find antique horse bits or rosettes. It was a fruitless trip, but I greatly appreciated the effort she made to do this for me. Later that evening, Paula and I did some more catching up. She was attending an invitation preview of a Sotheby's auction the next morning at eleven. The Duke of Baden was thinning out some art objects from his seven castles. It might be called a "castle garage sale." The preview was by invitation only. Paula had at least ten pounds of fascinating catalogues for the two week auction. She offered these to me. However, the thought of anything else to carry was too much. In fact, she also gave me a Bavarian hat that I really liked. However, I had to refuse it as it would be something more to carry.

Later, at Babenhausen, I learned that the Duke of Baden supposedly had made more than twenty million marks the first week of the two-week auction. This would help toward the enormous upkeep of these castles and their taxes, I am sure. Many of the aristocracies are having increasing problems keeping their costly estates. Even the day to day expenses, with Germany's rate of inflation, can be prohibitive.

I was to ride to the station the next day with Marai on my way to Gunilla's. Paula was to be at the auction at 11:00 a.m. Paula's son, Count Ronni Clary-Aldringen, and his wife, the Countess Tamara, picked her up the next day. This gave me a chance to greet Ronni whom I had not seen since the sixties. I liked them both. However, I had to turn down their offer to stay with them in Frankfurt due to our conflicting schedules. Hopefully, I will have a chance to visit with them all more extensively on my next trip.

Paula and I parted with the hope that she would come to my home for a visit the next spring. I feel that we have both forgotten the difficult times we had at my last visit. Marai von Bredow had the flu, but took me to the station, anyway. She waited with me until my train arrived. Bless her. She filled me in on how well she thought Paula was doing and other interesting things about her life. Even with laryngitis, Marai is quite a talker. After thanking her profusely for her kindness, it was time to board the train. I was looking forward to seeing Gunilla and the castle where, fifty years before, I had spent

many happy times. I would greatly miss Prince Friedrich Carl, her
husband and my good friend, on this visit.

Again, the train was a delight. It was clean and my seat was different in that it swivelled and could be adjusted for a more comfortable
position. Plus I also had a table that I could pull up for more comfortable reading. The car was open, not a compartment for only
about six, as the others had been. I had a large window through
which to watch the scenes that seemed so familiar. We had driven
this route often in the forties. There were no more bombed ruins, of
course, but things in the country had not changed that much. The
fields and forests were so pretty and green. It did not appear to me
that the forests were as clean of bushes and undergrowth as they had
been after the war. Then, a person could see through the trees, as
people gathered every bit of firewood. They had scavenged anything
that they could burn, except the trees. The deer and boar had little
shelter from the hunter then. Only one seemingly lonely *reheböcke*
(red deer) was to be seen. It brought back many memories of our
hunts, mostly at Babenhausen, but also at other areas.

I seemed to be a little mixed up on my geography, as usual. It was
surprising how quickly we came to Karlsruhe. This was a town where

Paula in her apartment in Baden Baden

Dad had been stationed at one time. Its' lovely church spires, with
the usual construction cranes near by, showed that they were carrying out the usual renovation. Then, very rapidly we were in Stuttgart.
At least I could see the hill where we had lived. The city was not as
pretty from the tracks and station. Even when it was so badly bombed
many years ago, it had still had an attractive landscape. It is shaped
like a cup, with the city at the bottom and parks and homes up the
sides. Many memories-however just a brief stop.

When we were under way again, I hurried to the train's restaurant
for a quick schnitzel. It was excellent. I began to feel very excited
about seeing Babenhausen and meeting Gunilla again. However, I
was afraid I was coming down with something, as I was getting a sore
throat. I tried to credit it to my imagination. I could not have caught
something that quickly from Marai, or could I? The conductor announced Ulm as the next stop, where Gunilla was meeting me for
the short drive to the castle at Babenhausen.

Gunilla had undergone hip surgery recently and so had said she
would be in the parking lot "waving my stick." I had told her that she
would recognize me by the white raincoat. I struggled in that hot
raincoat with that damn load of luggage up the usual three flights of
steps. I glimpsed her sitting on a bench looking as she had twenty
years ago. By the time I reached the landing, we were hugging each
other as old friends. It was so good to see her again.

She seemed to me little changed by the years. She still had her regal quality and that lovely voice of rich Swedish accent over excellent
English. She was in amazingly good health, considering her surgery,
and was even without her "stick." We somehow managed to get my
luggage in the car and I found Gunilla to be an excellent driver, no
nonsense. Many ask me what type of car she drives. I cannot say,
other than many Europeans seem to prefer the manual gear stick instead of the automatic shift.

I was not sure that I recognized the country fields that Gunilla
would point out as places we had hunted or visited. However, when
I glimpsed the old castle, Babenhausen, in the distance, I was again
in familiar territory. I missed the oxen and the cobblestone roads in
the villages that we were passing. Oxen are rarely seen anymore. Yet
Babenhausen still has its cobblestone streets in some places. This
town surrounding the castle remains small. Where they are building

Princess Gunilla Fugger in 1995

new homes, they are using the old style that retains the beauty of the place. Renovation, as seen in so many other places, was also going on at the castle. They had just painted it a lovely cream color. Over most of the building was a large section of new roof. Roofing this building would be like roofing my entire neighborhood!

Prince Hubertus was spending the weekend at the castle and his flag was flying over the roof. Whenever the reigning prince is in resi-

dence, the flag is flown. Hubertus, Gunilla's second son, had inherited the title of Prince, when his father, Friedrich Carl, died. Their oldest son, Toni, who I had known and loved as a youngster, did not get along with his father's ways and they had parted company. Very difficult for all, especially Gunilla.

Gunilla and I were talking about Friedrich Carl and his great love of sarcasm. I reminded her that Friedrich Carl and I had bantered this way a lot, much to the chagrin of the others. The Colonel especially did not like sarcasm, and certainly not from his daughter. Gunilla felt that Friedrich Carl was not as unmerciful to women as he was to his men friends. She mentioned several friends who would drive to see her and if Friedrich Carl's flag was flying, they kept on going!

We entered the grounds of castle Babenhausen through several openings in the surrounding walls. Then we drove over the moat and into the courtyard. I saw so many familiar places, figures, and entrances. At last the courtyard, the gardens, and the castle's inner circular drive. Gunilla no longer lives in the castle proper, but has had a wing remodeled, beautifully, into a lovely small home. As we entered her living quarters, I was impressed with the combination of very new and very old. Paintings of her ancestors, in lovely frames, cover the walls. The rooms have exquisite furniture from ages past and Italian slate floors. Leading to the upstairs is a gorgeously modern steel and marble spiral staircase. An open-sided fireplace in the living room adds to the atmosphere of comfortable elegance. French doors open to her garden, and the house and yard are full of her favorite roses. I struggled, again, with the eighty pounds of luggage up the stairs to my room. It was overlooking the courtyard. At last a respite from that load.

Count Markus Fugger, Gunilla's third son, was ill with the flu. While she went to check on him in his apartment, I unpacked and changed clothes. I had a lovely room with my own private bath nearby. No running up and down stairs to the toilet. A very large bookcase, from floor to ceiling, filled with excellent modern books, was a testament to Gunilla's love of reading. Nearby, a painting in its very heavy gold frame is of Gunilla's namesake. This was Queen Gunilla (Bielke), wife of King Johan 111, king of Sweden in the mid 16th century.

Count Markus Fugger-Babenhausen

I had known both Count Toni Fugger the eldest, and Hubertus the second son, as babies. Paula and I had tried to help toilet train "Hubi" by tying him to the leg of a bed while he sat on a "pot." He protested loudly while Paula and I were trying to make sounds of waterfalls, etc. We were not at all successful, and I apologize to Hubi. I think we had a few glasses of champagne before our efforts with this husky little fellow. Gunilla was pregnant with Markus when I left Europe in 1949 and then had two more children afterward. They are the Count Johannes Fugger-Babenhausen and Baroness Tatiana Rukavina. Gunilla is very proud of her children, as she should be. Toni often travels with her, Markus watches after her, and she visits Tatiana in Switzerland and Johannes at his home near Frankfurt.

When Gunilla returned from Markus, she explained he now had a fever. She had wrapped his legs in cold wet towels to draw the fever out! Well, I find the Europeans hold to many superstitions and old ways that we have long forgotten. Paula used to use a cold wet towel around her neck when she had a sore throat. I believe if it works, use it. I was feeling hot and had a sore throat by now. However, I did not mention it and hoped it would be gone by morning. It was not, so

perhaps I should have tried some of the old remedies.

We had a light supper prepared by Frau Hübl who comes every day to cook and do the housework. I should mention Gunilla's dog, Lexi, a Cavalier King Charles Spaniel. I get along well with dogs, but Lexi is a one-woman dog. The whole time I was there, if I spoke to her, she barked, growled, or glared at me with seeming disdain. By contrast, Markus' dog, Chicha, was friendly and a tail wagger. I offered to take Lexi out one morning when Gunilla was still in bed, but that dog just looked at me and would not budge. The only time she would have anything to do with me was once when she was disciplined. She had looked crestfallen. I said, "poor Lexi," and she came right over and laid her head in my lap. After that, it was back to the growling or barking. A fickle pooch.

Gunilla and I reminisced for a while that evening. We were both concerned for Paula and her health. Gunilla had not been aware of Paula's illness. However, we were both rather tired and Gunilla went for a final check of Markus. I went to bed. I took several aspirin, but the "thing" was getting worse. I seem to get some kind of illness every time I take a trip to Europe. I was praying this was not something serious.

It was so enjoyable waking up on this particular Saturday morning and looking over at the front door of the castle where we used to stay many years before. Markus would later take me through the now unoccupied rooms for a tour of memories. As I looked at the door, I remembered one early morning fifty years ago. Prince Friedrich Carl, my boyfriend Captain Michael Bressler, myself, and several others had gathered, bleary eyed, at 4:30 a.m. for a hunt. Friedrich Carl's man, Janni, was about as hung over as the rest of us. He accidentally, I think, fired one of the guns in the quiet courtyard where we stood. Before we could recover, it seemed, Gunilla appeared in her nightgown obviously very upset. Finding us all looking quite cowed, she gave us a resounding lecture before realizing how she was dressed. I am sure she must have blushed and she quickly disappeared. None of us laughed. We just hurried out of there.

Today, Gunilla tells a different version. We were making a "perfect row" and had awakened her with our noisy giggling and shouts. She heard the gun go off and was frantic that someone might have been hurt. Putting on her robe, but not taking time for her slippers,

she flew down the stairs. I would certainly agree with the latter. Seeing that we were all right, she automatically slapped the nearest person, which was poor old Janni. He really did deserve it though. I am
just glad I was not the nearest person. I was probably hiding behind
the closest car. Nonetheless, I do not remember it happening that
way. She says she then made a "dignified exit."

My throat was worsening, and I was beginning to cough. The last
time I had been to Europe, I had come down with near pneumonia
so this did not seem fair. Luckily, I did not feel too badly and I was
very glad to again meet Markus, whose fever was gone. That tells you
something about the old medical ways. He was fixing breakfast so I
helped and began to get to know him better. There is a lot of
Friedrich Carl in him, but none of the often unkind way Friedrich
Carl might approach some situations. Markus is a kind man, sensitive, and yet he can set one back on their heels with a direct approach to an indirect topic. If that makes sense! He is good at sarcasm, as Friedrich Carl and I were. He is the curator of the castle's
museum, and he also manages the unrestored part of the castle. His
apartment is in this latter area and he has some very handsome furniture.

After breakfast, Gunilla and I went shopping in the town. Everyone knows her and she feels they are her "family." The grocery store
was absolutely shining clean. Rows of cheese, sausages, breads, fruit,
etc., were neatly stacked. I was beginning to remember more of my
German. Nevertheless, the dialect often confused me and Gunilla
would have to interpret. I do well enough with the language to survive on my own but as mentioned previously, I am reluctant to speak
it. The town seemed much as I remembered it. Occasionally, in
those earlier days we would leave our games at the castle and wander
into the village late at night. If a party was going on somewhere,
Friedrich Carl would brazenly walk in and announce himself and his
guests. Sometimes I was a bit uncomfortable, but it always seemed to
work out. I think the veiled anger some hosts might have felt would
be when we ate some of their food. Most of us were careful about
this. Friedrich Carl was not.

Later that day Gunilla and I took the dogs, both barking in anticipation, and drove out to the fields where we had hunted. The farmers constantly mow the fields for silage. They look like large mani-

cured lawns with stands of trees on the slopes. It was beautiful and the dogs hunted through the ditches and trees.

While we were watching the dogs, Gunilla asked if I remembered a forester named Herr Anton Richter. I could not recall. She said we would be going with him and his wife, Maria, the following day to a church festival. It was to be a celebration of the finding of a carved wooden Madonna hundreds of years ago. When she had told him I was coming to Babenhausen for a visit, he told her a story about his first meeting with me. I was twenty-one and so was he. Friedrich Carl had planned a hunt for me—my first—and he had told an old forester to build a hochstand in a field. This was where a certain buck would show up at about 6:30 p.m. The foresters kept track of all of the deer on the property and knew their habits and the time of their arrival in a given field. This allowed Friedrich Carl to protect the best bucks, and let us cull the weaker ones.

The hochstands were about fourteen or fifteen feet high and usually had a railing on top for protection. Sometimes they had small lean-tos or huts on top. We would go out an hour before a buck was expected and sit and wait for it to appear. Rarely did the buck fail to appear, and it was always in the same place. I am sure I was excited when we arrived at the stand. Friedrich Carl, Anton, and I climbed up the rickety ladder to the platform.

As Anton told it, the old man had not had time to build the railing, and Friedrich Carl was quite angry about this. We sat very still and soon the buck came into the field. It always surprised me that the field could be totally empty and then, seconds later, there would be three or four deer standing there. It was magic. Friedrich Carl told me that this was the right buck and to stand up and shoot. I stood up, but must have teetered or paled or something. Friedrich Carl told Anton to hang onto me. Herr Richter had put his arms around my waist so that I could steady myself and shoot. Afterwards he said he told Friedrich Carl how much he had enjoyed having his arms around me. Friedrich Carl became furious that Anton would talk about his guest like that. I told Gunilla that I did not remember this and asked, "Did I get the buck?" Yes, I had. I could not kill anything today.

That evening we dressed for dinner and I wore my strand of pearls made of "pearl powder." My friend, Vera Stewart, had given

them to me from her trip to Hong Kong and they are quite pretty. Still, anyway one looks at them, they are not real. I thought I could get away with them as the pearl strand is knotted. The Europeans usually felt you would not waste knotted strands on faux jewelry. At least they felt this way in the forties. I thought I was all right until Gunilla came down in a lovely blue outfit with the most beautiful strand of pearls. They had a special sheen to them and were separated by rubies and sapphires. I shot back upstairs and put on my carved ivory necklace, retiring my faux pearls to the suitcase. The next day I told Gunilla how much I admired those pearls, and she said, "They are not real, my grandchildren gave them to me." We both had a good laugh when I told her what I had done.

We had supper and told so many stories about the old times that we kept ourselves and Markus well entertained. Gunilla told of one evening when Friedrich Carl and several of his friends were drinking in the great hall. As she rarely joined late night parties, this night she warned the men not to make noise or come down the hall near the nursery. Toni, then three, was ill. Her bedroom was across from the nursery. She decided to set a trap in case they started down the dark hall while she slept. She took a rope and strung it from a heavy chair across the hallway to the stove door on the other side. These stoves are used to heat a room and are tiled in the room with just an iron door in the hall side. The servants filled them with wood in the early morning hours before the sleepers arose. Sometime during the night, Friedrich Carl sent Rödle Kreuzer, his village friend, to get more liquor. Rödle was quite tipsy, he loved a good party. He rushed forward right into the rope, ripping the iron door off its hinges with a loud clatter, and knocking the chair to the floor, breaking it. This awakened everyone, including the children, who cried while Rödle lay on the floor in a state of shock. For once, it was Gunilla who had overdone it.

Gunilla decided to call Baron Pümi Laffert, who had lived at the castle near the end of the war. Also there, at that time, was his sister, Baroness Gundi Laffert. We had all been friends, hunting and playing together. Gundi had later died tragically of cancer. Pümi had married and was now eighty-three and living in Hamburg with his wife. He had always been a gentle, kind fellow who became quite funny and gregarious when he drank. When Gunilla called, he was

so happy to hear from her. After catching up on their lives, we talked. It was exactly like the old days and he sounded the same.

I could tell he had a few drinks because he was telling me that he had just come from his bath. He wanted me to know that he had perfumed and powdered himself and wished I were there to smell his essence! Eighty-three! Bless him. He said that he had received an announcement of my father's wedding to Bebe Jorgenson. That was in 1952 in Frankfurt. Bebe was a college love of Dad's and they had found each other again in Europe. Pümi said he had sent a telegram of regrets and said that he would look forward to seeing Dad at his "next wedding." I hope the Colonel laughed.

Gunilla also called Countess Sigi von Welczeck who was living in Munich. Pümi, her brother, had told us that she had not been well. Sigi was living in an apartment by herself. We were upset to learn that her health was quite poor and that she had fallen several times. She was having quite a struggle. I did not speak with her and do not know if she would have recalled our friendship. What a pity that such a beautiful lady, with such a colorful past, would be in such sad circumstances.

Finally to bed on my comfortable bench sofa. My throat was not so sore, but I did have a cough and felt perspiration pouring down my back. I took several aspirin, but could not get to sleep. I lay there thinking about the things that had happened on this day. Gunilla and I had taken a walk around the castle. A wedding was taking place in a garden area near the tennis courts. Gunilla said that young couples find it romantic to be married at the castle. I agreed. We walked to the moat, passing a hideous statue of a boar. It was life-size, with a water pipe sticking out of its mouth. This was supposed to be a great fountain that Friedrich Carl had ordered for the courtyard. Not a very good tribute to him I am afraid. Yet there was humor or sarcasm there somewhere. The moat in this area is in grass and lined with rosebushes and shrubs. There are steps leading down and then up and onto the area of the tennis courts. The swimming pool is to the right of the courts.

The pool is near the large wall around the castle. Gunilla related that after the war, Gundi and her sister, Countess Sigi Welczeck, and she decided to go swimming on a hot day. Because of the war and shortages, the other ladies had to make their swimsuits from scarves.

These scarves tended to float away as they swam. Gunilla began to feel as though they were being watched, although the wall is high. She carefully, not wanting to be noticed, looked at the trees along the wall. She saw there were four or five grinning American soldiers perched on the limbs, getting an eyeful. Without attracting attention, she whispered to the young women and they gathered their scarves, covered themselves, and returned to the castle.

I also remembered a time when we seemed starved for good times. Gunilla and Friedrich Carl had organized a party where we had to find our dinner. We were split into teams and were to go to five different spots to find the dinner courses. If we chose, for instance, the forest meister's hut, for the entree, and instead it was the salad, we had to go like mad to make up time and find the entree. Whoever completed the meal first, won the prize. I think Pümi, Gundi, and I were together, in one car. I remember Gunilla and Dad were in another. Together there were probably five groups of us.

We also had obstacles along the "course." At the swimming pool, one person on the team had to raft across. Another had to ride a horse around the pool at a full gallop. Everything, as I said, was at full speed. Pümi elected to raft, and I chose the horse. I made it around quite well but poor Pümi tipped over in his rush to get across the pool. Other guests, awaiting their turns, were yelling encouragement or laughing uproariously. Pümi eventually propelled himself to the other side. He was dripping wet, but we went rushing on to the next stop. We had a great time. To me, the difference between our parties then and now, was we always seemed to have a purpose. We did not just stand around talking, eating, and drinking.

Our team was lucky and we hit three correct stops. We arrived at the wrong one next, but driving at break neck speeds through the woods, we made great time. I cannot say the whole thing done at such a pace did much for the digestion. When we arrived back at the finish, we were just behind Dad and Gunilla, the winners. We jokingly suggested Gunilla might have known the route, but both she and Dad vigorously denied this. It was not until a year or so later that they admitted they had known it! I was reminded of the bridge game on the train when Gunilla's mother "peeked." Just a little bit of cheating! But it had all been very enjoyable. Finally, I drifted off to sleep.

The next day, as we walked after breakfast, Gunilla told me that a company of 150 young boys, ages fourteen to eighteen, were stationed at the castle,. This was toward the end of the war. They called them the *Arbeits Dienst*. The Nazis were training them to go behind the troops as support and to fight. If they panicked, as a young person might be expected to do in battle, and ran, they were shot. I have never forgotten a shelled, overturned armored German tank on one of the roads outside Stuttgart. Alongside the tank were the helmets of the dead boys, lying on the ground. These boys were only fourteen to seventeen years old. These were some of those same *Arbeits* Dienst's boys.

While at Babenhausen, the young boys often, carelessly, littered the castle grounds. The Nazi colonel in charge was very arrogant. Nevertheless, Gunilla was the mistress of her castle. She told him to have the boys cleanup the messes they were making around the courtyard. The colonel could have arrested her, or any number of painful things could have happened to her. However, he gave the order and things were picked up. Today, old men will show up at the castle and greet her, telling her they had been stationed there. They would ask to see the part of the castle where they were billeted. They remembered her also. It was good to know that some of these young people had survived. What stories they could tell.

Gunilla told of a frightening occurrence at the end of the war. As if the war, shooting and bombs were not enough, then they never knew who might come along and try to enter the castle. The German soldiers were shooting everything in sight on their retreat. The displaced people were starving and looking for a place to stay. It was a very uncertain time. There was relief when the Americans took over and things began to settle down. However, one day, some Jewish American officers came by the castle. Gunilla would always go to the door with at least two other people with her. On this day, Sigi and Gundi were with her.

These officers told the ladies that they had heard there were women in the castle. They then began to berate Gunilla and the others. The officers told them that they should be ashamed for raising their men to do such atrocities. None of the ladies was over thirty. That they should never have allowed their men to go to war and follow Hitler. They were quite verbally abusive. When these officers

were done, they told the ladies they would come back that evening and bring liquor. Gundi, Sigi and Gunilla were really quite afraid. However, Gunilla was able to arrange with another American officer to have guards stay at the castle to protect them.

This was Sunday morning and the church bells were ringing all over the area. Gunilla had warned me of their noise. Still, I found the sound lovely and even recorded it. The bells ring for an hour or more, not allowing the sleepers to overlook their trip to church. I remember seeing the castle church years ago. It was beautiful with its gilt religious statues, stained glass windows, golden altars, and nooks. After Gunilla and Markus returned from church, we changed into warm clothes for the Madonna church ceremony. The Richters were to pick us up. We had a hurried lunch in a restaurant in town where there was excellent food– raw salmon for me. Then we raced back to the castle to meet the Richters. I had been losing my voice, and now Gunilla said she was getting a sore throat. I tried to blame it on Markus, not wanting to think I had given her this certainly virulent virus.

The Richters are both very pleasant, and obviously think highly of the Princess. Markus was not going and we set out for the little church farther out in the country. As we drove through the fields, Gunilla told the story about the Madonna. It seems that several hundred years before, the master of Babenhausen, a knight of the family Rechberg, went out hunting in the woods. Suddenly his hunting dogs began to bark furiously so he rode to them to see what they had found. He saw they were barking at something half-buried in the ground. Dismounting from his horse, he discovered it was a carved wooden statue of the Virgin Mary holding the baby Jesus. He carefully dug the carving out of the ground and carried it back to the castle. When he arrived, he placed it in a hall cabinet. He would decide what to do with the statue later.

The next morning the knight went to the hall and found that the figure was missing. He queried his servants, but no one knew what had happened to it. A search was made of the castle, without finding it. Completely puzzled, the knight called for his horse. He rode back to where he had found the Madonna, and there she was in the same exact spot. He again carefully carried the statue back to his castle and locked it in a cupboard until he could show the statue to his

priest.

The priest arrived the next day and they went to the cupboard, unlocked the door, and the statue was gone again. Again they searched the castle and questioned the house staff. No one knew what had become of the statue. The knight and priest rode to the woods and found the Madonna where the knight had first seen her. This happened one more time and the knight then decided that the Madonna wanted them to build a chapel on the spot. He built a lovely, small church there as a place to rest the statue. Devoted Christians and pilgrims come from far distances to pray for special benefits and venerate this Madonna.

The gold and gilt alcove (or area for the statue of the Madonna) in the small church has its walls covered with crutches, canes, and other evidence of miracle cures. Many candles are specially lit for her, and she is certainly revered by this congregation. This is a special place for Gunilla to come during the week for prayers and meditation. It is quiet and absolutely lovely.

So this was the church where we were going today to celebrate the discovery of this figure many years before. A large crowd was already gathered when we arrived. By now, I was coughing and so was Gunilla. My damn coat was holding heat in. I felt I must have been well over 100 degrees. Poor Gunilla was shaking with a chill. I envied her. We sat in the front pew on seats that were about six inches deep. They were very old and designed to keep the sitter awake. A person would be so uncomfortable, sleep would be out of the question. I suppose if one did fall asleep, one would slide off that narrow ledge and be quite embarrassed!

The local parishioners put on the festival and were dressed in their lovely German costumes. They played various strange instruments that have been used for ages. Four German men, dressed in their *lederhosen* (leather pants) felt jackets, and felt hats with a tassel, sang with beautiful voices. As if to be sure of equality, several ladies sang with equally lovely voices. The choir was beautiful, and the minister gave short sermons that seemed well received. Again, because of the Bavarian accent, I could not understand what he was saying. The church, as always, was gorgeous. The lovely stained glass windows, the gilt-covered statues, and woodwork made the church a work of art. The whole atmosphere was of peace and beauty. I understand

why Gunilla would go there for quiet time.

Meanwhile, I was hotter than I can ever recall with no way of taking my coat off as we were packed in tightly. I could see Gunilla struggling not to cough. Despite our ills, it was a beautiful and colorful celebration and I thoroughly enjoyed it. But, I continued to envy Gunilla the chills as I sat in my "hot tent."

We went to the Richters' home after the festival for coffee and *apfel kuchen* (an apple pie/cake combination). It was excellent. The Richters' home sits in a rural setting overlooking the fields and forests he has managed as head forest meister. There were many deer and *hiersch* horns on the walls, but the most astounding part of the visit was Herr Richter's wood carvings. This man is a carver extraordinare. His carvings are about two or three feet high and of religious figures, with absolutely fabulous detail. He showed us a crucifix about eighteen inches high. It was done in a dark wood with some kind of wax treatment to lighten the body. The tiny hands showed the fingernails clearly. It was exquisite! A wonderful visit.

When we arrived back at the castle, Gunilla, who was chilled to the bone, went straight to a hot bath and then to bed. Markus and I, after checking on her often, made our own dinner. He is such an easy person to talk to and likes to hear about the times spent with his

At Richter's home, Anton, Maria and Princess Gunilla.

father. However, by now my voice was almost gone so it was an early evening. Before retiring, Markus asked if I would like some of the "immune stimulant" that he and Gunilla were taking. Markus, I suspect, is still into the holistic health regimes. I was willing to try anything at that point. He brought out a small bottle and poured a tablespoon full. Wondering how it might taste, I downed it. Ahhhh! It burned my throat all the way down. No wonder they call it a stimulant. A look at the bottle label showed it was about 50 percent alcohol. A pleasant way to get well.

The next morning, now Monday, Gunilla had a very sore throat, a cough, and a fever. Markus called the doctor. The hospital is just across the street from the castle and the doctor made castle calls. Gunilla felt badly that she had become ill and that we could not travel more. She was concerned that I might not be enjoying myself. I reassured her that I was having a wonderful time. The way I was

Wood carving of Herr Richter's

feeling made staying put just fine. I had coughed most of the night and was so hot. Nevertheless, I still did not feel badly enough to go down. Markus and I spent time together in easy chatting. He also took me to the museum in the castle. This gave me a chance to see how he has gathered and catalogued articles of Babenhausen history. I had shown them an old flyer for the reopening of the Fuggerei, a Fugger housing complex for retired workers and others. I had it in with some pictures I had brought along. In 1948, Dad and I had attended the occasion with Friedrich Carl and Gunilla. Markus asked if he could have it for the museum. Of course I gave it to him.

On the way to the museum, we met Princess Alexandra Fugger, Hubertus' wife. She seemed a very disciplined person who sized me up carefully. I do not know if I passed the inspection, perhaps. They had invited me to their wedding in October of 1977. However, I had been unable to attend. Her children are very well mannered and Leopold, the eldest, introduced himself and asked politely where was my home, etc. This was a brief visit as there is some distance between the family. I did not see Prince Hubertus this time.

The museum is quite overwhelming with the ancient artifacts of the Fugger family. They have history dating back to an entry in the records of Augsburg in 1367. Markus gave me a small book detailing the founding of the family. Of course, I was looking for horse bits and old horse books. Markus told me that they had sold the horse bits sometime ago. Sigh. The books that are there regarding horses were too old to be handled. So, I took pictures of them through the glass. I tried to pressure Markus into having them completely photographed for me. Markus accepts pressure well–it just goes right by him. I saw such beautiful crystal, porcelain, and furniture. What we Americans call antique is really new by comparison to the age of things in Europe. Lovely old paintings cover the walls of the museum. They are of Fugger ancestors painted by noted artists of the time. Some armor and trappings shown in these paintings were also present in the museum.

After the museum, we went up the double staircase to the grand room. I felt so many ghosts. There used to be a suit-of-armor at the foot of the stairs that had been tried on by many a party goer. It is now in another part of the castle. The reason I never had a picture of this suit is due to my own stubbornness. I had stopped to take a

picture one afternoon in 1948. I remember there were seven or eight people gathered around, so perhaps we had been on a hunt. Dad was with us and was suggesting how and where I should stand, etc.

Of course, the fact that I was a photographer did not cross his mind. I always resented his "help" as it had seemed to come too little, too late as far as my childhood went. At any rate, we began to argue and I let my stubborn streak take over. I would not do the photo as he suggested. As a result, I did it wrong and therefore have never had a picture of the handsome armor. Rather like a delayed adolescence at the age of twenty-two or so.

At the landing, on the way up the stairs, the baroque stag head mount with the enormous rack still hangs there on the wall. Then, up the last steps to the Grand room. Ancient tiles on the floor often clatter from the years of footsteps. Markus works to keep this part of the castle intact with its old paintings and furniture. Windows are opened to let fresh air in and to keep out the dank odors of age. I loved this old place, and still do, as it does not change even with new residents, furniture, or paint. Imagination can take one quickly back to the days of knights, ladies in long gowns for warmth, battles, and even the heavy boot step of a Nazi soldier.

We went through the rooms that I remembered and into one that had often been my bedroom. It is not used these days. How well I remembered this lovely Italian ceiling. Here were the cupids and angels with their heads, legs, or feet dangling in a three-dimensional style. The family had called in some Italian artist to make this room special many years before. I loved waking up in the morning and seeing those figures. We then walked down the long hall past rooms I knew for tea or dining. We went down the back stairs to where the servants quarters had been. These are now offices and Markus has his apartment there. His very handsome furniture and rugs make it a warm bachelor's apartment.

Later, I walked downtown and tried to find a shop to purchase gifts to take home for friends. However, there was only one gift shop and it had mostly souvenirs and nothing old. I had waited too long. The walk back was a little slow as I felt the "thing" coming on again. I also think I was looking ahead to my return trip and the effort it would take. I was feeling sadness that this all seemed such a brief stay. Hopefully, not a final one. Germany is like home to me. My

German ancestors were stirring, I guess. I think if I were younger, I would choose to live in Baden Baden, so metropolitan for such a small city.

When I arrived back in the courtyard, I met Alexander, Prince Hubertus' second son. Again, his manners and manner were charming as he introduced himself and asked where I lived. I think he must be about eleven or twelve years old. He had a small bucket and was picking pears from the vined trees on the castle wall. He offered me one and I took it upstairs to Gunilla's room where we shared it. It was excellent. She was feeling better but was not ready to join us downstairs. Again an early evening that I needed. My cough was worsening and my voice was just about gone. Gunilla was again concerned that she was not able to do more for me. I let her know that this was the best vacation for me since the forties.

We discussed the idea of writing this book together. Gunilla felt that as she had already started writing her own life history, perhaps we should work on our own. She said she was very willing to help me with names and places, as needed. I had to agree with her. I realized that I had spent most of my time in Europe at other places than Babenhausen. Paula had also offered to help. So often she was with us when we went to many northern castles.

On Tuesday Gunilla was able to be up longer. As she was feeling better, we spent a part of my last evening watching the outcome of the O.J. Simpson trial on her television. Markus and Gunilla were quite interested in the trial. They felt that the "not guilty" verdict would avoid a bloodshed with the African-American population. I was upset regarding the verdict, having felt that the evidence proved him guilty. However, they were not surprised. We then enjoyed a German horse jumping show. Gunilla was practically jumping the jumps with the riders, so I knew she was better. She loves horses and had been a very good rider.

I felt that Gunilla and Markus were more knowledgeable about our politics than I am about theirs. I did learn that Germany is having an expensive struggle coming together with East Germany. The economics and very poor environmental situation in East Germany was unexpected. Also, Germany is eager to put her capitol city back in Berlin, from Bonn. A tremendous expense of twenty billion marks. Yet, when most Germans are asked why they would spend that

amount, it is always, "that is where it should be."

Next morning Markus arrived to take me to the train. As usual, I had pressured to arrive at the station early. Nevertheless, as I said, Markus handles pressure quite well and we moved at his pace. Gunilla was still not well enough to come with us, so we said our good byes with promises to see each other again soon. It took her two months to get over this flu. The same for me. Hopefully, I can make a trip to Europe just once without coming down with something.

I had an enjoyable ride to Ulm with Markus, who I had come to really like. We had just about ten minutes to wait for the train. He teased me to come back and "stay longer" next time. This was about a remark that I had made earlier saying I had perhaps stayed too long. Markus helped me to the train and once again that heavy suitcase was heaved on board. He left after giving me a great bear hug and kisses. What a wonderful time.

The train seemed to fly toward Frankfurt and my mind was now occupied with the process of getting to the airport and to my motel. I had arranged to stay overnight in Frankfurt, then fly to London and home. Next time I will go straight through to London and stay over. It will make the return trip a bit shorter.

I arrived in Frankfurt with a lighter load as I had left soap, etc., at the castle. It was still a struggle to find the lower platform where the commuter train goes to the airport. The people were friendly, although a bit rowdy, and eventually, with my poor German, I was on my way again. It was about a twenty minute ride and then a seemingly twenty minute walk to the British airlines. I learned that for "security" reasons I could not check my eighty pound bag until the next morning. By this time, I was about done in with the luggage, sweating in that damn coat, and coughing my head off.

I eventually found a taxi to expedite things. The driver tried to get me to take a motel limo but I would not give in. He did, finally, and we went to the Novel Motel about eight miles from the airport. I say this only because the brochure said two miles. I did not have enough *Deutsche* marks for the taxi ride. So, I "persuaded" the taxi driver to take fifteen dollars (U.S.) a bonus for him. My motel was adequate, quiet, and the food was fine.

I called Gunilla to let her know that I had arrived safely. She had

the doctor in again and she did not sound too well. We both hoped she would feel well enough for her trip to Baden Baden. She goes there for the diets and baths. Gunilla was to let me know how she found Paula. We did not talk long because our voices were raspy. I again thanked her for such a memorable time. I was now looking forward to the long day ahead and just getting home.

I arrived at the airport that next morning, early as usual, and immediately checked the heavy suitcase. What a relief to let someone else carry it. I would stuff the "damn" coat into the overhead compartment until arriving in Seattle where it would be needed. Although both the coat and the luggage had been a pain, I had survived! Meanwhile, there were many interesting people to watch while I waited for my flight. The shops were full of foreign items, terribly expensive but fun to browse through. At this point, I felt that the rest of the trip was simply a matter of passing time until I reached my destination–the drive down the lane to my home in Aberdeen. What wonderful memories I would have to carry me through the "duration"!

EPILOGUE

This book has been in the thinking for a very long time. However, if I had known the complexities of having a book published I might never have started! I have attempted to report my memories of fifty years as precisely as my non precise personality allows. Therefore, if the reader finds mistakes, I would greatly appreciate hearing about them and they will be corrected in the next hoped-for edition. I have certainly learned that grammar, quotation factors, and spelling change with time!

These were the most fascinating days of my life, and I hope the reader will find them equally enjoyable. There is no forgetting the horrible things that happened in World War II. Perhaps we were premature in our friendships with the "enemy". However, everyone living in Germany at that time was struggling with the after-effects of the war and trying very hard to get things back to normal. Many of our friends are named in the groups that tried to oust Hitler at great risk to their own lives.

Apologies are in order for the quality of my photos. Although I was good behind the camera it seems I was not so good with the developing of the negatives. I found many had become faded or stained through the years. The computer has done its best to enhance them.

Disclaimer
I have searched every record available and hope that no one finds errors that are objectionable to them. Hopefully fact has not become fiction, nor fiction become fact.

ABOUT _the_ AUTHOR

Jean Walters Gayle is a psychotherapist in private practice in Aberdeen, Washington. This book was planned for many years. She was aided by the letters her mother and grandmother had saved from her time in Germany and by Princess Fugger and Countess Clary. She was a professional photographer in Europe and most of the pictures in the book are hers. Jean has three horses, warm bloods, at her five acre home. She has enjoyed a very active life including her professional career and she continues to have an interest in her community. Jean is a collector of antique bridle rosettes, museum quality horse bits and Meissen porcelain. Jean has also written articles about the rosettes, college life, and other items of interest that have been published in various magazines. She hopes to write another book about her father's fishing resort, Rancho Buena Vista in Baja California Sur, Mexico.

Author today with her mare, Eugenia Rex

ORDER FORM

The Colonel's Daughter
Jean Walters Gayle

DATE: _____

NAME: _____

ADDRESS: _____

CITY, STATE, ZIP: _____

TELEPHONE: _____

I would like to order:

_____ book(s) @$32.00 U.S. hard cover-limited edition
_____ book(s) @$18.00 U.S. soft cover _____
                                                  subtotal

Sales tax (WA State residents only)
add 7.8%   _____

Shipping & Handling   _____
(U.S. Add $5.00 per copy. Canada and Europe - $10 U.S. Postage)

Total Enclosed   _____

Send Payment with Order Form to
Three Horses Publishing Co.
P.O. Box 104
Montesano, WA. 98563

Tele: 360 533-3490   Email JGayle@Techline.com